The Philosophy and Aesthetics of Music

THE PHILOSOPHY & AESTHETICS OF

MUSIC

Edward A. Lippman

INTRODUCTION BY

CHRISTOPHER HATCH

University of Nebraska Press : Lincoln and London

Copyright © 1999 by the University of Nebraska Press
Manufactured in the United States of America ⊛
Library of Congress Cataloging-in-Publication Data
Lippman, Edward A.
The philosophy and aesthetics of music / Edward A.
Lippman : introduction by Christopher Hatch.
p. cm. Includes bibliographical references and index.
ISBN 0-8032-2912-7 (cloth : alkaline paper). –
ISBN 0-8032-7984-1 (paper : alkaline paper)
1. Music – Philosophy and aesthetics. I. Title.
ML3845.L567 1999 781.1'7–dc21 98-43967 CIP MN

Contents

Introduction

DWARD A. LIPPMAN's reputation rests most notably on his four books: *Musical Thought in Ancient Greece* (1964; reprint, 1975), *A Humanistic Philosophy of Music* (1977), *A History of Western Musical Aesthetics* (1992), and *Musical Aesthetics: A Historical Reader* (3 vols., 1986–90). Prefiguring the philosophical-aesthetic interests that they share was his dissertation, "Music and Space: A Study in the Philosophy of Music" (Columbia University, 1952). Thus he has long contributed to his chosen field of endeavor.

Until his retirement from teaching in 1988, the music department of Columbia University served as Lippman's academic home. Among his other duties there he offered graduate seminars in a wide range of philosophical areas, so courses as diverse in subject matter as phenomenology and the musical thinking of ancient China readily found a place in the curriculum. Under Lippman's watchful guidance, immersion in primary sources – in a profound sense, learning to read – became, for scores of prospective musicologists and music theorists, an essential stage in their training. In this way a historical sensibility might be developed and a vantage point gained from which the newest or currently most popular historiographical practices could be better judged.

Lippman's teaching was able to rely on example at least as much as on precept, for his unrivaled knowledge of the treatises arose from a fine sympathy with the authors' points of view and a willingness to sift the material in search of its underlying meanings. The care with which his writings, too, treat their topics shows just such respectful thoroughness. The ever-contentious bustling on the musicological scene has been powerless to distract him from his distinctive scholarly pursuits; a public display of scoring points with or against his publishing colleagues has held no attraction for him.

The Philosophy and Aesthetics of Music is composed of articles by Lippman that first appeared over a period of four decades (1953–94) in journals and Festschriften, both American and German. These twelve essays exhibit characteristic facets of his work quite apart from interrelated themes. The well-shaped form of his arguments possesses literary value per se, and the style of their expression often attains a quiet eloquence. Even in the absence of source notes, which in certain essays stems from their earlier existence as orally delivered papers, an undeniable authority is maintained as surefooted reasoning drives the discourse forward. Yet the book rather than the lecture provides the ideal vehicle for Lippman's meaty prose; deliberative readers, allowed time to test the written assertions and to ground them in their own experience, can in a sense join forces with the author.

The two initial essays neatly complement each other as the focus turns from the ideational to the physical dimensions of music. In chapter 2, marshaling the relevant scientific findings, Lippman demonstrates how music entails the intricacies of acoustics and physiology, whereas the opening essay concentrates on music's meaning. There "the aspects of music that may reflect external ideas or that may lead away from the immediate musical experience" are sought out. In an intellectual tour de force, an all-embracing conception of symbolism draws together extremely diverse subjects, ranging from notation to the music of the spheres. No mere inventory of specific symbolic modes, this article emphasizes the extraordinary complexity of music and with special subtlety delimits the unique nature of musical emotion: "Musical feelings have their own character: they are not the feelings we know and roughly name in our experience outside of music, and they do not lead in themselves to ideas or concepts of other feelings. Thus music may be an emotional experience and still not represent emotional contexts belonging to other areas of life."

Noteworthy in Lippman's approach is not only a generous definition of what is intrinsic to music but also a responsiveness to what, in changing historical and personal circumstances, has been considered so. His early investigations into Greek musical thinking may have strengthened his awareness of music's reach. In any event, the essay on the place of music in the liberal arts (chapter 5) clarifies its function as an explanation of mathematical relations, a counterpart to astronomy, and an influence even within the verbal categories of the trivium. The following essay (chapter 6) serves to disclose the beginnings of musical aesthetics. That is, in treating a variety of theoretical treatises on music, it disentangles predominantly aesthetic considerations from the "discussions of cosmic harmony, ethics, mathematics, science (acoustics, physiology, psychology), ontology, theology, and still other matters" that bulk large in systematic writings on music from antiquity to the eighteenth century and beyond.

A much narrower historical perspective governs several of the articles. For instance, the essays on Wagner's and Schumann's aesthetics (chapters 10 and 12 and chapter 9, respectively) take up what these composer-authors, on the one hand, explicitly advocated and implicitly approved and, on the other, cast into works of art. By highlighting the lapses and inner contradictions that burden Wagner's ideas, chapter 10 is unusually critical in tone, though historical explanations arising from both biography and more long-term musical developments soften this negativity. Written more than thirty years later, "Wagner's Conception of the Dream" (chapter 12) takes a further look at the central fissure in Wagner's theories: "the conflict of interest between absolute music and musical drama." Lippman now finds that "in Wagner's final theoretical conception, the drama has become a true image of life that is seen in a clairvoyant dream provoked by music," with hearing alone acting as "the instrument of the dream state."

The aesthetics of the elusive and inward-turning Schumann, for its part, presents some baffling puzzles. In chapter 9, Lippman painstakingly studies the composer's music as well as the verbal record (ranging from Schumann's poetic music criticism to offhand comments and memories), not to mention his absorption in literature. Through this means Lippman addresses the salient issues with regard to the meanings of his music and how they are to be explicated. Not all of Schumann's assertions can be reconciled, but the drift of his thinking, as unmarked as the path of a butterfly, is documented in telling detail. (Here as elsewhere, Lippman is a master of the apt quotation.)

Being gifted composers, Schumann and Wagner occupy a privileged position in speaking about the creative process. In Wagner's view the inspired composer works in what Lippman calls a "state of ecstatic clairvoyance," with music conveying the "insight of the deep dream to the waking consciousness." Schumann's stance concerning the creation of music, by contrast, leads Lippman to complete a "picture of formative influences on music by a theory of multiple causation," whose factors combine in all manner of ways. Yet whatever forces are at play during composition, the result is a transmutation of these factors. "Whether images provide information about the creative process or are poetic fancies partly determined by the listener, while it may be a matter of interest and curiosity, is in fact of no consequence with respect to the musical substance itself. As concrete entities of a visual or conceptual nature, cause and effect are actually of equal relevance; to the intrinsic character of music, with its strange generality, the one is as unimportant as the other."

Of course, categories of music exist in which the concrete entities cannot be confined to cause or effect but are, rather, integral parts of musical works. Obviously this is true of pieces that include sung words. Lippman treats vocal music in two contrasting essays. Chapter 4 concentrates on the distinctive joining of poem and melody in strophic song, whereas chapter 7 interprets the historically conditioned elements of meaning that are lodged in a single aria from Bach's *St. John Passion.* The doctrine of affections underpins this interpretation, which further indicates how symbolism operates in the aria through the deployment of modulation and occurrences of repetition.

As these two chapters demonstrate, questions concerning repetition hold an important place in musical aesthetics. Recurring patterns, broadly conceived, likewise figure largely in the subject matter of "Progressive Temporality in Music" (chapter 3). This study looks at its subject from sharply varied angles, defining separate temporal classifications yet also commenting, with great finesse, on the minutiae of selected musical illustrations. The compositions cited cover several centuries, so that one by-product of Lippman's discussion is a panoramic survey of rhythmic practices and styles.

To speak of style in this context is to remind oneself of Lippman's classic article "Stil," which appears in the encyclopedia *Die Musik in Geschichte und Gegenwart.* In the present collection the term *style,* with one of its everyday referents – the style of the individual composer – is dwelled on only in "The Formation of Wagner's Style" (chapter 11). At the heart of this subject is the process by which genius molds its style from earlier music, now transformed as new conditions arise and a new aesthetics is attained. Again, the contents of "The Tonal Ideal of Romanticism" (chapter 8) touch on style, but as something shared by a whole school of composers, since this essay describes the characteristic sound, the tonal ideal, of Romantic music and explores the meanings that it conveys. Lippman tracks the participation of German literary Romanticism in creating this sound ideal, which answers to a Romantic mode of listening that "is directed toward an invisible world. . . .

It suggests constantly . . . a world that is imperceptible even to hearing, yet to which only hearing can give access." That Lippman can face and control a paradox like this should indicate the intellectual hardihood evidenced throughout this book. His skill in handling difficult concepts is accompanied by other strengths, for he is a trained musician-historian who can bring the past to his readers with extraordinary immediacy. Combined with his historical awareness are keen musicianship and a knowledge of music that he draws upon effortlessly. Lippman may not often permit his musical enthusiasm to become overt, but however hidden, it adds to the persuasiveness of his highly disciplined aesthetic thought.

Christopher Hatch

The Philosophy and Aesthetics of Music

Part 1: Philosophy and Aesthetics

1

Symbolism in Music

SYMBOLISM entails a relation between two different kinds of experience, one somehow pointing to the other, and this is a type of relation that music presents in remarkable variety, for music is an extremely intricate activity. What is symbolic for the composer may not be so for the audience or the performer, and the historian also finds his own kinds of symbolism in music. Symbols even can be thoroughly personal: Robert Schumann delighted in private meanings, and there are special listeners and performers who have a marked synesthetic response to music, or who have strong associations with certain works, or in whom music produces visual images of some kind. We are concerned with such special significances only insofar as they exemplify general types of symbolism, evident in the normal musical experience.

But the complexity of musical symbolism does not end with the various persons concerned; it exists in the symbols themselves, for music involves not only auditory symbols – melody, harmony, rhythm, tone-color, structure, dynamics, and so on – but visual ones also, in its instruments and performers and notation. Many of these symbols are as extended as a whole musical work; others are brief word-painting.

The same considerable variety is also presented by the entities that may be symbolized: physical objects and motions, feelings and moods, abstract ideas and conceptions, and even music itself, both as a physical event and as an emotional experience.

Finally, the ways in which musical symbolism takes place, the routes that lead from one experience to the other, are again diversified in nature, and each of them may bring us to the final object of the symbolism either directly or in a number of steps. It is these various underlying relationships between symbol and object that appear to offer the most instructive basis for securing a broad understanding of musical symbolism, and this suggests that we seek out the aspects of music that may reflect external ideas or that may lead away from the immediate musical experience.

THE SYMBOLIC PROPERTIES OF NOTATION

Musical notation is probably the most important visual aspect of music, and it embodies two different types of symbolism, both of which are generally inactive for the audience, but exist for the composer and performer and historian. Primarily, musical notation represents the sound of the music, much as written language symbolizes speech. This type of symbolism is inevitable; it is always present when we possess written music, for there are essentially no instances of musical notation that do not imply a heard music. Equally fundamental is the fact that this symbolism subsists wholly within the music immediately present: it leads neither outside of music nor to other musical works or other parts of a single work. The most common bases of notation are visual and auditory equivalences which are more than arbitrary, for intersensory connections are involved in the representation of pitch along a visual dimension, and auditory duration is projected at least partly in terms of visually perceived length. Tablature, on the other hand, symbolizes sound only indirectly, for the immediate objects of the symbols are certain tactually experienced positions, and these in turn call forth the eventual auditory object of the notation. Whatever its type, and for all its intersensory basis, written music is scarcely an exact symbolization; in fact, it is often but an indication of the sounds to be realized in performance or in imagination.

In addition to its normal musical object, notation is able to represent extramusical entities – abstract conceptions as well as actual things and events – but this type of symbolism is not inevitable; rather we must be informed about its object by means other than the musical notation proper, or we should not know what was being symbolized, or even that there was any symbolizing present. With the help of a text, however, unfilled and stemless note heads can be seen to represent pearls or teardrops, blackened notes come to symbolize darkness, and a wavelike melodic pattern can stand for the rippling of a brook. The wavelike outline is so closely related to the sound of the music that in this case the visual symbolism is reinforced by an auditory one, and the object becomes apparent to a listener as well as to a singer. In no case, however, is it easy to prejudge a notational symbol as purely visual: appreciative audiences may hear a great deal more than we might imagine, and listeners have often been performers also. Sharps and flats, favorite visual symbols, can easily be heard as well as seen, even by a listener who has never looked at the musical notation.

THE REPRESENTATIVE FUNCTION OF SOUND

Auditory as well as visual sensations are nearly always interpreted as symbols of external events, and heard music will invariably represent the tonal sources and the motions of musical performance, in a symbolism present to everyone but the performer himself. Both static and dynamic entities may be conveyed symbolically: music may be dominated by an unchanging reference for as long as the symbolization lasts, sometimes for an entire composition, or it may take advantage of its unfolding nature and present us with a moving and developing object. Thus the basic representative symbolism of sense perception does not mean only that the sound of a trumpet represents a trumpet – that musical sounds symbolize singers and instruments – but also that the particular sounds of any given trumpet passage represent a trumpet being played in some particular fashion. From the dynamic point of view, music is the symbol of a series of events: of a succession of tensions and efforts and motions.

Although the virtues and the variety of musical symbolism are due to the fact that music easily frees itself from the primitive function of representing its sources, this very representation is often important to musical experience.[1] Spatial interplay between segments of a performing group, as in antiphonal and polychoral practice and in the concerto and the symphony, is directly dependent upon the local relations of the musical sources. And the simple recognition of different instruments as such is often constitutive of the conception of music for small groups. In fact it is only in the exceptionally oriented Romantic era that the objective individuality of the performers was neglected in favor of the withdrawn, introspective response to music; and even here, virtuosity was a contemporary manifestation of the other extreme. Also, whenever a singer or an instrument is itself used symbolically, the music must be especially active in representing its source. Thus in opera, where the singer becomes part of a dramatic representation, and in musical hunts and battles, where the horn and the trumpet become part of a musical picture, it is the singer and the horn and the trumpet themselves which the music must make prominent. But aside from the role it plays in music, the representative function of sound is an example of what is probably the prototype of all symbolism: a later evolved aspect of experience stands for a more basic complex; sensory impressions symbolize an underlying and important reality.[2] The light and the mechanical vibrations proceeding from an event are really parts of the event, and in this relationship symbols have a natural origin, part serving to recall whole and effect representing cause.

IMITATION OF SOUNDS

The principle that makes music a natural symbol of the events of performance enables it also to symbolize other objects and happenings, provided that they are not silent ones, for music need not sound only like the singers and musical instruments that produce it. Like the natural or normal representation, imitation is concerned with presenting physical entities; but as a kind of deceit, it is active only when the composer practices it. Certain traditional objects of imitation have a long history, some in both vocal and instrumental music: brooks and fountains and raindrops, the sounds of birds and other animals, vendors' cries and women's gossip, bells of every description, and the thunder and cannon fire of storms and battles. Perennial subjects, however, should not blind us to the generality of the technique; any audible occurrence may be imitated, even as unlikely an object of musical attention as the sound of snoring.

A somewhat different possibility exists totally within the field of music, for one instrument or voice may imitate another. Pizzicato violins have often represented a lute or a guitar, and the piano occasionally tries to sound like a music box. The organ has attempted to imitate every instrument (not to mention the singing voice), while, conversely, orchestral wind choirs will strive to sound like an organ. And when musical hunts and battles forgo actual horns and trumpets and use only characteristic melodic material, they move from the symbolism of literal representation to that based on imitation. Trumpet arias and keyboard *battaglie* announce their battle calls even without imitating tone-color, and the same is true of *caccie* and *chasses,* which use voices and instruments respectively to imitate the horn. It is also possible for one voice to imitate another: opera is full of disguises and of comic imitations in which one person tries to sound like another, and even in nonoperatic vocal music, a narrator will often temporarily assume the role of one of the characters in his narrative.

But more important than the possibilities that have been mentioned is the instrumental imitation of singing, either fully melodic or declamatory. In the imitation of vocal melody, instruments obviously may have recourse to tone-colors approximating those of the singing voice, but there may be a second path open to them also in the procedure of copying a specifically vocal style. For just as a flute or a clarinet can imitate a trumpet by making use of a passage characteristic of that instrument, so it appears possible for an instrument to imitate the voice by duplicating a style peculiar to song. Such symbolism would not be associative – it would not simply consist in the reproduction of a melody known to be vocal – but instead would be the representation of an idiom that was native to the voice in some particular historical context. The extent and persistence of specifically vocal styles are relevant factors here; vocal style may exist, but we must avoid the error of presupposing that it is changeless. There is an excellent instance of the imitation of song in the slow movement of Brahms's Second Piano Concerto: the distinctly vocal sound of the solo cello is due partly to association of the melody with that of an actual song, but it is due also to what is unquestionably imitation, both of the tone-color of the voice and of a characteristic vocal style.

The symbolization of singing is much less equivocal when an instrument imitates recitative rather than song, for in spite of a wide range of types, recitative is a more sharply defined province than is vocal melody. The speechlike patterns of rhythm and of intonation that characterize declamatory singing continue as a telltale feature of its instrumental imitation, although without the aid of prior association, there is as little likelihood of conveying a particular text here as in the imitation of formal vocal melody. What is involved is really a shift to a different field of expression: instrumental recitative, as we find it in Beethoven, for example, seems to represent the desire for a new concreteness or a new eloquence. But in the opus 135 Quartet a programmatic indication tells us just what words the music will symbolize, and in the Ninth Symphony there is an interesting reversal of the more normal procedure – we hear the actual recitative after its imitation. With Wagner, of course, it is a regular feature for the recitative to precede its symbolic restatements by instruments, and with the help of this prior association, we hear the very sound of the declamation just as distinctly as if the text were present.

Does vocal music symbolize speech? One phenomenon seems as fundamental as the other, and this supports the notion of a common origin rather than that of a dependence; but if we except primitive cultures and examine the evidence more closely, we meet numerous examples in which it is obvious that singing represents speech. When it does so, imitation of sound plays a large part in the representation, and singing is modeled upon speech either throughout, as in recitative, or in isolated moments of expressiveness or realism. Word-dominated music, where it is an expression of a self-conscious art, is as much a symbolization of speech as it is a new product or a heightened speech.

FORMAL RESEMBLANCE

In representing musical instruments or in imitating the sounds of the external world, music symbolizes by presenting the auditory part of events, but it is evidently incapable of becoming this kind of symbol for objects that make no sound. Yet silent events and things, and happenings whose sounds are not distinctive enough to represent them, can be symbolized in music by a resemblance of form, a similarity or even an identity of structure. Music, itself auditory, is forced back upon relatively indirect means in representing nonaudible things. It becomes an analogue or an allegory of the event represented. Such symbolism is less spontaneous than the imitation of sound; it is apprehended by a conscious act of intellect.

It cannot be pretended that symbols of this type can act unaided; they would be without significance in nonprogrammatic instrumental music. But from the standpoint of quantity such music is after all not of predominant importance, as an unprejudiced examination will reveal. Even in Western music, we are at once impressed by the vast wealth of vocal music and opera, and of dance music and ballet, and of the endless varieties of programmatic music. Thus the field within which symbols are generally effective is scarcely a restricted one.

A simple formal equivalence is that of number: a single person can be represented by a single voice, or two people may be symbolized by a two-voiced setting. Similarly, number of voices can represent any instance of a small integer, any small group of things, and even a number itself. Number in its temporal form, as a repeated tone or a repeated pattern, may represent the same objects, but it is more properly adapted to symbolizing a succession of occurrences. The representation of two or three people by two or three singers is really more than an equivalence of number: the formal similarity runs deeper and includes a spatial correspondence between people and singers, between external positions and the positions of musical sources.

Besides equivalence of spatial and temporal number, another basic formal relationship between music and other events is that of motion, and indeed the term itself is fully applicable to music. The motional experience that music contains is intrinsically quite similar to our experience of physical motion, and it follows almost as a matter of course that one readily falls into correspondence with the other. Thus music can depict real events insofar as they are constituted by motion, and it can depict objects by representing the motions characteristic of them. A prolonged tone or chord will represent a stationary object or a changeless state, while a musical change of a given rapidity is a natural symbol for an external happening of related speed.

The sinuous motion of snakes, the trembling of the earth, and the gentle and regular rocking of cradles – all have been cast into musical symbols innumerable times, and music has similarly depicted the undulating waves of the ocean and the pitter-patter of separate raindrops.

Any form or formal characteristic in music will have an unlimited number of symbolic possibilities; even intentional formlessness – aimless voice-leading or deliberately incorrect writing – has served as a symbol of confusion or chaos. Especially suggestive formal features are those of repetition and of sequence, of diminution and augmentation, of inversion, of antiphony, of the octave-relationship, and of the major-minor relationship. Canonic structure has often symbolized adherence to rule or plan, or rote repetition, or strictness and legality, or the simple physical relation of following, and these applications are far from exhaustive. The sonata and the symphony sometimes appear to contain a formal analogue of some dramatic situation, and the structural basis of much program music is to be found precisely in its resemblance to some extramusical course of events.

Even the fundamental tonal relationships that underlie music have been found elsewhere, or really everywhere, for the whole universe has been compared structurally to music in the widely disseminated idea of a musical cosmos. There is no response to music involved in this symbolism, nor any special symbolic formulation on the part of a composer. Instead, it is music as a whole that is symbolic: not an individual work, but the very material of music, and the idea of music apart from its sound. The object of the symbol also is no sensible manifestation, for music is the counterpart of a conception rather than of a visible universe. It is quite in keeping with its nature that cosmic symbolism has existed for the philosopher and not really for the composer or the performer or the listener.

While symbolism by means of imitation of sound is restricted essentially to representing physical events and objects – and really only audible events and objects – symbolism based on pattern seems capable of representing not only a wider range of objects and happenings but also of representing ideas themselves. It does this by exemplifying the structural characteristic that an idea embodies: lack of order, for example, or speed, or threeness.

INTERSENSORY RELATIONS

Symbolism based on formal resemblance depends upon a fully conscious appreciation of small or large structural features; it is a type of symbolism (if we set aside its stock of conventional or traditional symbols) that typically presupposes a logical or reflective response to music. In contrast, symbolism occurring by means of intersensory relationships is dependent upon a response to music that, ideally, is spontaneous and follows psychological and physiological laws relating hearing and vision or hearing and touch. Not so much the structural aspects of music come into play here, for these are almost always consciously apprehended, but rather the elemental attributes of tone: pitch, volume, brightness, tone-color, loudness, and so on. An ascending passage will represent an ascending visual motif, tones that are felt to be large will symbolize large visual objects, and bright tone-colors will summon up bright visual impressions. Although grounded in a primitive interrelation of the senses, such symbols have in certain cultural settings been thought out or devised and have called forth a similarly detached response. And we must not fail to notice again the development of traditional symbols, in which the original heterosensory reaction is equally inactive.

Intersensory relations are responsible for what is probably the most persistent symbol in music: the representation of high and low and of up and down through pitch. High and low pitch can represent not only physical position and visually perceptible ascent and descent but also abstract conceptions which are somehow associated with physical high and low, such as God and angel, and hell and death. In whatever period of Western music we look, we find this same spatial symbolism. It is used for the Resurrection, for the fall of man, for the stars and the heavens and lightning, and for the depths of the sea.

Visual and auditory are extremely close in the case of lightning, and we readily can come to feel that lightning actually emits sound. The tonal symbol is based on the brightness of high tones and also on rapidity, here an intersensory rather than a formal feature of resemblance. The musical version of lightning and thunder fosters a confusion of the senses, and it is only with effort that we recognize the participation of two different types of symbolism: one based on intersensory response, and the other on imitation of sound.

It is Wagner's great sensitivity for relations between the senses that is responsible for the effectiveness of many of his leitmotifs. The representation of fire, for example, or the symbolization of the Rhine is dependent neither upon imitation of sound nor upon formal correspondence but upon the heterosensory outcomes of the music; the fascinating strength of the motifs, their perfect suitability, is the result not of an intellectually perceived resemblance but of a felt likeness, a much more primitive connection. The prelude of *Das Rheingold* is a complete sensuous experience of a river – tactual as well as visual – expressed in sound only; scenery is truly superfluous here, for it cannot make the water more real or vivid. The shining sword is captured by the brilliant tone-color of the trumpet, while the qualities of gold are expressed by the mellow tone-color of the French horn.[3] And the remarkable success with which the dragon Fafner is depicted is due in large measure to the slow-acting and ponderous tones of the tuba. Even the slow and tortuous and ungainly musical motion does not in this instance appeal to reason but becomes a matter of sensory qualities rather than of formal properties in its similarity to the physical locomotion.

Outstanding instances of intersensory symbolism are the representations of water in both the piano music and the orchestral works of Impressionism. Sight and touch are conveyed in auditory terms, and the appearance and feel of water are present in astonishing variety. Fountains and rivers and oceans and waves and spray and rain are depicted in all their aspects; they seem to be everywhere, if not as explicit models, then as unconscious ones.

EMOTIVE RESPONSE

We have been concerned thus far with things and happenings of the external world, with the symbolization of physical entities or of abstract conceptions associated with them. When we turn our attention to the subjective sphere of emotions and feelings and moods, we meet with a relatively complex state of affairs, and there is a welcome tangibleness about our usual point of departure in the properties and effects of music. Musical experience is emotional, and thus music is to some extent comparable to situations that produce emotion. There may be an aesthetic response to music that is characterized by contemplation and noninvolvement, but we also can remain detached and unmoved by events in life apart from music. The possibility of becoming merely a spectator is no argument against the relevance of emotion and feeling in either case.

    Let us not fall into the easy trap here of assuming that because musical and extramusical events both evoke emotions, they must both evoke the same emotions. As a matter of fact, emotions are peculiarly specific to their causes; they are fully dependent upon attendant circumstances. It is no more possible for a musical composition actually to arouse an instance of love or jealousy or sadness than it is for the stimulus of such an emotion to arouse the very emotion produced by a musical composition. The music is the outward circumstance, the specific cause, attached to the peculiar emotion to which it gives rise and to which it lends its detailed characteristics. In a somewhat similar fashion, other situations will produce and color their own special emotions, and these have even been grouped under rubrics that refer really to the causal happenings rather than to the forms and qualities of the emotions themselves. There are tendencies in music toward similar groupings of emotions: opening sonata movements in C minor furnish an example. Also, many nineteenth-century character pieces for piano belonged to what were really families of musical feelings: the external reference even of such a term as *nocturne* is only a slight part of its significance.

The connection of emotions with the more palpable circumstances that bring them about has another important corollary, for it really places the feelings conveyed by music in a world apart: these feelings are not just aroused or excited, nor do they simply follow after the music as other feelings follow their nonartistic stimuli. Instead, musical feelings are molded and patterned by music; they conform to it as closely as the sound of music conforms to musical notation. And unlike the comparatively uncharted feelings outside of art, they are highly differentiated and finely structured – the product of the composer's painstaking formulation.

The musical symbolization of emotions will provide innumerable examples of the dependence of emotion on associated physical manifestations, for music always symbolizes a situation rather than some supposedly abstract emotion; we are really still dealing with events or, at any rate, with their effects. The specific character of emotion does not affect the possibility of symbolism, however, for we cannot deny the existence of resemblances; musical emotions are doubtless similar to others. These similarities are in pressing need of closer examination. Music is not comparable to other events in any immediate way, and since a comparison can thus not be based directly on causes, we must have recourse to feelings and moods themselves. The problem of classification and resemblances here is one that will have to be deferred, but the lesson Hanslick taught has been well learned: one and the same musical passage can symbolize with equal felicitousness two emotions outside of music that appear to be of diametrically opposed natures, at least in respect to their external circumstances.

In Baroque times, many of the melodic and rhythmic patterns known as figures were symbols acting by means of emotive response, for these figures represented not only objects and motions but also emotions, or usually emotional categories, which were called affections. This was a pervasive symbolism, with a long history, a deeply rooted doctrine, and a wide employment. The entities that were represented were static, so that sections of compositions and also whole compositions were dominated by a single figure; there was little attempt to represent developing or changing emotions. The patterns used as symbols had their basis in the evocation of a feeling akin to the generic type being symbolized. A figure representing the affection "sadness," for example, arouses a natural response quite consonant with an instance of extramusical experience that we would normally designate as sad. But the figure, which is as much intellectually apprehended as it is felt, remains a specifically musical-emotional experience, taken only by convention to convey the affection it is said to represent. The distinction is important; we must not suppose that the affection is exactly evoked by a musical pattern, for an abstraction or a category cannot be evoked. In a rationalistic setting, the conventional element of this symbolism becomes dominant. Direct response recedes in favor of symbolism in its restricted sense – knowing, or conscious recognition of meaning. The conventional nature of the figures explains their efficacy even in non-programmatic instrumental music; the familiar patterns carry their affections with them, and emotive response to the music is aside from the point. It is only in the hands of a master that this symbolism escapes the desiccant action of rationalism; Bach's symbols act by arousing feelings and emotions, and they are adapted to the particular emotional situations of their texts. Individualized emotions, rather than abstractions, are symbolized.

Not only melodic patterns but chords, or instruments, or also whole passages or works arouse feelings and moods adaptable to symbolic purposes. Every chord, even every interval, has its own emotional character, strongly dependent, of course, on its context. And each instrument can become symbolic of a characteristic realm of emotional experience: trombones awaken their own feelings and moods, and so do horns, or a flute, or the organ.

Chromaticism is an important example of symbolism that acts largely by means of emotive response. It has a formal basis as well, for chromaticism bears the same relation to diatonic music that unusual events do to normal ones, but this is a relatively minor factor in the effectiveness of the symbols. Whether we read Greek theorists or those of the Renaissance, we learn that chromaticism is the vehicle of the extraordinary and the strongly emotional. It represents a different brand of music running alongside the ordinary diatonic kind. And music itself, from the Renaissance to the nineteenth century, offers abundant proof that this special nature of chromaticism is not merely imagined. In the dramatic madrigal of the sixteenth century, in the *nuove musiche,* in the *lamento,* in the Baroque figures, and still in Mozart and in Wagner, chromatic melody and chromatic harmony are the inevitable symbols of pain and sorrow and ecstasy, and especially of great suffering. Many of the motifs of this symbolism remain unchanged for centuries.

Like chromaticism, any scale or melodic pattern whatever will excite specific feelings and moods, so that it is at least possible that the modes and the melody-types so widely found outside of the Western music of the last few centuries have served symbolic purposes in their application to particular functions and texts.

Symbolism based on emotive response is applicable not only to representing emotions but also to representing physical objects and happenings. Even when our attention goes to emotion itself, we are usually forced to recognize a concrete context: emotional experience is most often embedded in some actual situation. But it may be our declared intention to represent the physical world, and we may then choose to do so indirectly by seeking to duplicate the emotions it arouses. This is the route of what is often called poetic or subjective program music. Physical entities can be symbolized by imitating the sounds they produce, by copying them structurally, or by creating a heterosensory equivalent; but symbolism can also be "more an expression of feeling than painting." A natural scene not only has objective characteristics which can be copied consciously or reproduced according to the laws of sensation; it evokes feelings and moods as well, and these can be approximated by our response to music. Still more in conformance to Beethoven's precept than the *Pastoral Symphony* itself are the symphonic poems of Liszt and Debussy and Delius, which present the external world through its impact on our internal life, rarely seeking either detailed description or detailed narration.

A procedure the exact opposite of this will make possible the representation of emotions by almost any symbolic method, for psychological states are not only outcomes of physical situations, but usually produce physical expressions of their own, such as sighs or hesitant steps or determined activity – objects accessible to pictorial types of symbolism.

Besides the representation of external emotions by musical experience, music appears to contain an emotional symbolism within itself which is not a matter of choice but is invariably present, for the sheer sound of music is a symbol of musical experience,[4] somewhat as musical notation is always a symbol of what we hear. Only original and primitive reactions are totally without symbolic reference, but every human experience is complex enough to contain internal symbolisms, and music is certainly much more than a patterned surface of sounds. A symbol must direct us somehow to another phenomenon, which we call its meaning, and we can guess that music conforms to this requirement, if only because we have come across examples that sound mistaken or meaningless. Music is symbolic when it makes sense – when it produces a response that is true to native or acquired ways of feeling. Also, it is only on the basis of symbolism that we can account for the causal aspect of musical development: there is no reason for any one historical trend or occurrence instead of another if the sounds of music have no significance.

When we consider the relation between musical emotions and the sound of music to be symbolic, we do not thereby admit that every stimulus is a symbol. There still must be a re-presentation: the object of a symbol must have some degree of independence. Now even if musical experience is peculiar to music, it is not completely dependent upon the particular musical work that produces it, for besides their agreement with the makeup of our feelings, musical materials have a history and an environment; they are not chance combinations of tones. The sound of music that is removed from our cultural tradition is not readily symbolic for us in the way that we are considering, because the experience it creates has no separateness, no past connections, but we are quite able to see significance behind every turn of phrase in Bach and Mozart.

Thus, apart from the intentional symbolism of external emotions, music possesses an internal and natural emotional symbolism, and this will become prominent when music draws heavily upon existing material, just as it will tend to vanish in extremely novel works. Recent times have been especially occupied with the resuscitation of past musical expression: Stravinsky in particular will don the robes of Pergolesi or of Bach or of Tchaikovsky, or he will assume the tone of the Viennese waltz or of American vaudeville music, convincingly representing all these styles with symbolically charged fragments of melody or ornamentation. But this historically minded symbolism is by no means restricted to modern times: the world of Beethoven's Ninth Symphony is invoked by numerous nineteenth-century composers, in the case of Mahler through an unfortunately large-scale appropriation of material; also the sacred vocal polyphony of the sixteenth century was continually imitated in later times; and the sixteenth century itself often reproduced earlier styles. There may be a part-for-whole symbolism here just with respect to the sound of the music, but the important point is that this type of borrowing emphasizes the symbolism of musical emotions by what is presented to hearing. All imported material, especially when it is the product of previous elaboration, is a ready-made symbol of the specifically musical feelings it embodies; it is symbolic even if symbolism is not its express purpose.

Painting and poetry also possess an internal emotional symbolism, but they usually have an external reference in addition. This relation to reality is not unimportant: only because music is unhampered by external connections is it able to achieve its direct expressiveness of our inner life. Yet music is not completely different from other arts: it may not primarily reveal the impact of the outer world upon our feelings, but it is concerned with past music – not only with specific compositions, but with the whole heritage of material – and this preformed matter plays the part in music that the real world plays in literature and the representative visual arts.

Language offers still other parallels of the internal symbolisms that we find in music. Written language is analogous to written music. And just as speech is chiefly a vehicle of propositional thought, so the sound of music primarily conveys feeling. Also, the ideas presented by language are colored by the sensible material in which they are realized; they may even be inconceivable without it; and this is equally true of musical emotions. Yet music can hardly be about our emotional life in general, for then why should it happen to be tonal? Why tone if we are not dealing with a specifically tonal experience? But then why is logical thought expressed in words when it is not inherently verbal? The role of words in reasoning is apparently comparable with the role of music in feeling; it is certainly incorrect that we cannot think or feel in other terms than these, and the only matter that calls for explanation is the eminent suitability of language and music to their tasks.

Unfortunately, the purely musical symbolism of emotions that we have been considering has given rise to the mistaken idea that music always represents emotions as they are known elsewhere. Now in the conceptions of music current in the early seventeenth century, for example, the idea of representing emotions and feelings belongs to the field of vocal music, and more especially to the field of dramatic vocal music, where it is clearly most meaningful. It is one thing to talk about the representation of feelings when they are expressed by a protagonist of dramatic action and quite a different thing to talk about representing feelings in the relative vacuum of nonprogrammatic instrumental music, for feelings have to be pinned onto somebody. The loss of concreteness and the lack of clarity begin when a specifically dramatic doctrine is expanded into a general principle and applied to other kinds of music. We can continue to give meaning to the idea in any vocal music, for the feelings involved can belong to the author of the text; and even in instrumental program music it should be evident that the music symbolizes our reaction or the composer's reaction to whatever extramusical matter is described by the title. But what are the external emotions represented in a sonata? And whose emotions are they?

This idea of the universality of emotional symbolism is unique: no one ever maintains that music is always saying something about external events or physical objects, and yet when emotions are concerned, programmatic music and nonprogrammatic music cease to be distinguished clearly. There is little more reason for believing that the emotional character of music inevitably points to some extramusical emotion than there is for believing that music consists exclusively in a representation of sounds known in other connections or for believing that musical forms are necessarily reminiscent of other structures. Emotive response is no doubt more closely attached to the sound of music than is recognition of form or a synesthetic reaction, but even if feeling were an essential constituent of musical experience, this experience would not thereby become symbolic of any other. Yet the confusion arises precisely because music has a sensuous appeal; we always are able to respond to it emotionally, and the composer tends to test his ideas and formulations in terms of this response. The joys and griefs of his life are not represented in his music, but this does not put an end to the question of emotional symbolism, for it is also true that his specific response to music is the very touchstone by which he selects and organizes his ideas, and this process can accurately be described as symbolic. The essential point is that this symbolism is internal and not programmatic. Musical feelings have their own character: they are not the feelings we know and roughly name in our experience outside of music, and they do not lead in themselves to ideas or concepts of other feelings. Thus music may be an emotional experience and still not represent emotional contexts belonging to other areas of life, for the emotions it formulates are not identical with those accompanying extramusical experience, nor does the one kind necessarily remind us of the other.

PRIOR ASSOCIATION

The symbols considered thus far have all been "natural" ones: where they have not actually been part of their objects, they have borne some likeness to them. In the case of imitation of sound, this likeness was a factual one, apparent to sensation. In the case of formal resemblance, the likeness was a question of analogy, of conscious relationship. In the case of intersensory qualities, the symbol was not like its object by way of perception or of understanding, but invoked a more primitive likeness, subconsciously apprehended. In the case of emotive response, the likeness was a felt likeness, even eluding analysis.

Standing in contrast to these types, symbolism based on prior association is an extrinsic affair, unconcerned with any kind of likeness. It is the importation into a musical composition of musical material that through past use has come to represent something, be it happening, emotion, or abstract conception. Just how the imported material has acquired its symbolic significance is a matter of some consequence, for if the symbolism is a natural one, we have no need of the prior association. The material brings its meaning with it, then, but it does so by no internal suitability to its symbolic role, nor by any resemblance between symbol and object, but purely by the fact of association. This is a very general method of symbolizing, as easily able to convey abstract notions as events or feelings.

It is chiefly on the basis of associative symbolism that symbolism in general is often denied importance in music because it is thought to be at odds with beauty: we have symbolism, it is said, only when our response to music is not a natural one and we are concerned with what the music means rather than with simply enjoying it. But the fundamental character of symbolism at once reveals how limited an idea this is; the vast range of symbolic experience makes an occasional conflict with musical interests relatively unimportant.

Vocal music and dance music and liturgical music are all somewhat similar in the way they are able to become symbolic by association, for functional music in general, when it is divorced from its use, will frequently recall the whole occasion of which it is part. Thus a melody to which words have been sung will tend to remind us of these words, dance music will represent the dance it has accompanied, and the music used in any rite or ceremony can become symbolic of that ceremony. This will happen even where there is little suitability of the music to its use, by the mere fact of association: functional music is everywhere symbolic of its function, for one of the fundamental means by which symbols come into being is a compression or substitution in which part stands for whole. Of course there are often connections between symbol and object other than association; the symbol must show some evidence of its use, although not to the same degree that it does in an internal symbolism. Some formal similarity, for example, is at times inevitable: the rhythmic patterns of a dance and its music cannot fail to resemble each other, and the structures of a poem and its musical setting must somehow be related.

A symbolic technique based on prior association must assume a knowledge of the particular connection that is being recalled. Most listeners will associate the melody that they hear toward the end of Schumann's *Two Grenadiers* with the idea of a victorious France, but other allusions are not so easily recognized. Bach will occasionally import a chorale melody into a work in order to symbolize the ideas of its text. Such an imported melody, or melodic fragment, may appear in the course of a recitative, sung to other words than the original; or it may be performed on an instrument in the midst of a formal movement distinct from the chorale in musical material. Usually the foreign nature of the chorale melody, and the manner of its announcement, makes us at once aware of a symbolic intent; but if we lack knowledge of the chorale text, the symbolism fails to achieve its true effect. Within music itself, a melodic quotation will be an associative symbol of the musical work from which it is taken; but here also we must know the association to grasp the meaning.

Keys appear to exemplify a symbolism based upon prior association, for they seem to define musical contexts, to represent orbits of musical-emotional experience. They are symbolic because they refer to some previously existent entity: the use of a particular key summons up a specific emotional field previously existing, even if it is one that was created within the sphere of music itself. Thus the choice of a key by a composer symbolizes the encompassing mood within which his work is to unfold. Certainly the major keys have a completely different gamut of expressive possibilities from the minor, but here we are dealing with a phenomenon found in any modal system: there is an objective difference in the modes, and the symbolism proceeds by means of emotive response. But beyond this modal distinction, E minor was different from A minor or D minor for the Classic and Romantic composers of symphonies and piano sonatas, and every key seems to have had its individual significance (varying somewhat, of course, with the composer). The keys of Mozart's operas are allocated with their specific expressive worlds in mind, and Wagner chooses keys with even more care for their emotional import.

The keys offer different technical possibilities to the various instruments, and they may even possess traces of characteristic melody-types. But while these factors may have played some part in the development of specific meanings, they are not a complete explanation: the symbolism of the keys continues to present a problem because the keys are patently very much alike and are even indistinguishable by the average listener. Furthermore, historical changes in pitch imply that one key could become acoustically identical with another one not far distant, and therefore vastly different in connotation. The significance of the keys can thus hardly be due to pitch; and its origin is really not to be sought in the nature of the keys, which is so largely constant from key to key, but in the nature of music. For the symbolic heritage of the keys is merely one aspect of a traditional body of material: it is the joint result of the influence of past works and the prerequisites of creative thinking. A composer cannot write music that is novel in too many respects, and whatever material he starts with will carry with it some suggestion or re-presentation of the experiences it has produced in the past; it is symbolic at the outset because of its previous associations.

To the cultural historian, association will tend to make all music symbolic of a historical period, or of a world outlook, or of some particular contemporary expression of art or science or philosophy. It is a matter of considerable import whether this symbolism is just associative, and whether it is not also due to common emotional character, or to attributes identical in different senses, or to formal resemblances, or to some other natural relationship or likeness between music and its companion phenomena. If such connections do exist, then music is really a source of historical insight and information for a historian able to see its significance. Musical structure would seem especially likely to reveal fundamental ways of organizing material, and thus fundamental modes of thought.

We should not leave the types of symbolism that have been described without realizing that they are no more than an inventory of possibilities of which only a characteristic group actually exists at any time. An outlook that is objective and rational, for example, will make symbolism a deliberate procedure, a matter of conscious comparison and analogy which seeks out formal correspondence. In such a climate, even symbols with an intersensory basis will be treated in a formal way, and symbols originally dependent upon emotive response will exist only if they have become conventional. On the other hand, a subjective orientation can make even structural similarity an affair of direct heterosensory response. Symbolic types are all servants of historical factors.

But besides this varying selective action of history, tradition exerts a constant transforming influence upon symbols. Universally operative, it has the same effect upon all symbolic types, deadening their original mode of activity so that they all run down to the level of convention, where symbols are simply known to have certain meanings and there is no awareness of a *tertium comparationis* or a connecting path between symbol and object. The symbols might as well be arbitrarily assigned, just as words appear to be when they are not informed with poetic insight. To consider conventional symbols a separate type, however, is to miss the principle behind our typology: the symbols must still have some basis, and if it is no other, this basis will be simply association.

Another qualification to which our scheme is subject is that the types of symbolism it proposes often do not completely describe the path connecting symbol and object. Since music is almost always powerless to represent a specific external object, it can only point in a general direction, or rather, in several directions, the different responses it simultaneously creates all remaining unconsummated by definite objects. The object of a musical symbolization must be independently represented or presented – by a program or by dramatic action or by scenery or by words. But as soon as we specify this intended object, the music reveals unsuspected richness of significance. Each of its aspects develops a concrete and appropriate reference, and every side of our experience appears to bear on the one representation. The independence of the experience vanishes, but by that very fact the door is opened to innumerable symbolic relationships. For although musical symbols acquire their extramusical meaning through some explicit object, they will make their own use of their new concreteness and, instead of referring to this object directly, may become figurative and express a related image or idea or mood. At times we may be able to distinguish two objects of the symbolism, implicit and explicit: the melodic motion may clearly symbolize waves, for example, when the text refers to the sea. We should then have a concealed figurative relation complementing the musical symbol, and the complete process would consist of a chain of symbols. Similarly, hidden but literal figures may be added to any musical symbols, all of which are themselves figures of one sort or another.

The most striking difference between our analysis and what it analyzes, however, is a kind of simultaneity which leaves no part of musical symbolism unaffected: neither the people involved, nor the symbols, nor the objects represented, nor the types of symbolism.

For one thing, at the very moment that the listener is transmuting his auditory impressions into musical and extrinsic feelings and events somewhat like those incorporated in sound by the composer, the performers are deriving from the notation a more or less close approximation of the music as it was conceived. At the same time, some of the listeners may be finding their experience informative with respect to the place and times in which the music had its origin.

Also, the very symbolism we are considering is really a composite rather than a simple phenomenon: music simultaneously presents us with melodies and rhythms and harmonies, with tone-colors and spatial arrangements and forms and dynamics, even with two or three melodies at once. And this still omits its development in time, which can increase the number of its elements almost without limit. All these aspects are interrelated, of course, but they are all independently capable of symbolic reference, so that a great number of factors or components may easily be present in any example of musical symbolism. Thus a musical symbol actually tends to be a group of symbols with members presented both simultaneously and successively.

Again, the categories into which we can divide the various objects of musical symbols are not sharply separated: emotions and moods are generally the concomitants of physical situations, and they are often attached to abstract notions as well. Abstractions have their eventual basis in concrete experience, both factual and emotional. And music itself, often an object of symbolization, is both a physical manifestation and a sensuous experience.

Finally, we do not respond to music in a compartmentalized way – here emotionally, there intellectually, another time synesthetically, and so on – nor does the composer write it, or the performer perform it, according to any single abstract mode of conception or comprehension. Instead, a musical experience will consist in a certain amount of sensuousness, some degree of apprehension of structure, at least an occasional awareness of the past associations of the musical material, and possibly also a correlation of notation and sound, or a realization of the activity of instruments, or tactual and visual projections of the music, or even a recognition of imitated sounds. The makeup and the configuration of the experience will differ at different times, both in history and in our private development, but it cannot exactly conform to an analytical type. The basic illustration of this complexity of response is found in the circumstance that music can scarcely avoid evoking emotions, whatever other response it may be calling forth at the time. In this characteristic, music is not unlike any other sphere of human experience: most visual and tactual and intellectual experience has its emotional side; events and objects and concepts have their emotional implications; and language frequently points to the emotions connected with external action or conveys feelings through their physical manifestation in behavior. Thus there is very often a double burden imposed upon music that seeks to portray physical events or abstract ideas, for it must represent feelings as well; and the texts with which vocal music deals are almost always an expression of feelings as well as an objective symbolism. The common areas of musical symbolism – dramatic action, natural scenes, descriptive and lyric poetry – have a nature quite in accord with that of music, and they are well able to make use of the many-sidedness of musical response. The emotional components of events are especially attractive and accessible to music no matter what it sets out to symbolize. For although music contains an internal symbolism of emotions, its own emotional qualities will easily fasten onto represented things and become specific symbols of the feelings connected with external happenings. Whatever resemblance our musical experience may bear to other matters is made explicit by the outside reference.

NOTES

From *The Musical Quarterly* 39, no.4 (1953): 554–75, by permission of Oxford University Press. This article was first presented as a paper during the 1952 meeting of the American Musicological Society at Yale University.

1. A detailed discussion of this point is contained in the author's microfilmed doctoral dissertation, *Music and Space: A Study in the Philosophy of Music,* Columbia University, 1952.

2. The nature of symbolism is very well explained by Alfred North Whitehead in *Symbolism, Its Meaning and Effect* (New York 1927).

3. The musical tones also represent the trumpet and the horn themselves, and in turn, the associated silver and gold colors of these instruments become visual symbols acting together with the intersensory ones. Even this simple example reveals the complexity of musical symbolism.

4. Arnold Schering and Susanne K. Langer are two outstanding investigators of musical symbolism who seem to subscribe to a conception of this sort. Schering's numerous articles on musical symbolism deserve mention as the most valuable and suggestive contribution to the field, even though toward the end of his life he permitted his imagination to run wild.

2

Spatial Perception and Physical Location as Factors in Music

1. THE SPATIAL CAPABILITIES OF HEARING

I T MAY NOT seem possible for spatial perception to play any role in an auditory art, but hearing is not the only sense involved in music, and – surprising as it may seem – even hearing is capable of providing considerable spatial information on its own account.

When sound energy reaches us from some object, there are differences in what the two ears receive, and these differences serve as cues to the direction of the object. With a source somewhat to the right, for example, the energy will reach our right ear a little while before it reaches our left. Also, the high-frequency components of the energy will be more intense at the right ear, for the head blocks these off somewhat from the left.

These binaural differences are not dependent to any great extent upon the distance of a source, so that our knowledge of distance – a knowledge that we can secure monaurally – must be based upon other cues. We know the distance of a source because the sound energy it emits suffers certain changes as it travels to our ear.[1] Some of these changes are extremely subtle and are restricted to transient and impulsive components of the sound. But it is certainly obvious that there is a decrease in intensity and also that there is a change in the intensity pattern, since high frequencies and abrupt components are more liable to be lost. What is more, sounds of high frequency and initially great intensity will reach us sooner than others, and the farther we are from the source, the more out of step they will be.

The perceived characteristics of sound that change with distance are by and large quite different from those due to varying dynamics in musical performance. When the effect of a distant trumpet is called for in Beethoven's *Fidelio*, for example, it is not sufficient for the performer to play the passage softly; he must remove himself some distance from the singers and orchestra in order that the quality of the trumpet tone be the desired one. *Forte* and *piano* will never be mistaken for near and distant sources, but still it is dynamics which creates a convincing near and far in music; a loud melodic line will unmistakably stand forth from its softer accompaniment, and when we call this accompaniment a "background" or say that a passage (especially a repeated motif) "fades away," our feeling is due to a history of literal spatial experience.

Nevertheless, when we are not dealing with the feeling of motion brought about by the strongly suggestive effect of a motif repeated at different degrees of loudness, softness can even suggest nearness, especially if it is accompanied by high pitch. Here it is the small volume, the fineness, of our sensations that gives us the impression of nearness, for only large objects can be perceived from a distance. And similarly, musical detail, in the shape of complexity and speed, is readily associated with nearness. But in these things we are no longer dealing with actual localization.

To a degree, however, pitch does represent a clue to the distance of a source, since it is less likely that high-frequency sounds will succeed in reaching us from great distances, and we do naturally expect, in consequence, that distant sounds will be low or dull. We know the nearness of a thunderclap from the rumble of distant thunder partly by the difference in the frequency structure of the sounds, and it is exactly this difference, apart from the difference in durational characteristics, that is reflected in the very words *clap* and *rumble.* The suggestiveness of pitch in music, though, is scarcely determined by this consideration, for the relationship can easily be obscured and even reversed; for example, high tones can suggest physical height and therefore great distance rather than nearness. At any rate, a decrease in loudness will decidedly take precedence over pitch in the suggestion of distance.

Auditory space perception is of course not limited to localization or the perception of position, but like vision, is capable of a number of more complex types of apprehension. Hearing is quite able to inform us about the motion of an object, for example. This type of perception forms a counterpart to the visual perception of motion, except that in vision the field is usually filled with objects which act as a reference against which the shape of the path can be measured as well as the speed with which it is traced. But in the case of paths traced by a light in otherwise complete darkness, the resemblance to hearing becomes striking. This resemblance extends to the details of the perceptions: forms tend to approach the circle, for example, and they manifest distortion depending upon the power of our perception in various directions.[2] A circle traced by a buzzer in the dark appears to be an ellipse, wider than it is tall, for our ability to determine direction is greatest in the horizontal plane.

The true auditory counterpart of vision would be the simultaneous perception of different positions, and we can indeed achieve an awareness of constellations of objects by means of hearing which is comparable to the perception of vision. Our world as revealed by hearing alone is full of external – and distant – objects which are various in location. We can convince ourselves of this at nearly any time by merely closing our eyes and taking stock of what we perceive by means of vibratory and auditory sensations alone. Just as in vision, there is the general effect of a variety of objects differing in location, while we reserve the power to single out whichever we choose and determine its position more accurately. Although there exist no scientific measures of unaided auditory ability in this respect, there is no reason why experiments cannot be devised easily to supply the objective basis we lack. The only apparent difficulty would be to eliminate the information given by vibration.

Auditory perception of shape and of size has practically never received treatment or even mention, and understandably so, for it cannot be pretended that unaided hearing has much ability in these respects. With regard to the shape or form of an object, the sound emitted gives little information directly. In most musical instruments, the object as a whole does not vibrate, so that our perception of its shape must depend upon its relationship to the actual source. The resonant properties of a soundboard or of a quantity of enclosed air are not very informative, and accordingly, our auditory perception of the shape of a string instrument is based entirely on inferential knowledge. The picture is much the same with other musical instruments: we must first infer from the quality of the sound that we are hearing a particular instrument, and it is really by this means alone that we know the details of its shape. If a sound source vibrates as a whole – as it does in idiophones and in most nonmusical sources – the situation is only slightly improved, and we still scarcely can secure information as to its shape, beyond the mere knowledge of regular or irregular form. Generally, then, whatever vague idea we may derive of the shape of an unfamiliar source by hearing depends upon the constitution of the sound emitted, musical sounds and tones indicating simple, regular shapes, and noiselike sounds indicating more complicated shapes, but even this relationship holds only in the instances when the source object is identical or closely allied with the actual sound producer.

In contrast to what we must therefore consider to be our practically complete inability to judge the form of a vibrating object, auditory perception of size appears to be possible within limits. The sound waves from an extensive source apparently exhibit no properties very different from those of the waves emitted by a smaller source. The shape of the wave front will differ, tending on the whole to be less curved with larger sources, but our perception is based on the information gathered by two point receivers, and this type of reception obviously can give little clue as to wave-front shape: a given time or intensity difference is dependent only to a negligible extent upon this characteristic. Thus our specifically space-perceiving mechanism remains unaffected by the size of a source, and size perception must rest on clues of another kind. Its basis actually can be found in certain intrinsic properties of sound.

The normal physical properties of materials are such that large objects have long periods of vibration. In addition, the rapid acceleration of large objects that would be demanded by a high-frequency forced vibration or an abrupt motion calls for an excessive amount of force. Therefore in general it is physically impossible for large sources to produce high-frequency sounds or sounds with strong high-frequency components. Even in the case of impulsive sounds, we cannot expect the high-pitched click we can produce by snapping one fingernail past another to be produced by thunder. The source event in thunder is too extensive for such frequency components; the large volume of air simply cannot be moved rapidly enough. Of course, if we are at a considerable distance from thunder or from cannon fire, high-frequency components are absorbed in travel before they reach us; but even when we are quite near, the sound furnishes an unmistakable index to the size of the source. The difference in size between a popgun and a cannon is at once apparent from the sounds they produce; and the regular gradation in size of orchestral instruments in accordance with their pitch indicates that size perception may even be capable of measurable distinctions. The scale of a musical instrument is in fact no less than a tonal yardstick of a series of lengths.

Whatever the speed of motion, however, and whatever the frequency, forced or free, it takes a good deal of energy to set large objects moving or vibrating and to maintain their vibration, so that large sources are limited not only in respect of the pitch of the resulting sensations, but also in respect of the loudness of these sensations. Thus loudness would seem to furnish another clue to the size of a source, large sources being in general incapable of producing loud sounds. But with large sources there usually go quantities of power sufficient to excite them. In practice, therefore, we judge by pitch alone, for loudness is grounded only in considerations of energy, which is widely variable, and in fact widely varied in musical practice, while pitch has not only this basis, but the more intimate connection with size determined by natural frequency. Thus loudness is evidently a poor indicator, but pitch seems to furnish a reliable cue – our only auditory one – in the perception of size. It is a datum that is not intrinsically spatial, but one whose connection with size is so fundamental that it does not vary or fail to be significant.

2. THE INVOLVEMENT OF OTHER SENSES

Although up to this point we have treated hearing as an isolated mode of apprehension, it is really a complex activity involving more than one sense. It is even bound up with bodily orientation, for this is achieved in part with the aid of external perceptions and it provides in turn the condition for accurate perception. In the case of our reaction to an unexpected sound, for example, we turn suddenly to confront the source in an action that is at once both bodily orientation and perception, and whose object is the full deployment of both hearing and vision. The auditory perception of spatial characteristics is auditory only because the ear leads the way, not because it acts alone. The ear itself, as a double organ, appears to present concrete evidence of the connection between orientation and perception, while its intimate connection with the musculature of the eye is the strongest indication of the cooperative nature of perception itself. The examination of a hypothetical act of "pure" audition is doubtless of some usefulness as an analytical method, but it contains the grave danger of distorting the true situation, for the ear may not act in isolation in the same way that it acts in its normal context of cooperative activity and organic adjustment.

It would therefore seem to be most valuable to form a picture of auditory spatial perception as it actually occurs: to determine what activities enter into the process, and to understand the role of each. From this point of view, head movements are of central importance. They show auditory perception to be an activity rather than a passive reception of information. It is the immobility of the ears which necessitates head motions and which at the same time reveals the ears to be less adapted to spatial perception than the eyes, whose fine and precise mobility offers convincing testimony of their great concern with space. Furthermore, the movable ancestors of our ears indicate that in auditory localization we are dealing with what is almost a vestigial function of hearing. Our ears largely play the part of sentinels in calling our attention to activity which needs investigation; the more exhaustive determination of the happening or object is reserved for the keener perceptive power of the eyes. The outlying parts of the retina play a similar role for the fovea: the image of motion or of a bright source falling upon the peripheral part of the retina acts as a stimulus calling forth a motion of the eyes toward the object and often a motion of the head also. The function of this reflex action is to facilitate the investigation of the object by causing its image to fall upon the most sensitive part of the retina, just as by head motion we bring a continuously or repeatedly sounding auditory object directly in front of us where its perception seems to be more adequately accomplished, even in terms of hearing alone. Thus our turning toward a source is calculated to bring our ears into maximum use: they are most sensitive in almost every respect, including that of localization, when they inspect a source that is straight ahead.[3]

It has been claimed in both visual and auditory perception that these motions serve as an index of the location of the object in question; that we come to know its position by means of the motion necessary to bring it into clear view or into clear "auditory view." This is even turned into the thesis that motion is essential to our knowledge of the spatial layout of our environment. There is much to be said for the idea, for it is at once apparent that a motionless observer will be poorly informed as to the existence of objects beyond those in his immediate frontal field of view, and our so-called knowledge of space is no more than an awareness of objects, or often merely of perceptions to be secured as the result of such-and-such activity. After all, alignment of the body for equilateral stimulation is probably as old as bilateral symmetry, and there is no doubt that hearing is a direct descendant – an orienting motion. Thus localization even as a passive perception might seem to involve adumbrations of such orienting motions. The existence of actual motion sensations in static localization is of course not the case; our perception is simply that of an object in a particular place, and we cannot countenance the idea of a sensation that is too weak to be sensed. It is true, however, that we assume the aid of motion in bringing about the efficacy of binaural differences and of other properties of sound stimuli as spatial cues; the development of the implicit behavior of static localization from an earlier explicit pattern is quite logical.

When we locate a source of sound by turning toward it, there may be more involved in the process than a large-scale single motion of the head. Often there is a series of rapid and successively smaller motions of which we are not aware,[4] but which constitute increasingly accurate adjustments of position to secure equal bilateral stimulation. Although these adjustments are made with respect to a particular object rather than to gravity, the whole activity is no less literally one of orientation.

Besides enabling us to localize sources of sound by means of binaural equalization, head motions provide data that give the location of a source without the necessity for us to face it directly.[5] The reason for this is that as we move our head, the binaural differences in the sound stimulus change, and we can tell by how they change and by how fast they change just where the source of sound is. In this process, cues from our eyes and our equilibrial organs and from the muscles involved in the head motion all act collectively as a base against which the changes in the binaural data are measured. Thus the change of binaural differences becomes a cue supplementing binaural differences themselves, and we doubtless engage in complex exploratory motions of the head just for the purpose of securing this supplementation.

Head motions are especially important because static localization is often ambiguous, and it is chiefly capable of right-left discrimination. Movements of the head enable us to distinguish more readily between up and down and front and back, and in general they permit us to select out of many possible directions for the sound source the one that is correct.

The possibility that parts of the inner ear other than the cochlea play some role in the localization of sound sources has received a remarkable amount of attention, and indeed, it is natural that where a spatial ability is in question, the organs of equilibrium should be considered. Several isolated clinical observations have tended to support the necessity of normal vestibular functioning for auditory localization, and thus to indicate in a general way that our equilibrial organs play a part in localization. Objections suggest themselves at once, however. For one thing, vestibular malfunction may involve a defective cochlea; and for another, the observations in question are not very numerous, and unfortunately quite haphazard in the measurement of localization ability. But even if we were to demonstrate that an impaired equilibrial functioning affected localization adversely, we should still not have touched upon the real problem of determining the precise role of the vestibular organs.

After bodily rotation, we are subject to systematic errors in auditory localization, and this effect seems to provide another general indication that localization and equilibration are connected. But "auditory nystagmus" – an illusory motion of sound sources that is quite similar in form to its visual counterpart – may simply show that hearing conforms to the dictates of the eyes rather than to those of the equilibrial organs.

Whenever head motions are involved in localization, of course, the equilibrial organs must participate in controlling the activity, coordinating the movements of muscles and providing a base that gives meaning to changing auditory data. This has been mentioned in part above, and it hardly requires demonstration. But going beyond this normal participation in kinetic localization, many direct approaches to the problem are based on the theory that the equilibrial organs are sound receptors, responding to vibration stimuli, and although this type of theory has been the center of a surprisingly large body of controversy, it does appear that the saccule, although not the utricle or the semicircular canals, responds to body-conducted vibrations, and that it may not have an equilibrial function at all.[6] Sounds of great intensity produce involuntary reactions – reflex motions of the head and the eyes – of the same type that occur when our equilibrium is disturbed, and they can also produce dizziness, so that we can almost credit the feeling of being "carried away by music" with literalness. These effects on the center of motor coordination entail a mode of response basic to lower levels of development but relatively unimportant in man, coming into play only exceptionally in response to abrupt stimuli which may represent danger, and for the most part supplanted by a deliberate localization activity which involves higher neural pathways – as our response to music and speech does in general. Thus primitive vestibular responses to sound appear to be only peripheral in the complete picture of human response to sound phenomena – they occur only with intense sounds and where there is a question only of direct reaction – but it is not impossible that they have a bearing on the effect of music, just as loud sounds do in general. There appears to be continual recognition by perceptive listeners of an elemental background which is a constant accompaniment of the various higher levels of musical significance, and which always threatens to take the upper hand in the listening experience. Dynamics would seem to occupy a peculiar place in music; sudden loudness may be frightening in a very literal way, and crescendos may threaten to overpower us by injuring our hearing. It is a matter of common experience that if we reduce the loudness of music (as we can most readily in a phonograph or radio), we affect our response critically; the music becomes less demanding, it loses the greater force of its hold on our emotions, and can become rather insipid altogether, even though objectively the formal nature has remained unchanged. Indeed, human response to loud sounds is a fear response – one of the few active even with the undeveloped state of the nervous system with which we are born – and the pattern of adult reaction to loud sounds appears to be indistinguishable from any reaction of fear.

It has even been claimed that motor responses to sound vary with the intensity and frequency of the sound, and the attractive but extremely fanciful idea presents itself that there may be some indissoluble connection between melody and motion – that every melodic pattern may have its specific motor reflexes,[7] as it does seem to have in certain pathological cases. It is tempting at any rate to attribute the effectiveness and the spatial outcomes of rhythm to an effect of sound on the equilibrial organs, and we should certainly arrive at the explanation of many important phenomena in this way. If the pressure of the endolymph in the equilibrial labyrinth maintains muscular tone, it is only a small step to the conclusion that impulsive stimuli may activate the muscles. It would then become apparent why rhythm is counted among the primitive elements in the effect of music and why the response to marked rhythm is so compulsive. Here, perhaps, is the highly welcome key to the reflexlike beating and foot-tapping that accompanies march music and dance music; and here, also, may be the basis of the more contrived patterns of dancing. Even the kinesthesis experienced in response to music, which is often so subtle and so involuntary, would find a direct and largely unsuspected solution. And we should be able to account for the testimony of primitive music that the original meanings and effects of music are motor rather than auditory – a matter of participation and overt reaction combined. The whole spatial suggestiveness due to rhythm – which music does undoubtedly possess – is offered an extremely attractive explanation in the vestibular efficacy of sound, but in default of decisive evidence, what may become fact must remain a tentative hypothesis. We are certainly not entitled to close the door to this type of consideration, nor in general to dispose of the antecedents of musical experience in pat fashion by insisting on the novelty and autonomy of music. Of course music represents a level of experience that is markedly different from practical response, and that must be considered in its own terms; but we shall never arrive at a full understanding of its place if we sever it from the rest of human experience and from its context of organic reaction. We must recognize its distinctive character; but its nature is partly constituted by any meaning sound may have, however removed and unrelated this may seem. That is why the distinction between the psychology of tone and the psychology of music is not to be emphasized too strongly; it may be an aid to analysis, but it should not be taken to imply an irrelevance to music of the effects of tone and of the results of experimentation.

Although there can be no quarrel with the direct vestibular effect of sound, this effect is evidently not the foundation of everyday auditory localization, for localization normally is more deliberate, it occurs more with the help of conscious mechanisms, than such an explanation would demand. But even if vestibular reactions play no part in localization, the possibility remains that the equilibrial organs may inform us about direction by the very means that the cochlea uses. Binaural differences in saccule stimulation could act like binaural differences in the stimulation of the cochlea. The mechanism of bilateral equalization can certainly be applied as readily to the saccule as to the cochlea; perhaps more readily, for it concerns localization as a motor response. Applying this conception to the saccule, of course, seems to add nothing radically different to the conventional picture of localization, but it does fit in well with the vestibular context of equilibrial function and of motor adjustment, and at the same time it conforms to the probability that the saccule responds to vibration. Binaural differences in labyrinthine stimulation enter into orientation reactions – in any curvilinear motion of the body, for example, labyrinthine pressures become unequal – and there is no reason why time or intensity differences in stimulation by vibration should not furnish cues in the case of localization. Such a situation, however, would suggest that localization has a dual nature, and interestingly enough, this does seem to be the case. There appears to be a localization reaction in specific response to intense sounds, and especially to abrupt or noiselike ones – a reaction which occurs reflexly and which partakes of the nature of bodily orientation in its adaptive character and its immediacy. Opposed to this stands the more usual process of localization, occurring in response to all sounds except those of startling nature, and more under conscious direction. The neural connections of the saccule and of the cochlea are such as to suit them precisely to these two tasks, and the evolution of ear neurology shows that a degeneration of subcortical neural pathways accompanies the decreasing importance of the reflex type of localization. Vision continues to participate reflexly even in more conscious localization, its role insured by the persistence of subcortical neural connections to the eye muscles, and the two kinds of localization possess a common element in the goal of investigation and visual fixation.

Along with the development of the special vibratory receptors of the ear, our body has retained a general sensitivity to vibration,[8] and this sensitivity must certainly be included in a summary view of auditory perception. Indeed, it is even capable of becoming more than a practical aid: we know from the experience of deaf people that the vibratory sense makes possible a kind of musical enjoyment where hearing is totally absent, although we should do wrong to credit this enjoyment with the refined aesthetic character and the great subtlety of audition. Both solid-borne and airborne vibrations affect the sense of vibration, but as in the case of the saccule, solid-borne vibrations seem to be of chief importance. At any rate, the vibratory sense is a distance sense, like hearing and vision, and it acts in intimate conjunction with hearing in revealing the direction of a vibrating object; even careful observers will tend to attribute to hearing what they come to know by vibratory reception. We can exclude hearing, however, and any two parts of our body in contact with a solid object – our feet on the floor or our hands resting on the arms of a chair or the top of a table – will permit a surprisingly accurate determination of direction. Vibratory sensations must also be of some help in the size perception that we usually take as auditory: vibrations are more likely to be communicated to us through the ground in the case of extensive sources because these are more often in contact with the ground; and vibrations are more likely to reach us through the air in the case of small sources because of their greater intensity. What is more, different parts of the body may respond preferentially to different frequencies of vibration, and because frequency is an index of size, this bodily localization may indirectly point to the size of the vibrating source: sharp noises (proceeding in general from smaller objects) often seem to make our head vibrate, and we feel low-frequency sounds in the middle of our body.

That vision participates in auditory perception has already been mentioned, and indeed, vision is so much our dominant sense that it never can be completely set aside. In everyday affairs, the evidence of our eyes is virtually uncontested by hearing, and this is only a consequence of the superior utility and precision of vision and the extreme lability of auditory perception. If we invert or dislocate the visual field optically, sounds will follow suit and soon appear to come from the new locations of their sources.[9] The dominance of vision over hearing is of course sufficiently obvious in ventriloquism, or in the sound film, or in television. In all these cases, the visual object becomes immediately and unequivocally the apparent sound source also, even though the position of the actual source may be quite different. It is vision, then, that is the final arbiter of perceived events, the standard and the verification to which the data of the other senses are referred. Thus we can readily understand that visual experience will continue to play an important if unanalyzed part in our listening to music, even though in this activity a new orientation has entered and there is no longer any question of the perception of objects as a goal. The musical experience is quite different according as the eyes are closed or open; according as the room is light or dark; according as we listen via phonograph or radio or are physically present at the performance. It is a matter of some moment still in music that we normally tend to fixate a source of sound which has our attention; in default of an actual performer, we will look at the front of a loudspeaker cabinet. But it is peculiar to music that we can actually engage in independent perceptual activity while we listen; and it does not transform the experience, but only colors it differently, when we inspect the interior decoration of a concert hall instead of the behavior of the performers.

In opera, of course, and equally in dance, it scarcely seems necessary to insist upon the importance of vision; but because of the phonograph and the radio, a kind of emasculated experience has become common in which "opera" and "ballet" are known with the visual element excluded, and live performance is so rare that it represents a peculiar novelty never adequately grasped. No one makes the mistake of considering dance music an acceptable version of what is experienced at a performance, but recorded and broadcast opera is customarily taken as equivalent to the original. Of course, the most important feature of the individuality of the characters is represented in the music itself, and in this respect opera is vastly different from ballet; but the vocal side of the happenings are a poor substitute for the actual visual presence of the action. The substitute is particularly weak because traditional single-channel reproduction almost completely eliminates auditory localization. But the situation would be little improved even with a perfect sound system, not only because opera is a visual art, but also because music itself employs our normal sensory apparatus, and hearing involves our eyes as well as our ears.[10]

NOTES

From *Acta Musicologica* 35 (1963): 24–34.

1. Reverberation also helps us determine distance, but the present discussion will deal only with direct sound.

2. Our considerable ability to perceive paths of motion by means of hearing is revealed by A. Tuzuki in "Über die zweiohrige Wahrnehmung der Be-

wegungsbahnen," *Japanese Journal of Psychology* 13, 1938.

3. For very weak sounds, however, our acuity is greatest when the source is on the aural axis, and for such sounds this position will be preferred, especially – as is true in darkness – if vision cannot be of aid in the perception.

4. A. Gemelli, "Il Meccanismo dell'In-

fluenza dei Movimenti della Testa sulla Localizzazione dei Suoni," *La Ricerca Scientifica* 13, 1942.

5. There is an excellent discussion of head movements in H. Wallach, "The Role of Head Movements and of Vestibular and Visual Cues in Sound Localization," *Journal of Experimental Psychology* 27, 1940.

6. A basic experiment in this field is that of Ashcroft and Hallpike. See "On the Function of the Saccule," *Journal of Laryngology and Otology* 49, 1934. The vestibular effects of sound are systematically investigated in G. v. Békésy, "Über Akustische Reizung des Vestibularapparates," *Archiv für die Gesamte Physiologie* 236, 1935.

7. P. Tullio, "I Reflessi Orientativi nello Studio delle Attività Mentali," *Rivista di Psicologia* 34, 1938.

8. The definitive work on vibratory sensitivity is D. Katz, "Der Aufbau der Tastwelt," *Zeitschrift für Psychologie,* Ergänzungsband 11, 1925.

9. The basic investigation of this type is G. M. Stratton, "Vision without Inversion of the Retinal Image," *Psychological Review* 4, 1897.

10. The present study suggests that the role of thing-perception in aesthetics might well be reexamined, especially since aestheticians have so unquestioningly based their thought on "semblance," or "distance," or in general, on the isolation of art from the world of practical interests. Purely from the point of view of aesthetic experience, the biological meaning of perception should be carefully evaluated rather than discarded; but also, much of what modern aesthetics has gained in the concept of autonomy it has lost in respect of the larger metaphysical and ethical attachments of art, where the attempt to construct new foundations has been only partially successful. Similarly, while we cannot doubt the radically different nature of systematic and historical musicology (see my review of the IMS *Report of the 8th Congress* in the *Musical Quarterly* of October 1961), there may yet be broad questions in which science and history can achieve a profitable partnership.

3

Progressive Temporality in Music

THE FEELING that music is progressing or moving forward in time is doubtless one of the most fundamental characteristics of musical experience; yet it manifests such a remarkable range of variation in its prominence and its quality that at times it seems to be absent altogether. Temporal progression or temporal process is hardly evident, for example, in the first movement of Webern's Symphony opus 21, where we seem to perceive a pattern of tonal interrelationships for which a presentation in time is almost incidental. And again, is not the revery of Debussy's *Nuages* or the lassitude of parts of the second act of *Tristan* without any conspicuous property of forward progress? Or what are we to say, to take still more extreme types of music, about compositions renouncing tone altogether as a material in favor of sounds undefined or ill-defined in pitch, or in favor of various kinds of impulsive sounds? Here we may find a series or succession of audible events, to be sure, but often very little feeling of temporal progress or flow. Indeed the successive sonorities may seem instead to move backward into the past, a process to which the sounds are subjected, not one which they generate.

Before trying to account for the genesis and significance of musical motion in time, let us examine it with respect to its perceptual dimensions, since an analysis of such a kind will not only provide insight into the basic organization of music but will also serve as a guide to any explanatory hypothesis. A distinction can doubtless be made between the sheer forward propulsion of music and the presence of a logic of continuation: the first is composed of continuity plus some degree of inertia or insistence; the second is more a matter of consecution, of the degree of conviction or necessity with which phrases or parts of phrases follow one another. And we can perceive music as moving forward, whether languidly and passively or with determination, without the feeling of a logicality or necessity in the sequence of musical events or phrases, although to be sure, the reverse is not true – that the experience of logic can arise in music without some basis in temporal succession.

These two types of temporal progression would seem to be grounded in a contrast of musical style, in the contrast, namely, between a continuous style and an articulated one, between a section of an Ockeghem mass, let us say, and a movement of an eighteenth-century symphony. But continuity and articulation in themselves do not give rise to propulsion and to necessary consecution. There is little propulsion in Debussy's *Nuages;* and the successive phrases of a song, for example, or its successive strophes, may succeed one another without any feeling of logical necessity. Additional factors always seem to play a part: a steady rhythmical pulse, certain harmonic progressions, certain melodic tones that press toward resolution, certain interrelationships in the melodic structure of successive phrases, or of successive parts of a phrase. Indeed the most compelling temporal progress will doubtless depend on more than one of these factors. They are very various in nature, but all nevertheless seem to contribute to the same end. Can this mean that in the efficacy of all of them there exists a common property? And might this common property be repetition of some kind? It could then be the expectation that repetition may produce, or the expectation it satisfies, or the satisfaction produced by recognition, which as the immediate cause of a feeling of rightness, would also constitute the proximate basis for a feeling of necessity, whether propulsive or logical.

Repetition can in fact be found without difficulty in two of the musical features we have proposed. Steady rhythm is obviously always grounded in the repetition of a unit duration, or in the repetition of a given duration that separates accents or stresses. And clearly even in rhythmic patterns as such, an urgent forward pressure will recur in every upbeat. Melodic interrelationships are based either on literal repetition, perhaps connected with antiphony, or on literal recurrence, or else on approximate repetition such as sequence, elaboration, or resemblance. Serialism has opened our eyes also to the importance of other types of repetition, or really types of symmetry, which play an axiomatic role in the structure of serial music. Indeed inversion and retrogression and so on are found in many varieties of music.

But does repetition of any kind play a part in harmonic and melodic impulsion? Is resolution in some way repetition? It does not in any way seem to be but apparently represents an altogether different basis for temporal progress. The progress it supports, however, is a type closest to continuity; it is a matter of direct (or postponed) continuation rather than of the succession of segments or phrases, which is a more properly structural type of interrelationship. But how is the forward force of resolution produced? The best we can do with this problem in the melodic sphere is to trace it to the feeling of a central or primary tone in melody, as opposed to an auxiliary tone or to a constellation of such tones. The spacing of auxiliary tones with respect to the primary one is a determinant of the strength and direction of their force toward resolution, and contiguity in particular seems most frequently to produce the most prominent resolving tendency. Melodic resolution, then, will not be an instance of repetition but a force of closure or return or completion. The forward impulsion and consequent continuity it produces will be a force toward finality or relaxation. Perhaps dependent upon this, or in any event related to it, is the impulsion to novelty, the growing need during the course of a melody to sound those tones in the melodic repertory that have up to then been unused, or used the least. Here the logic or in any event the rightness of melodic succession is grounded in the satisfaction of filling out, of new perceptions, of complementation.

Harmonic resolution has called forth both melodic and purportedly harmonic explanations. Given a descending cantus in Western polyphony, and granted the psychological need for opposed motion rather than for simply intervallic or chordal enrichment based on melodic duplication, B–C was an inevitable accompaniment of D–C. And given the demands of terminal consonance, F–G (or G–G) can likewise be deduced in the case of three voices. Four voices and a changed perception of consonance will call for F–E in place of F–G, a change favored by the attraction of proximity, and for G–G as well. Thus harmonic resolution becomes a consequence of melodic resolution, and really also an intensification of it, in turn capable of becoming an accompanying reinforcement of it. On the other hand, a downward bass leap of G to C is additionally explained "harmonically," for even the single musical tone of G (since pure tones are not used in music) will include – at least in respect of a "subliminal perception" – all of the melodic tendency tones demanding resolution, but neither of the prominent resolution tones C and E. Harmonic resolution, therefore, will have a double explanation and for this reason, again, a considerable force. And if the cadence is indeed the prototype of all harmonic resolution, as Rameau believed, it will provide an account of harmonic progression in general, at least within the framework of Classical tonality. But then repetition will play a role even here, and add increasingly to the force of resolution a larger factor of expectation and logic that will strengthen not only the individual resolving force of each harmonic progression but the general consecution of the music as well.

It is possible, then, that the variety of types and degrees of temporal motion in music arises – in an analytic rather than a cultural sense – from the variety of active causes and the variety of their combination. Thus it would seem sensible, in the further pursuit of our problem, to consider concrete examples of different musical styles and to submit each of them to examination with reference to the factors we have postulated.

Before doing this, however, we can formulate our initial consider-ations more systematically, as a guide. Let us say that three types of tem-poral progress can be distinguished in music. The first is that of sheer continuity, or also, of succession in itself. The second adds to the first the phenomenon of motivation or impulsion, and this may be either constant in its intensity, or continuously increasing or decreasing, or variable in some less regular fashion. The third type manifests the prop-erty of logic, a kind of necessity that is structural in nature, depending upon articulation, with concomitant relationships of pattern either within phrases or between them. These relationships are the basis of co-herence but also, within the framework of our present investigation, the basis of a necessary consecution.

Instances of continuity or succession seem to present us with tem-poral progress in itself, with what is in fact the fundamental property of all lived experience. At most, they seem merely to clothe this property in tone or sound, as the most appropriate or compatible sensuous me-dium for its expression. It is unusual, however, to find examples of mu-sic, particularly in Western history, in which qualities of feeling do not superimpose motivation, impulsion, or foreboding on continuity or succession, or in which configurational interrelationships do not super-impose logic on them; but often the superimposition is not striking enough to mask the underlying basic manifestation of temporal prog-ress as such. The prelude of *Das Rheingold* adds at most an increasing motion to continuity, but at first no feeling of intention or increasing intensity; what we have primarily is a fusion of passage and constancy – a compound that seems simply to reveal in tone the fundamental qual-ity of consciousness. Even in the single trumpet tone, on the other hand, that opens the *Rienzi* Overture (and that recurs elsewhere as an important motif of the opera), the crescendo produces a feeling of growing motivation, so that propulsiveness, our second category of temporal motion, is to some extent combined with the first. The opening of Debussy's *Nuages* is another instance of an almost uncomplicated continuity. The simple, floating figure conveys a uniform temporal flow into which various types of repetition inject a quietly pulsating motivation and an element of succession.

Clearly rhythm and loudness will have a great deal to do with the presence of qualities of motivation. Rhythm particularly is an important determinant of which types of temporality are manifested by a given piece of music. A comparison of the first two preludes of the *Well-Tempered Clavier* will serve to illustrate this consideration. Both pieces are built on a constant sixteenth-note pattern and both have more or less the same harmonic structure for many measures. The motion in both is lightly modulated by passing impulsions of harmonic force and resolution, and starting in the fifth measure in both, sequential repetition adds similarly subordinate elements of succession and of logic. Yet the prominent qualities of motion in the two preludes are radically different. The first flows quietly along in a continuous way; the second has a driving intensity that is conveyed by succession rather than continuity. The distinctive effect of the C-Minor Prelude depends to a considerable extent on speed and loudness, although the character of the key plays a role as well. In addition, of course, the detailed nature of the figuration in each prelude is of the greatest importance. The arpeggiation figure of the C-Major Prelude does not interfere with its continuity but rather turns this continuity, as opposed to that of sustained sonority alone, into a flow – a quality doubtless underlying the traditional wavelike symbolism of repeated triadic figuration. The figuration pattern of the C-Minor Prelude, on the other hand, has a sharp character that produces successive stresses particularly on the high points of pitch and in general causes the tones to stand apart in a succession rather than flow together in a continuity.

Continuity and succession, however, cannot always be separated easily or completely. In Indonesian gamelan music, for example, above a certain level of rapidity there is a kind of bubbling character which is at once a continuity not far from that of sustained tone, and yet also a succession. In the regular marking of temporal intervals by the prominent instruments of punctuation, on the other hand, succession has an un-equivocal and striking manifestation.

Succession in general is conveyed not only by individual tones or chords but by any repeated pattern that is short and rapid enough to become a perceptual unit more than an internally articulated musical idea or phrase. One of the most familiar instances of succession can be found in the repeated cadences and chords that frequently conclude the first and last movements of Classical symphonies; indeed these are occa-sionally carried to such lengths that the initial expectation of contin-uance can give way to an expectation of cessation and then even to a growing curiosity as to just when the conclusion will become a fact.

Repetition is not always of the same effect, however; the variety of musical manifestations that are all accurately described by the single concept comprises a broad range of phenomena, some quite different in character from others. In the fundamental case of exact repetition, of course, the quality of succession will generally become manifest. Rela-tively short patterns may then suggest the rippling of waves or the turn-ing or rolling of a wheel. Yet as the melody or section repeated becomes longer – in an extended melody of a strophic song, for example, or in the repetition of the statement of a sonata movement – the property of succession will emerge less readily or even not at all. A single repetition, unless the repeated element or pattern is exceptionally striking and brief, will hardly set up the feeling of expectation of succession. Con-ceptual and cognitive factors will obviously play a role also, in many cases; the repetition of the statement in a sonata movement, however brief it may be, cannot initiate an experience of succession, for we know that no further repetition will take place.

Musical propulsion, which in general is superimposed on continuity or succession, is more elusive and more various in its quality. It also arises from several different causes. A simple increase in loudness im-posed on any continuous sonority will produce an impetus and an expectation, and the rate of the increase, which we can take to be con-stant, will influence the quality, whether of foreboding, curiosity, or fear, although other factors are of greater importance in this respect, such as the pitch and harmonic constitution of the sonority or the suc-cession. The crescendo leading into the last movement of Beethoven's Fifth Symphony has an entirely different character of futurity and pro-pulsion than the one that opens the Ninth Symphony, and the primary cause of this difference is not the different rates of the crescendos, but rather the low-register third and the ominous drum taps of the one and the strangely elusive open fifth of the other.

Regularity is a particularly widespread and effective cause of the inertia of motion. It is conspicuous in keyboard toccatas and preludes and études from the Renaissance to the twentieth century. An irresistible momentum is set up at once – to take a striking example – by the powerful arpeggios of Chopin's C-Minor Étude (opus 25, no.12), where the regularity of succession extends from the individual notes to the accents at the bottom and top of each rise and fall, to the repeated harmonic units that make up each arpeggio, and to the repeated rise and fall itself. These regularities are joined by the dynamic swell of each cresting wave of sound and by each rise in pitch as well, which add the further regularity of a periodically pulsating forward force grounded in these different principles and enlisting the aid also of the literally physical inertia of the pianist's arms and body. An equally convincing momentum is established in much Baroque music by the motoric regularity of sequential figuration, abetted by loud or moderately loud performance and similarly enhanced by the participation of bodily muscular activity. Here the resolving force of harmonic progression by descending fifths contributes a potent additional impulsion. An impressive nineteenth-century example – again in C Minor – of the power of regularity is provided by the opening of Brahms's First Symphony.

Increase in speed will act very much like increase in loudness; it produces an even more insistent sense of a propulsion, of a hurtling forward, that cannot be halted or obstructed. Often accelerando is combined with crescendo. Beethoven makes conspicuous use of the acceleration of both rhythm and tempo toward the end of the Fifth Symphony, with crescendo acting characteristically as a natural reinforcement.

Rapidity of succession in itself will also create a future-directedness, and this will be more pronounced in loud passages and more subdued in quiet ones. Thus the fugue of Bach's organ Toccata in D Minor (BWV 565) and the ghostly third movement of Chopin's B♭ Minor Piano Sonata are very different in their quality of impulsion, but in both cases rapidity is the cause of an unremitting expectation. With slower rates of succession, momentum and expectation will decrease and disappear. The musical features responsible for propulsion would seem to bear a relation of decisive importance to bodily and mental processes, such as heartbeat, breathing, and speed of locomotion; but in all its instances, succession bears a strong resemblance to physical inertia and contains a tendency of continuance directing us to the future with some degree of insistence.

Given a certain regularity, then, the propulsiveness of a succession will be enhanced by a crescendo (which has the same influence on a succession that it has on a continuous sonority), by an increase in speed, and by a rise in pitch, although the effect will be conspicuous only if an appropriate degree of loudness is present. It is characteristic, as our Chopin example suggests, for the factors producing propulsion to act jointly, and this remains true for a final factor, which is that of increasing motion. Although motion can be increased by an increasing rapidity of succession in general, what it designates most specifically is the animation of melodic figures. Familiar examples are the prelude of *Das Rheingold* and the opening of the Ninth Symphony, in both of which an increasing forward force goes hand in hand with an increasing animation.

In addition to these steady increases (or decreases) of propulsiveness there are others that are momentary and fluctuating. These are largely the forces of melodic and harmonic resolution, which produce impulses pointing to immanent satisfaction. Generally melodic instability is associated with harmonic dissonance, and the connection of the two gives added impetus to the forward force. Ornamental and dependent tones are attached to tones of primary importance and stability, to points of rest after the impulse toward resolution, so that melody is composed of two types of tone, principal and auxiliary, of which the former is associated with harmonic consonance and the latter with dissonance. The interplay and balance of the two change in response to the musical style; we can see in the *Tristan* prelude how subtleties of rhythm and chordal quality combine with linear tendencies to produce impulsions of varying force that lead often only to relative resolution; the music is continually pushed onward as peaks of dissonant energy are time and again released into flowing troughs of melody that lead always to new concentrations of dissonant force. There is thus an ebb and flow of propulsion arising from the give and take of dissonance and consonance, of tendency tones and their resolution.

Momentary impulsion can also be produced by spurts of rapidity, by impulsive crescendos, and by sudden rises in pitch, generally all combined in brief and rapid upward scales or arpeggiated patterns leading irresistibly toward a climactic chord on an accented beat. In sum, musical propulsion comprises steady or accumulating forward forces, and two variable types of force that often act in conjunction: the fluctuating impulses of resolution and the impulsive surges that drive into the stability of strong accents.

The third fundamental kind of temporal progress in music is what we may call logic of consecution. It is based on structural interrelationships between or within phrases, which comprise a large variety of types of repetition and modified repetition but also an equally large variety of types of resemblance and contrast and reaction. The simplest relationships are those of literal repetition and of sequence. Now if the repetition of a pattern follows the preceding statement of it without pause, if the pattern is repeated often enough, and finally if it is short enough and rapid enough to be encompassed in entirety by the specious present, then the repetition reduces to succession and belongs to the first category of temporal progress. In the case of somewhat longer phrases, however, and especially in sequential repetition, the general expectation of continuance can become more a feeling of inevitability. In late Baroque music this inevitability is reinforced by a strict regularity of rhythm and by a harmonic progression of descending fifths which is associated with a melodic sequence that descends by scale steps, each phrase extending over two fifths. (See example 1.) The combination of factors in progressions of this kind produces a compelling logic of consecution.

Example 1. Bach, *Well-Tempered Clavier,* vol.1, fugue 24.

If repeated phrases are separated by noticeable pauses, however, whether between short phrases or between the strophes of a song, the effect becomes one of rhetorical emphasis; the logic of consecution recedes in favor of an effect concentrated in the phrase itself, which becomes more insistent in its message. This is particularly evident in

Example 2. Wagner, *Der fliegende Holländer*, act 1.

sequential repetition that rises step by step. The example from Wagner above (example 2) can be contrasted with the passage from Bach in example 1.

. . . A second important type of repetition is the adoption of the closing motif of one phrase as the opening motif of the following phrase. This technique produces a powerful logic of consecution that can be extended indefinitely in a kind of chain, as in example 3 from Beethoven's Piano Sonata opus 10, no.2, and in a more extended passage from the last movement of Brahms's second piano concerto, seen in example 4.

As opposed to more or less literal repetition, types of resemblance and contrast and response, which are found both within phrases and between them, are much more difficult to analyze, especially because the variety they introduce is further complicated by changing relationships to melodic and harmonic forces of resolution. They are also difficult to define, since we are no longer dealing with the unequivocal resemblance created by repetition or even, at times, with resemblance at

Example 3. Beethoven, Piano Sonata opus 10, no.2.

all, but with a kind of compensatory consequent whose logic resides in its dissimilarity to the opening formulation. Most important of all, logic of consecution is generally fused with propulsion in a composite overall property of temporal progress which will include continuity also. As a rule, however, the three components can be separated, at least from an analytic point of view. Where repetition is modified or absent, finally, we are sometimes confronted more with coherence than with temporal motion, and if coherence alone is in evidence we have obviously left the sphere of our present problem altogether. Let us consider the theme of

Example 4. Brahms, Piano Concerto no.2, last mvt.

Beethoven's D-Major Cello Sonata as an example of these more complex relationships of temporal progression. (See example 5.)

Clearly the convincing consecution in this theme is no longer due to relationships of simple repetition. The logic is undeniable, but it rests on more subtle connections. The last two of the three sections of the theme are doubtless convincing simply because the first section, the opening three notes, acts as a kind of introduction that sets up an expectation. This is due importantly to the extra duration of the third note and to its upward inflection to the sixth step of the scale, a degree

Example 5. Beethoven, Cello Sonata, D Major.

that calls for more to follow. The expectation is satisfied by the faster and more definite configuration of the two following phrases, which through this character alone represent a logical continuation. Are notes 5, 6, and 7 also a response, in diminution, to notes 1, 2, and 3? The ease with which we can hear this to be the case certainly suggests that it is a logical property intrinsic to the melody. The third phrase follows so logically from the preceding one because it has an unmistakable resemblance to the second, and it continues the downward response to note 3. The upturn at the end of phrase three is again a formal relationship that has an intrinsic logic, since the third phrase is thereby made decisive; it is not just related formally to the second, but also makes something happen just when it seems proper for something to happen. This logic is reinforced by the masculine termination of note 17, which contrasts intentionally and strongly with the feminine cadence of phrase two on notes 10 and 11. The effect is particularly convincing because the two cadences are both on the dominant, so that note 17 insists on what notes 10 and 11 have already said and makes the statement definite and emphatic. Thus there is a built-in formal logic of succession in these opening sections of Beethoven's theme.

But united with this are equally important and equally natural properties of propulsion. These are due chiefly to rhythm. The first impulse occurs in the passage from note 4 to note 5, doubtless because of the acceleration of motion that takes place at the onset of the prevailing quarter-note pace of the theme, and because of the rising progression to the accent. This forward impulse is followed by a much more powerful one on notes 8, 9, and 10. Some of the impulsive intensity here is created by the rhythmical parallel to notes 4 and 5. But clearly the intensification rests on more than this resemblance, for added propulsion is produced by the two eighth notes and by the still more insistent force of resolution that is created by the dissonance of note 10. Thus at the very instant when we expect the propulsion to reach its goal, a new impulse is added. The outcome is a still further and more generalized accumulation of forward force in phrase three, an increase which rests essentially on the progressions to the two accents of the phrase. Notes 12 and 13 acquire an insistence by repeating the upward step of notes 4 and 5, additionally emphasizing the effect by replacing the third with the more decisive interval of the ascending fourth, a cadence that is confirmed by the new, stable sense of the tone A, which stands in striking contrast to its sense in the preceding measure. And the progression of notes 15, 16, and 17 is the culmination of the successive impulses to the first beats, not only because of its purposeful ascent but also because of its strategic terminal position, which is reinforced by the length of the final tone; the progression seems to reap accumulated benefits of strength and finality from the whole variety of formulations of the impulses that preceded it and from their gradual growth in force.

The second phrase of the theme has the definite future-directedness of a scalar succession. Is this sense of impending future an example of continuity or of logical consecution? Both would seem to be involved, for a scale not only sets up an expectation of continuation but also contains a type of structural interrelationship that makes its progress logical – even consecutive in a preeminent sense. Indeed a scalar succession underlies the directedness and the coherence of the theme as a whole, for the outcome of the initial upward motion to the tone F♯ is a restoration of stability that really carries us downward stepwise for more than an octave to the terminal E. The approach to this E from below and by way of its leading tone definitively halts the scalar descent, while the long duration of the tone endorses it as a new point of stability.

The play of significance in the three As of the theme, notes 1, 10, and 13, contains still another structural logic of consecution. Note 1 is the platform upon which the theme unfolds; this foundation is attacked by the momentum of the descent of phrase two and gives way to the tone below; the decisive ascending fourth with which phrase three opens then restores it as a center of stability, whereupon it leads downward courteously and of its own volition to the dominant of note 17. After the transformation of the sense of the tone A in note 10, the restoration of the original sense in note 13 becomes a logical fulfillment. The theme in sum is a wondrous concatenation of logical relationships, propulsive forces, and tendencies of continuity, remarkable both in its cohesiveness and its temporal motion. Every note, with its particular duration and particular position, plays a vital role in the economy of the whole.

The property of forward-directedness in music can be regarded not only in a positive sense, as to how it is produced and enhanced, but also in a negative one, as to how it may be controverted or diminished. Any logic of consecution, for example, in the absence of appropriate structural interrelationships such as scalar motion and types of repetition,

Example 6. Schumann, *Humoreske.*

may simply not be in evidence. An illogic of consecution may even be set up in its stead, as in example 6 from Schumann's *Humoreske*. During the first five measures here, confusion if not chaos seems to prevail. In the fourth measure a temporal circle of no progress seems to be closing, in the return to the opening pattern. We grasp fleetingly at the hypothesis of an initial three-measure phrase that is about to receive its complement, but with measure five this possibility is replaced by the feeling of incoherence: a strange four-measure phrase that goes nowhere has been succeeded by a breakdown of intention or an apparent failure of compositional technique. It is only with measure six that a new possibility of progressive coherence begins to make its appearance, and in measures seven and eight this possibility becomes a certainty. The second four measures are seen as a variant of the first four, although they still lack a convincing logic of consecution; the eighth measure in particular, creating a cross-relation as it starts, seems to be placed there arbitrarily and hardly as a continuation of the seventh. With the third four measures, however, all incoherence disappears, and the two preceding phrases in retrospect take on the character of an ineffectuality that is essential to the unexpected expressiveness and growing conviction of measures ten to twelve. (It is doubtless characteristic of Romanticism that increasing expressiveness is set against an unvarying background regularity.)

The logic of consecution here is particularly compelling because it appears suddenly and with rapidly increasing force after a passage in which logic was artfully destroyed. Each of the measures ten, eleven, and twelve, especially after five is accepted as an exact repetition of one, is heard in comparison with its earlier unconvincing counterparts, so that against the lack of purpose of measures two, three, and four, and of measures six, seven, and eight, we hear three variants of these measures presented in measures ten, eleven, and twelve – three different and increasingly ingenious departures from the preceding statements of phrase one and phrase two. The expressiveness leaps forward strikingly measure by measure, powerfully abetted by the propulsiveness of measures eleven and twelve, which are so astonishingly different in effect from their earlier parallels. Yet Schumann carefully sustains the ambiguity and the suggestion of incoherence. The repetition of the last measure of each phrase suggests the classical consecution technique illustrated in examples 3 and 4. But the echo dynamics attaches each repetition to its original as an extension. Such a relationship, however, would deprive the measures that follow in each case of a logical beginning and would reduce them to only a fragment of a phrase. Yet the slyly inserted "extra" measure of the first ending of the period is a final touch that supports the claim of direct repetition as a part of the phrase – but as the opening part! – rather than as a coupling of two phrases. But the coupling, of course, is improbable from the beginning because the final measure of the phrase repeats the opening measure, thus turning a progressive chain of phrases into a succession of self-contained groups. On the other hand, the repetition of the passage that

Example 7. Webern, *Symphony,* opening measures.

begins with the first ending really does suggest a new articulation, the measures grouping by twos, but now starting a measure before the beginning, as it were, and concluding with an extraordinarily effective three-measure phrase. This casts a new light on our initial feeling of confusion and illogic. We should have grouped the measures by twos from the beginning, we now feel, and the whole point of the passage must be not confusion but shifting articulation, a play with perceptual organization, a perfect expression, in fact, of the whimsey of *Humor.*

But instances of music can be found, even beyond this, in which logic of consecution, propulsiveness, and even continuity seem entirely lacking or purposely eliminated. Such a possibility was indicated at the outset, in the case of Webern, as illustrated in his Symphony, of which the opening measures are shown in example 7.

As we can see at a glance, every feature of music that makes for continuity and propulsiveness and logic is here systematically excluded, from sheer tonal persistence and scalar progression, to forces of resolution and almost all perceptible varieties of repetition. (The canonic structure and the large-scale repetition of the first section produce no conspicuous properties of temporal motion.) One must find enjoyment, as in much traditional Chinese and East Asian music, largely in the succession of single tones, in the relationships of individualized pitches and tone-colors. In a triumph of constructional speculation over "natural" or spontaneous formulations, the most fundamental properties of musical experience have been dispensed with to create a radical break in the prevailing Western tradition and an extreme kind of music even in the context of world history.

Our investigation has thus far been applicable to monophonic music, to homophony, and to accompanied melody, for in these types of music there is a single determination of rhythm, articulation, and form in general. But what can be said of continuity and propulsion and consecution in polyphonic music, where we are confronted with higher degrees of structural complexity? There is no doubt that two or three melodic lines can be perceived simultaneously, and it would seem, therefore, that the directed temporality of these lines can also be perceived simultaneously. But polyphony is not thereby disposed of, for two questions remain. First, there is the question of overall properties. Has the composer had recourse to simultaneity solely for the sake of the interplay of two or three distinct musical experiences? Or are there not some truly joint properties that result from the combination, and among them a resultant directed temporality? Second, are the melodies in fact perceived, or are they intended to be perceived, simultaneously? Do not one or more recede in perception and act as a background for a single prominent melody, thereby reducing the polyphony to homophony? Or do not the melodies alternate their roles, now one and now the other coming into prominence as the remaining ones are reduced to an accompaniment? Let us examine the principal types of polyphony in turn with these questions in mind.

Polyphony with a sustained or pulsating drone is perhaps both the simplest and the most widespread type. The drone fuses with the flow of consciousness, which moves calmly toward the future leaving at the same time a residue that trails back with equal speed into the past. With time, the progressive motion into the future grows increasingly inevitable; there is a kind of increasing momentum even though the forward velocity does not change. The propulsive character of the melodic part is also heard in its own right. If the sectionalization of this part is unobtrusive, if no kind of repetition or internal resemblances are evident, and if there are no propulsive rhythms or melodic forces, the future-directedness will be similar to that of the accompanying drone, relatively constant but more active. The degree of activity and energy of the forward motion will be dependent solely on the speed of the melodic succession, and would become more rapid or more languid only if faster or slower passages were inserted, and in direct synchronization with these changes in speed.

But here the first effect owing to the joint action of two voices comes to our attention, for even without any distinction in the melodic voice itself between principal and subordinate tones, the presence of the drone pitch will give to the duplicates and octave duplicates of this pitch in the melodic voice a striking importance, so that any approach to the consonances of the unison or octave or double octave will create a leading-tone effect and a consequent momentary intensification of future-directed force, which will then decrease suddenly to a value below the prevailing one when the consonance is reached. There will often be some similar effect when fifths and thirds and even sixths are approached, particularly if the preceding tone is a half-step away and if there is a pause on the consonant interval. If the melodic voice possesses its own tendencies toward principal tones, the influence of the drone pitch or pitches will of course have to be added to these, with a resultant reinforcement of the closure phenomena. It is also clear from the principles we have appealed to that any type of repetition, recurrence, or resemblance within the melodic voice – any pattern that recalls, even through contrast, a past pattern – will have the same effect on forward impulsion in drone polyphony that it would have in a purely monophonic setting. And apart from any specific interactive effects, the very presence of two forward-moving parts would seem to enhance the propulsiveness of both.

The temporal flow of parallel polyphony – such as we find in ninth-century organum or in the music of Debussy, for example – whether constant or variable in its force, would seem again to represent an intensification of the corresponding properties of a single melody, provided we can assume that the formal characteristics which produce these properties are the same for all the melodies of the polyphonic compound. The duplication of the effects can only intensify them. But there is a factor of tonality involved also, in the broad sense of a tonal center, so that even if the melodies are strictly parallel, the propulsive forces of one will differ from those of another (except in the case of melodies separated by one or more octaves). Thus instead of reinforcement, there will be competing possibilities for a tonal center, and whichever is selected, on the basis, say, of acoustic or perceptual prominence, will be weakened as a center by the competing presence of the other. At the same time, the effect on any leading-tone tendency will be ambiguous: there will be the reinforcement of parallelism in itself, but also a different significance in the subordinated melody that will weaken the reinforcement, for a leading-tone to a secondary center has a different propulsive quality from that of a primary leading-tone. This complexity will be somewhat lessened if no single tonal center is established, and two different tones, for example, retain equal claims as centers, but a thoroughgoing simplicity can exist only if there is no tonal center at all, and the polyphony is reduced to an enriched monody, characterized at most by local tendencies. But while this kind of reduction can be found in impressionism, the medieval formulations of parallel polyphony modify the parallelism so as to subordinate one of the melodic lines.

In polyphony composed of two or more independent melodies we have a still more complex situation. There can be little doubt that each constituent melody retains the characteristics of its temporal progression and that each is still perceived in its own right regardless of the other melodies unfolding simultaneously. To be sure, although this remains true at least for three melodies, it represents a challenge to musical perception and calls for exceptional diligence. That expectation can be divided into two or three separately flowing channels of consciousness may perhaps represent a physiological mystery, but it is evidently a psychological fact. Yet there is intercommunication and mutual influence as well; there is a unifying total consciousness along with the streams of individualized experience. A single melody may stand forth or tend to stand forth quite often as a result of its distinct register and its relatively sharp melodic and rhythmic profile. The other melody or remaining melodies will then content themselves with the repetition of a pattern established during an earlier occasion of prominence, so that they do not continue to demand much attention. Or the regular rhythm of a running pattern will foster the same easy apprehension. In high classicism, on the other hand, and in the medieval motet as well, this stratified polyphony calls for a truly equal attention to the participant voices. On the other hand, the temporal properties of progress and propulsion and logic that belong to each melody will generally be modified to some extent by the melodies accompanying it, although a coincidence of progressive rate or cadential resolution or logical structure can of course also produce an additive effect. Clearly it is only an examination of the individual composition that can yield a close description of the types of continuity, propulsion, and consecution that are present, and of the changes in each. In the fourteenth and fifteenth centuries in particular, the polyphony of diverse melodic lines often assumed a special form in which the voices were of unequal importance. This can manifest itself in two different ways. In the case of a single predominant melody in the upper voice, the other part or parts will play the role of an accompaniment, so that the significant melodic forces have a single determination. In the case of a two-part discant structure to which one or two additional voices have been added, there is again an inequality, in which the basic discant melodies are the two chief participants in the interplay of temporal forces.

Imitative polyphony represents a special case of polyphonic diversity which is a simplification with respect to temporal properties. For one thing there is generally a basic two-voiced structure again, but now this is set up when the second voice enters with the subject, and this structure is subsequently repeated essentially unchanged except for the interchange of parts. The result is an articulation into sections, each having essentially the same content, so that repetition on this level is inevitable, with its usual outcome of increasing forward momentum. This larger property is accordingly added to the temporal forces within each section as such. These considerations apply to the melodic interchange of the thirteenth century (*Stimmtausch*), to the imitative polyphony of the Renaissance, and to the Baroque fugue, although not so much to the *caccia* and the *chace*, where the temporal interval of imitation can be extremely long and where sectionalization and repetition may not be conspicuous.

Mensuration canons are another problem entirely, since they call for all the attentiveness of stratified polyphony, plus the additional effort demanded for recognition of the melodic identity. The relative interference of the different voices, their obscuration or cancellation of the configurations of progressive force of each, will also be at a maximum.

All types of progressive temporality in music must necessarily be grounded in the temporality of consciousness itself, which they will either make more conspicuous and develop, or perhaps conflict with in some way. Any auditory object, such as a tone of a given duration or a melodic phrase, is generated by the automatic intentionality of consciousness acting on, and in response to, a complex of changing elementary auditory data. Given the appropriate intentional act, which may be either universal in occurrence – physiologically determined, let us say – as in the case of a sustained tone, or culturally specific, as in the case of a melodic phrase of a particular style, the auditory object will come into being. Another type of intentionality, practical rather than aesthetic in its operation, will produce the singer or the musical instrument that underlies the purely tonal objects. But after occupying the specious present, the tonal objects will fall away, perhaps displaced by new ones in a series that comprises the performance of a musical work. They fall away through a stage in which their auditory image is still vivid, into a memory in which they are no longer actually imaged but from which they can be recalled or revived by a second appearance of the same object or by a related object. Their presence in memory is manifested through their power to act on subsequent perception whenever they are relevant.

One of the peculiarities of this temporal process is that we can describe it in two ways that seem diametrically opposed but are at times actually equivalent. We feel that the perceived objects are receding into the past as we remain in a present into which there well up ever new auditory objects, but we feel also that the music is moving forward into the future as we move along precisely with it. What determines the greater appropriateness of one or the other of these two descriptions seems to be the nature of the auditory objects themselves. A series of separate objects will move back into the past while we remain in the present, and a continuously unfolding object will move forward and carry us with it. Rapidity accentuates both effects; the speed of the backward or forward motion is directly dependent on the speed of the music. But if consciousness is so labile, so influenced by its auditory objects themselves that it has no characteristics of its own, it can hardly become a basis of explanation for musical structure, to which it will simply adapt itself and conform. In fact, however, the two opposed descriptions are probably applicable simultaneously to any musical passage of either type, so that they can be taken either alternatively or jointly as a basis for the understanding of musical structure. Certainly in the simple case of a sustained tone, the two descriptions are both equally accurate; either one will commend itself to us as we consider it.

It would seem, then, that musical continuity, as in the instance of Debussy's *Nuages,* would rely directly on the intrinsic character of consciousness, on the falling away into the past and the motion into the future, both at a speed, however, that is determined by the speed of the music. Every repetition of a phrase makes the falling away evident, while within each phrase the motion forward is more prominent. Musical propulsion, however, adds to this natural forward flow a special impetus that seems due more to the music itself than to the normal workings of consciousness. Regularity and speed seem to superimpose an intensity on the motion and at the same time emphasize the forward direction while suppressing the backward one. Crescendos have the same effect. And the impulsive force of accents, of short bursts of rapid notes on upbeats, and of melodic and harmonic resolution provides additional propulsion that is still more clearly attached to the auditory objects themselves, which carry us, nevertheless, along with them. Finally the logic of consecution that is due to the relationship of successive patterns to earlier ones, to relationships of repetition, resemblance, and divergence, rests on the retentive powers of memory and particularly on the retention of vivid images of patterns heard immediately before. A newly sounding motif or phrase not only makes sense because of its relationship to what has just preceded but also follows this in a convincing manner because it follows *from* it in some sense. The preceding image is the basis of logical consecution, just as the trace in memory is the basis in general of formal coherence, which makes use of recurrence and resemblance after the intervention of time and of other musical material.

Thus the fundamental process that governs musical structure would seem to be one in which the patterns falling back into the past continue to be present either in images or in their influence on later perception. Music is a play of new patterns against retained older ones, a play in which an astonishingly close comparison of new with old permits the most various and subtle formal interrelationships. The slightest change is registered as well as striking alterations on the one hand and quite distant formulations on the other, in which the connection of new with old runs the risk of going unperceived.

This process of comparison can take place, no doubt, only if a record of what has passed is somehow preserved in the brain, in a durable synaptic pattern that is readily traversed. But how this pattern is found to be relevant to incoming ones, how the relationship is discovered and the detailed comparison made, will doubtless elude precise explanation for a long time to come. In the case of exact repetition or exact recurrence, a mechanism of superposition suggests itself, the new pattern fitting precisely over the old. But more complex relationships cannot be accounted for by such a ready scheme of comparison. Some type of scanning activity must also take place, a search for patterns relevant to the incoming ones which would seem to depend on a varying large-scale flow of chemical and electrical activity that continuously brings new areas of the cortex into attention until the connections of relationship are made and with them the coherence of musical form established. Most puzzling of all is the preservation of the temporal succession and rhythmic properties of a phrase that has been converted into a spatial pattern. Without such a neural record, of course, the immediacy of recognition and comparison would disappear, and with them the coherence of music. But physiological speculation apart, the comparison of present perception with what has been retained is doubtless the most fundamental process of musical form and underlies in particular the experience of progression through time, whether of continuity, of propulsion, or of logical consecution. A dynamic understanding of music derived from this fundamental point of view would act as a necessary corrective to the various techniques of static analysis that have dominated musical theory for so long; for the purportedly "objective" tabulation and comparison of the facts and features of structure operate with inert units that have been drained of their qualities of life and thus of their living contribution to the larger life in which they are imbedded.

From *The Journal of Musicology* 3, no.2 (1984): 121–41. © 1984 by the Regents of the University of California.

4

Reflections on the Aesthetics of Strophic Song

An Addendum to *Das deutsche Lied*

T HE FORM of the strophic song – the repetition of the same music for all the stanzas of a poem – is encountered with such frequency and in so many times and places that its very prevalence seems to call for some explanation. Strophic song is found in oral tradition as well as in notated music. It is found in choral as well as in solo song. It occurs in Antiquity, in the Middle Ages, in the Renaissance, and in more recent times up to the present: It is essentially universal in all the various types of jazz, in church hymns, in national anthems, and in convivial songs. It is found in the Renaissance chanson, the lute song, the Lutheran chorale, the German polyphonic Lied, in song accompanied by the harpsichord and from the eighteenth century on by the piano.

What is the reason for this curious predominance? It is too widespread and too diversified to be accounted for by the influence of one local type upon others but would seem to arise directly from the nature and value of the strophic form itself. Repetition is certainly a feature of melody that is so fundamental that it can be avoided only with difficulty and with conscious effort. If it is not equally prevalent in poetry it is at least a feature that can be called characteristic. At times melodic and poetic repetition occur together, as they do in refrains. But music clearly has a much greater propensity for repetition than poetry, a propensity that is attested to not only by strophic song but also by the use of only a single melodic phrase or pair of phrases to sing a whole series of poetic lines, which produces a stichic rather than a strophic form, as in antiphonal psalmody or in the chanson de geste.

Thus we find melodic phrases or melodies accompanying a variety of texts in the course of their life and even melodies that endure for many centuries in more or less the same form or in a series of easily recognized variants. Such melodies, in oral or in written form, are applied to widely different texts, often in different languages. Generally no orginal or initial version can be determined, and we have simply various realizations of an archetype, religious or secular in turn. Beyond this, a narrative impulse or the desire to sustain a mood or a quality of feeling can give rise to an extended text and perhaps also to a stanzaic one and thus to a strophic song.

In the sphere of aesthetic purpose and identifiable composers, the stanza set first will often represent the most satisfying interrelationship of words and melody: later stanzas will contain violations of accent·or meter, or fail to reflect the proper grouping of words needed to make sense. Indeed enjambment between stanzas simply cannot be conveyed in strophic song.

As far as the content, or substance, of a text is concerned, there are still more difficult problems. It is rarely possible in most narratives – in ballades, for example – to sustain the same speed of action, or the same atmosphere or quality of feeling, throughout. The repetition of the same music will be appropriate, however, only where some significant object or activity in the poem is prominent continuously or where the mood evoked is unchanging. (Lyric poems, of course, generally present the requisite continuity.) Sometimes a brook or a river is a constant feature in a narrative, both visible and audible, or the scenic setting is the same throughout, or some activity – the turning of a spinning wheel – persists from beginning to end. As far as mood is concerned (and it is nearly always a factor) the musical repetition of each stanza not only permits constancy but often produces an intensification that rises to considerable power.

Quite different in nature is the repetition of a melodic phrase made up largely of a reciting tone. Usually opening and closing formulas will be added, and perhaps a medial inflection as well, which divides the tonal pattern into two parts that are roughly equal in duration but contrasting in function. What results is not really a stichic melody so much as a subservient tonal formulation that acts simply to emphasize the articulation and logic of the text or to enhance its audibility and carrying power. But even in authentic melodies, and indeed in music in general, repetition of one kind or another is rarely absent. Sometimes it is confined to a characteristic rhythmic pattern and often it allows for rhythmic or melodic changes, but repetition, whether varied or strict, is clearly ubiquitous in music, while it is relatively rare in prose and poetry. The striking difference would seem to rest on the different natures of the two media. For sensuous pleasure and the qualities of feeling that are attached to chordal progressions and to melody thrive on continual repetition and recurrence, just as every pleasure does, while what verbal art in itself presents (recited, say, rather than sung) are stories and ideas and images. Words can convey the sensuous beauties of vision and hearing only by description and by the sonorous beauty of verbal formulations in themselves.

When melody and words are combined in song, the melody tends to occupy the foreground of attention and to obscure or suppress the meaning of the text. Unless the melody is devoid of interest or is little more than the intonation of speech, a conscious effort is required to retain our awareness of the words and their meaning. This effort decreases in succeeding stanzas of a strophic song, since the melody becomes increasingly familiar and makes way to some extent for attention to the text. At the same time, the repetition of the melody not only represents a normal musical practice but also provides a foil that facilitates our grasp of the changing ideas and images of the text. In refrains, the periodic recurrence of words and ideas becomes enjoyable rather than tedious, for melody – easily stepping into the foreground of attention – conveys its own pleasure as well as the pleasure of the tonal-verbal composite, and for both of these, repetition is a natural ally.

Before we examine the relationship of words and melody in song, however, we must make a basic distinction, for there are two types of song, which are radically different from one another in nature. In one of these it is possible to separate the words from the melody, so that each can be considered independently. In the second type this kind of analysis is not possible because the combination of the two is intimate rather than external; the verbal and tonal constituents form a unity in which words and melody no longer exist as such but only in the modifications that are produced by their process of unification. This dualism of types is most clearly defined in respect of origin: a separable song is essentially a chance product of the juxtaposition of text and melody, while an inseparable song is a carefully planned combination in which considerations of compatability and of the qualities of the whole are a constant concern. Now the succession of stanzas that enter into a strophic song obviously will present no compositional or aesthetic problem if the text and melody are separable. An intimate interrelation of text and melody, on the other hand, can be secured only through a concern with integration that can hardly be repeated with equal success in every stanza. Thus many songs achieve a remarkable unity of text and melody in only one stanza (usually the first) but a more or less imperfect one in others. There are poems, of course, that present little or no difficulty because they have no significant changes throughout – lyric poems, for example, or ballads in which the impact of individual events is less important than a predominant atmospheric quality, for example, or than the unremitting rapidity of the action. But apart from poems of these kinds, a strophic musical setting cannot easily do equal justice to every stanza, although precisely this purpose was adopted as a guiding principle toward the end of the eighteenth century in Germany. In practice also, the dualism of separable and inseparable often does not exist in pure form, for a separable text and melody will be drawn together to some extent if only as a result of their association in perception, while in a unified song, the text or the melody alone can often be held responsible for many qualities of the song as a whole.

In the later eighteenth century the relationship between the poet and the composer of a Lied was conceived in terms of equivalence and mutual respect – a relationship that remained the same whether the poem was written before the melody or the melody before the poem. In either case the greatest care was taken to match the melody to the preexistent words or the words to the preexistent melody, especially when alterations in either seemed to be necessary. Fundamentally also, the poem of a strophic song is best if there are not too many strophes; with more than a half-dozen, say, the repeated melody will tend to become tedious, even if the text is engrossing or dramatic. But varied events or radical changes in emotional character or mood cannot be adequately expressed in a strophic song in general, since it serves primarily the ideals of singability and folklike quality, both of which call for a degree of restraint in melodic expression: for a limited range and regular rhythm.

During the same period in which the equilibrium of poem and melody was achieved, however, the through-composed song became more prominent. It provided an alternative that went well beyond the flexibility practiced in the performance of strophic songs, such as changes in the color of the voice, in the character of the declamation, in the dynamics of the accompaniment, and even in the tempo. But strophe-to-strophe changes in performance were hardly comparable to through composition, for this at once permitted an essentially unlimited freedom to the melody and to the accompaniment of the song to express all the changes of meaning and feeling that the words were correspondingly enabled to embody, to remove entirely the threat of the tedium of melodic repetition, or even to assume a relationship not of the equivalence of music and poetry but one in which music was complementary to poetry. It might express the feeling, for example, that underlay the overt action and the explicit verbal content. By way of complementation, then, the earlier ideal of balance was displaced by the newer ideal of expression, and this fostered an indefinitely expanded variability, scope, and detail in the text. And since every poem, particularly in the early nineteenth century, is immersed in an ineffable atmosphere of qualities and connotations that entirely elude the formulations of language, the roles music might conceivably play, the contributions it might conceivably make to a Lied, can hardly be numbered. As a result of these changes, the song, even when it retained a stanzaic text, no longer had a stylistic sphere of its own but could import elements of other genres, such as powerful emotions, dramatic quality, dialogue, and recitative.

Around 1800 also, the sonority intrinsic to language became increasingly prominent, both in prose and in all varieties of poetry, including the stanzaic poetry intended for song. Somewhat like music itself, verbal sonorities could even be elaborated into a second art of sound, as we can see in this poem of Clemens Brentano.

Der Spinnerin Lied

Es sang vor langen Jahren
Wohl auch die Nachtigall;
Das war wohl süßer Schall,
Da wir zusammen waren.

Ich sing' und kann nicht weinen
Und spinne so allein
Den Faden klar und rein,
So lang der Mond wird scheinen.

Als wir zusammen waren,
Da sang die Nachtigall;
Nun mahnet mich ihr Schall,
Daß du von mir gefahren.

So oft der Mond mag scheinen,
Denk' ich wohl dein allein;
Mein Herz ist klar und rein,
Gott wolle uns vereinen!

Seit du von mir gefahren,
Singt stets die Nachtigall;
Ich denk' bei ihrem Schall,
Wie wir zusammen waren.

Gott wolle uns vereinen,
Hier spinn' ich so allein,
Der Mond scheint klar und rein,
Ich sing' und möchte weinen![1]

In spite of the exceptional artistic value of the patterns of juxtaposition and recurrence of sense and sounds and images in this verbal composition, the poem is clearly musical only in ways which are figurative. It may seem to be an ideal text for song, but converting it into melody, no matter how successful that may prove to be, will inevitably cancel out its verbal "music," as though the strength of literal melody does not permit a weaker rival to exist alongside it. But it is also possible exceptionally for music to be rendered impotent by the strength of poetry. This has been painfully evident in the case of Goethe's *Über allen Gipfeln ist Ruh'*. In all the numerous settings of this poem, the natural and usual dominance of music is replaced by helpless subservience. As a result, the would-be Lied has invariably found an obscure end.

Interest in the sonorities of language was joined shortly afterward by a new concern with the sonority of the piano as well. For the technical developments in the structure of the piano – notably double escapement, heavier construction (one-piece cast-iron frame), greater string tension (required by the thicker strings needed for loudness) and cross-stringing – radically enlarged the capacities of the instrument and transformed its tonal quality. Of all the musical results of these changes, we are presently concerned with the richer quality and prolonged intensity of tone, since it is these which support the enhanced lyricism that brings the piano closer to the voice and creates a feeling of kinship between the two. On occasion this feeling gives rise to characteristic special textures, of which one is the assumption of the melody of the Lied by the piano, which frees the voice from this role and permits it to adopt a more declamatory style if desired. Another such special texture is duets of piano and voice, which can be either polyphonic (parallel melodies or diverse) or antiphonal (question-and-answer phrases or a series of statements with a refrain after each). The enhanced lyricism was the basis also of types of interplay and interchange that were of remarkable variety as well as intimacy or subtlety. Prominent examples of these are Schumann's *Der Nussbaum* and Wolf's beautiful *Um Mitternacht.*

Turning now to the relationship of words and melody in song, we find that the metrical and rhythmical characteristics of both the text and melody of a song are relatively well defined, so that their combination is easily perceived and comprehended. This is true, moreover, whether the text and melody are separable, which nearly always means that each has had a prior, independent existence, or whether they constitute a unity. In contrast, however, the meaning and feeling expressed by the words and especially by the melody are more difficult to grasp and to specify, even if the words and melody are separable. The words may not present a clear, conceptual meaning but perhaps instead a veiled or ambiguous one, or a meaning with overtones of other and possibly opposed mean-ings. Beyond this, the words may have largely or exclusively the kind of "meaning" that resides in sonorous values rather than in concepts or ideas, or in feelings that can be named.

Still more elusive is the meaning of the melody in itself. For a melody has a quality of feeling which is specific to that melody and not to be found elsewhere in the realm of human experience, whether within music or outside it. This "meaning" is really a train of musical feelings which cannot be designated or described in language, or even suggested by the sonorous qualities of words. Yet when a poem is sung to that same melody, the specific quality or feeling of the melody immediately becomes the feeling of the poem also, in a transfer that takes place when there is even the slightest degree of kinship of feeling between melody and poem. The feeling quality of the melody in itself, however, is not simply transferred to the sung text, for there is really an interaction of the melody and the text in which not only are the words (considered, let us say, as spoken) transformed into song, but the melody also under-goes a subtle transformation of its own, in which the flow of feeling is modulated in a second process: by the fusion of tone and verbal sonority. As compared with the relatively uninflected course of melodic feeling in a performance by an individual musical instrument or by the human voice without text, the course of feeling of a melody sung with words has an intensity and complexity of emotion that raise it to a new level of musical significance. At the same time, the melody undergoes a series of minute alterations as a concomitant of its assumption of words: its rhythm is influenced by the rhythm of the words, its tone color changes continuously in response to the fluctuations of the verbal sounds with which it is fused, and the meanings and feelings incorporated in the words are transmuted into the intensified expressiveness of tonal relationships.

The bond between melody and words in a perfectly unified verse or stanza contains the key to the aesthetics of the strophic song. For strangely, this bond that seems to be unique in its strength and in the peculiar mutual appropriateness of the paired components is only one of an indeterminate number of similar bonds between the same melody and other poetic verses. These alternate bonds have an equal strength and an equal mutual suitability of melody and words. It is thus entirely possible to find different sets of poetic lines, each of which seems ideally appropriate for combination with the same melody. How can this be?

The only explanation that suggests itself is a very strange one, namely, that the specific feeling of the melody is changed instantly by the influence of a different text and now seems just as ideally suited to the new words as it had been to the old. The only alternative to such an immediate response would be a melody whose quality of feeling prior to any connection with words seemed specific but actually was not or actually assumed a general nature as soon as it was joined to words. In the one case there is an abrupt change of feeling, in the other, an abrupt change from specific to general that is more puzzling because the melody must be thought of in itself even though it exists only in its union with a text. There is a further puzzle as well: What kind of generality does a melody possess in its union with a text if it can unite equally well with a number of different texts?

Many answers to this question have been proposed. For Boyé, writing in 1779, emotions are expressed by the imitation of their external signs: the imitation of "attitudes, gestures, inflections of the voice, exclamations, sighs, sobs, finally by words and the manner of articulating them."[2] But musical tones, Boyé argues, are not really able to imitate either inarticulate cries or the indefinite, natural inflections of speech.

What we are moved by in song is the content of the text and "the feeling of the actor." Of course, the melody must be suitable to the words. In the well-known air from Gluck's *Orpheus*, however, suitability is "entirely neglected." Boyé cites the text:

> *J'ai perdu mon Euridice,*
> *Rien n'égale mon malheur,*
> *Sort cruel, quelle rigueur?*
> *Rien n'égale mon malheur.*

"The style of the song," Boyé resumes, has been found so gay that a very jolly contredance has been made of it. The words that follow would be much more appropriate:

> *J'ai trouvé mon Euridice,*
> *Rien n'égale mon bonheur,*
>   *Quels moments!*
>   *Quels transports!*
> *Rien n'égale mon bonheur.*

However, when Monsieur le Gros performs this piece the way it stands in the opera, that is to say, with the words "J'ai perdu mon Euridice," he has the ability to correct its defects by tones so pathetic, that the tears flow, that hearts melt at the terrible situation that he feigns to experience.[3]

Music may possess various characteristic qualities, Boyé concedes, but it cannot imitate the affections of the soul, just as the façade of a prison may have a sombre character, but it does not express the feelings of the prisoners within.

Much can be said about this argument. If music can be naive, virile, majestic, sprightly, langorous, gracious, and melancholy, as Boyé grants, why does it not express, by that token, "affections of the soul"? Can a distinction really be made in music between characteristic qualities and affections of the soul? Or between the feelings in the melody and the feelings of the singer? For the air of Orpheus has been found gay, as Boyé tells us, while the performance of it by Monsieur le Gros makes tears flow and hearts melt.

A partial explanation of this paradox has been offered by Eduard Hanslick, who says about the melody in question that "music more assuredly possesses accents which more truly express a feeling of profound sorrow."[4] From a historical-stylistic point of view we can say that the classical ideal of eighteenth-century France together with the character and restricted range of Rococo feelings have lent a gentle and even a neutral quality rather than a tragic one to Orpheus's lament. To some extent, then, this represents a generality of musical feeling against which there would then be set the more specific feeling defined by the text and the dramatic situation.

Included in Schopenhauer's *The World as Will and Representation* when it was published in 1819 was a view of music that proved to be unusually attractive to the aestheticians of the nineteenth century and of considerable interest to those of the twentieth as well. What this view entailed for the relationship of music and words in song can be seen from his theory that music "never expresses the phenomenon."

But only the inner nature, the in-itself, of every phenomenon, the will itself. Therefore music does not express this or that particular and definite pleasure, this or that affliction, pain, sorrow, horror, gaiety, merriment, peace of mind themselves, to a certain extent, in the abstract, their essential nature, without any accessories, and so also without the motives for them. Nevertheless, we understand them perfectly in this extracted quintessence. Hence it arises that our imagination is so easily stirred by music, and tries to shape that invisible, yet vividly aroused, spirit-world that speaks to us directly, to clothe it with flesh and bone, and thus to embody it in an analogous example. This is the origin of the song with words, and finally of the opera. For this reason they should never forsake that subordinate position in order to make themselves the chief thing, and the music a mere means of expressing the song, since this is a great misconception and an utter absurdity. Everywhere music expresses only the quintessence of life and of its events, never these themselves, and therefore their differences do not always influence it. It is just this universality that belongs uniquely to music, together with the most precise distinctness, that gives it that high value as the panacea of all our sorrows. Therefore if music tries to stick too closely to the words, and to mould itself according to the events, it is endeavouring to speak a language not its own. . . .

Accordingly, music, if regarded as an expression of the world, is in the highest degree a universal language that is related to the universality of concepts much as these are related to the particular things. Yet its universality is by no means that empty universality of abstraction, but is of a quite different kind; it is united with thorough and unmistakable distinctness. In this respect it is like geometrical figures and numbers, which are the universal forms of all possible objects of experience and yet are a priori applicable to them all, and yet are not abstract, but perceptible and thoroughly definite. . . .

For, as we have said, music differs from all the other arts by the fact that it is not a copy of the phenomenon, or, more exactly, of the will's adequate objectivity, but is directly a copy of the will itself, and therefore expresses the metaphysical to everything physical in the world, the thing-in-itself to every phenomenon. Accordingly, we could just as well call the world embodied music as embodied will; this is the reason why music makes every picture, indeed every scene from real life and from the world, at once appear in enhanced significance.[. . .] It is due to this that we are able to set a poem to music as a song, or a perceptive presentation as a pantomime, or both as an opera. Such individual pictures of human life, set to the universal language of music, are never bound to it or correspond to it with absolute necessity, but stand to it only in the relation of an example, chosen at random, to a universal concept.[5]

This theory was further described in the second volume of *The World as Will and Representation,* published in 1844, and then in essence presented again by Richard Wagner in his essay *Beethoven* (1870) and by Friedrich Nietzsche in *The Birth of Tragedy* and *On Music and Words,* both of 1871.[6]

In his *Vom Musikalisch-Schönen* of 1854, Hanslick contends that music can represent only the dynamic properties of feeling; it can reproduce the motion that accompanies mental activity in accordance with the factors of speed, slowness, weakness, and increasing or decreasing intensity. "But motion is only one property, one component of feeling, not the feeling itself."[7] In this view, what music conveys is not feeling but only the dynamics of feeling, only the patterns of change or motion abstracted entirely from the qualitative whole.

It follows that a given pattern of dynamic change may be common to a number of different feelings that may differ sharply from one another in character or even to a variety of different manifestations that have no connection with feeling at all. A pattern of dynamic change, however, may have a feeling character of its own, even when it is not embodied in a melody but is conveyed by verbal recitation alone. Finally, there is also a common type of song that seems to contain no quality of feeling at all. Examples of this kind can be found among Protestant hymns. The text and melody of such a song will almost always be separable rather than unified, and the justification of the song will lie in its function rather than its beauty.

Susanne Langer describes the relationship of words and music in song in terms of a "principle of assimilation" (*Feeling and Form*, 1953). The words of a song, she maintains – or really the verbal materials of a song, both sounds and meaning – are transformed into musical elements; "they help create and develop the primary illusion of music, virtual time" (p.150). What follows from this seems to be the unimportance, or relative unimportance, of the poetic value of the words. Poetic value, in fact, would seem to represent an obstruction to a successful song; and we have mentioned the idea above that when poetry is of unusual value in its own right it will be unsuitable for use in a song, very much as though it will resist the addition of any further artistic expression. It can similary be remarked how inferior to the poem are all the musical settings of *Über allen Gipfeln ist Ruh'*, and it seems likely that the more perfect a poem is, the less it will tolerate the addition of music, a circumstance that is really a corollary of the principle of assimilation, which calls for annihilating or at least subordinating the poem.

On the other hand the principle of assimilation would seem to make it almost impossible for any song to be an "ideal combination" of music and poetry, for this would seem to entail an exceptional degree of beauty or expressiveness in both the music and the poetry taken individually.

It also seems indisputable, however, that songs of extraordinary qualities of beauty and expressiveness can employ poetry of routine quality or worse, so that the inferior text is "redeemed" by the music and the principle of assimilation finds a striking exemplification. In a similar way, poetry that is misunderstood or poorly understood can nevertheless give rise to songs taken to be of exceptional beauty or expressiveness, although it is certainly possible in such cases to find fault with a positive evaluation that is unqualified.

An interesting variant of Schopenhauer's theory was presented by Viktor Zuckerkandl in 1978, in his *Man the Musician* (vol.2 of his *Music and the External World*). Here the words are even less important than they are in Schopenhauer's theory, where they represent only a particular instance of the universal forms of the Will that are given by music. For Zuckerkandl the words are essentially superceded or really fused into a larger whole in which emotions play no part. His conception is best stated in the discussion of the German "folk song" *Death the Reaper*. In considering the passage "Die silbernen Glocken, Die goldenen Flocken, Sinkt alles zur Erden" Zuckerkandl writes as follows:

To the singer, these words do not suggest anything like an endless falling of bright, fragile shapes. In fact, he sees nothing at all, imagines nothing; nor does he "empathize" with all those things, including himself, that must fall to the ground. He simply is this falling and the falling is he. He does not observe the falling; he "lives" it and the falling "lives" him. In the layer of meaning opened up by the tones, things that are separated meet; speaker and spoken word, 'person' and 'thing' come into direct contact. It is as though a door had opened through which the speaker's living goes out to what has been said, and what has been said enters him as something that has a life of its own, as an 'I'. Although neither of the two swallows up the other, the antithesis 'I' and 'it' is transcended.[. . .]

What we have here is not – far from it – the result of a particular emotional effort; it takes place below the layer of affectivity (this is the way singing "with feeling" inhibits rather than furthers the process). But if exactly the same tones which fit so uniquely specific words that they bring to light their innermost meanings can just as uniquely fit different words, producing the same effect – if the same musical effect – if the same musical phrase can hit different marks with the same accuracy – it is clear that words, which emphasize what distinguishes one thing from another, cannot play the decisive part in this process. The whetting of the blade, the falling of the flowers, the transience of all things earthly, the falling ascent to the heavenly garden – each of these is sung to the same tones, each is made equally alive by the same melody.[8]

It would appear, in sum, that the theoretical consideration of the strophic song contains a justification and an explanation of its remarkable diffusion and persistence as well as the implicit suggestion that its flexibility and universal receptiveness made recourse to through composition unnecessary. But alongside this aesthetic theory the Lied itself went its own way and represented a practice whose developmental course was rather different from what the aesthetic theory of the strophic song would imply. For through-composed songs so far outstripped strophic ones that in the nineteenth and twentieth centuries the strophic song was relatively rare in the field of serious art and was to be found largely in popular music and in special areas such as children's songs or cradle songs and songs based on traditional poems and on folk dances. Of the fairly numerous strophic songs composed by Brahms, for example, almost all have origins of this kind. In contrast, the use of strophic form in Schumann's *Berg und Burgen* is part of an imaginative conception that could in no way have been foreseen – an expression of creative novelty that reveals an unsuspected possibility of a form that had apparently been exhausted and superceded. This remarkable Lied, one of the opus 24 Heine group of 1840, is quite similar both in its character and in the conception of the piano part to the quiet lyricism of the second Romance of opus 28, written the year before. The melody (marked *Einfach*) is a distillation of the content of the first stanza of the poem. The awakening of the "secret feelings" of stanza two leads to the crucial split that is the theme of the poem and that culminates in the figure of the river as a likeness. This process described in the poem produces a progressive change in the meaning of the music. Instead of continuing to mirror and enhance the poem, the music gradually becomes ironical, and this quality is also taken on by the surface of the stream as well as the face of the beloved, both of which come increasingly to falsify and even mock their own depths.

Thus a new possibility of the strophic Lied discovered by way of compositional practice can be contrasted with the values of flexibility and universality that are rationally uncovered in it by way of aesthetic theory.

The principal way most of the qualities and properties of the strophic Lied persisted into the future was in the form of strophic Lieder in which small changes had been made – alterations, or modifications, of which there are innumerable kinds. A stanza might be set in major instead of minor, for example, or in a different key or different meter. Doubtless the oldest and most common of these alterations – but also probably the most drastic of them – was to be found in the ballade and the romance, in which a dramatic or decisive incident had always served as a dénouement or a conclusion that broke the strophic pattern (and at the same time pointed to the future). The powerful impact of such a close had the obvious prerequisite of a series of preceding strophes that was long enough to establish the expectation of continuance.

In general, the number of strophes in a Lied has a considerable importance in itself. If there are two strophes, alterations made in the second will automatically and immediately be noticed and compared with the corresponding original passages even though these themselves cannot be recalled. The changes will generally have a descriptive or symbolic purpose. If there are three strophes, the first two produce a certain need for novelty. From this impulse there can originate the refreshing novelty we find in the *Abgesang* of the Bar form, for example, to mention the most prominent instance of a ubiquitous form that is manifest as early as the ancient Greek ode.

On the other hand, when a strophic song exists in the nineteenth century without any notated departure from regularity, there is a possibility it will display, almost as a raison d'être, some surprising innovation or an exceptional degree of beauty. This is certainly the case in Schumann's *Im wunderschönen Monat Mai* and in Wolf's "almost strophic" song *Um Mitternacht,* with its haunting refrain.

In the inexhaustible fertility of history, finally, the question of the relationship of melody and words was superceded by the appearance of a type of tonal speech in which it was no longer possible to discern any dualism. It was not possible even to speak of melody and words, for that would seem to entail their having some kind of existence as separate entities. This new manifestation, however, appeared in the mature operas of Wagner and the Mörike songs of Wolf, which are essentially outside the sphere of strophic form.[9]

NOTES

From *Festschrift Walter Wiora zum 90. Geburtstag* (Tutzing: Hans Schneider, 1997), pp.173–85.

1. Clemens Brentano, *Werke,* vol.1 (Munich: Carl Hanser Verlag, 1968), p.131.

2. See Edward Lippman, *Musical Aesthetics: A Historical Reader,* vol.1 (New York: Pendragon Press, 1986), p.285.

3. Ibid., p.290.

4. Eduard Hanslick, *The Beautiful in Music,* tr. by Gustav Cohen from the seventh German ed. (New York: Liberal Arts Press, 1957), p.34.

5. Arthur Schopenhauer, *The World as Will and Representation,* tr. E. F. J. Payne (Indian Hills CO: Falcon's Wing Press, 1958), vol.1, pp.261–63.

6. See Edward Lippman, *Musical Aesthetics: A Historical Reader,* vol.2 (Stuyvesant NY: Pendragon Press, 1988), pp.357–93.

7. Eduard Hanslick, *Vom Musikalisch-Schönen* (Leipzig 1854), p.16.

8. Viktor Zuckerkandl, *Man the Musician* (Princeton NJ, 1973), pp.40–41.

9. Even *Um Mitternacht* is not a strictly strophic song.

Part 2: Historical and Critical Studies

5

The Place of Music in the System of Liberal Arts

I N T H E medieval system of liberal arts, music has its place as one of the quadrivial sciences – arithmetic, geometry, music, and astronomy; but its position in the group shows a curious variability. It is the last of the four disciplines in the definitive scheme of Martianus Capella around 400 A.D., but more often it appears as the second or third study; in reduced formulations, when arithmetic is omitted and only three sciences are mentioned, it can appear as the first.[1] To the extent that this variability is not due to chance, its explanation must be sought in the internal structure of the quadrivium and in the interrelationship of the constituent studies. This quest will take us to Pythagorean and Platonic sources, for it was within these traditions that the quadrivial concept of the branches of mathematics was formulated and developed.

According to the Pythagorean Archytas of Tarentum, a pupil of Philolaus and a friend of Plato, the mathematical sciences are related because they all deal with the two primary forms of being (which we can take to be multitude and extension).[2] In listing these sciences, Archytas puts music in the last place, a position that may point to its culminating status, for it is in the field of music that he expresses his special admiration for the work of mathematicians. He affirms also that the arithmetic, geometric, and harmonic means all belong to the subject of music, so that arithmetic and geometry would appear to be presupposed and more basic studies. If we consider music to be the science of relative quantity, it will obviously comprehend both arithmetic and geometric relationships; thus it will logically occupy the third or fourth place in the quadrivium. But actually music is restricted in principle to rational ratios; it is the science of relative *multitude,* and although rational relationships can always be stated geometrically, geometry has a peculiar interest in incommensurable line segments and thus possesses a greater generality than music. Since it is closely connected with arithmetic in particular, music will become the second quadrivial study, or – fused with arithmetic – the first of a group of three. It would seem, alternatively, that the rational ratios of music might be considered a special case of the more general geometric study of proportion, and that music might consequently be placed after geometry; but this would be an arrangement suggested by a modern rather than an ancient perspective.

Astronomy is somewhat different from geometry in its relationship to music, for while it also makes use of musical proportions, these become a peculiarly characteristic part of the science; unlike line segments, the heavens bear an inherent resemblance to the world of consonance and musical intervals, and for this reason, even apart from the factor of rhythm and motion that is common to both spheres, music is frequently placed either directly before or directly after astronomy in the quadrivium.

A closer inspection of the actual subject matter of the discipline of music confirms its complex interconnection with the other branches of mathematical science. As one of the *mathemata* music was represented by harmonics, and Archytas was one of the major figures in its development. His work in harmonics, explained in part by both Ptolemy and Boethius, can be represented fairly by the Euclid *Section of the Canon,* written about 300 B.C., just as the arithmetic known to Archytas can be represented by the arithmetic and harmonic books of the Euclid *Elements* (books 7–9). Considered not as the whole study of proportion but more accurately as the study of proportion insofar as it relates to musical intervals, ancient harmonics depends directly on arithmetic. It deals with the compounding and dividing of consonances in accordance with the postulate that they correspond to multiple and superparticular ratios. The ratios of the consonances are determined and then used as a basis for deriving the ratios of the entire tonal system. The central concern of the science is the insertion of arithmetic, harmonic, and geometric means between two given quantities. Archytas is responsible for the basic proof that neither one nor more geometric means can be inserted in a superparticular ratio, so that by and large, and except for the fundamental articulation of the tonal range into octaves, the division of intervals must proceed on the basis of the arithmetic and harmonic means.

But more fundamental for the broad ramifications of music than its close dependence upon arithmetic was the fact that the consonant ratios which were known to Philolaus and Archytas in terms of the comprehensive progression 12, 9, 8, 6 were all contained in the integers 1, 2, 3, 4 – the holy tetractys of the Pythagoreans – which had basic ontological importance. In addition, the Pythagoreans conceived the very constitution of number, and thus of the world, as resting on the harmony of two fundamental constituents, the monad and the dyad (or the limited and the boundless). In spite of his opposition to the Pythagorean and Platonic hypostasis of number, even Aristotle acknowledged paired contraries and their harmonic combination as basic principles in philosophy and science; but it is Plato who most fully appreciates the general role of music and who at the same time deepens the theoretical basis of the interconnection of the *mathemata*. Music becomes the final discipline because it is the most general and it best explains the whole nature of mathematics. Its position as the last discipline emphasizes not only its concern with relation but also its connection with motion: it becomes the counterpart of astronomy, as the motion of both number and figure. Plato insists upon the universal relevance of music, writing in the *Laws*: "Moreover, as I have now said several times, he who has not contemplated the mind of nature which is said to exist in the stars, and gone through the previous training, and seen the connection of music with these things, and harmonized them all with laws and institutions, is not able to give a reason of such things as have a reason."[3] Indeed it may very well be music that is responsible both for the unity of mathematics and for its ethical value. A vibrating string is an audible unity of number and length, of arithmetic and geometry, while the moral and emotional influence of music suggests that its corresponding mathematical study may possess ethical powers of its own.

In the *Republic*, Plato emphasizes the ethical value of the *mathemata*,[4] a view that was of vital importance in defining the function of the liberal arts. The ethical concept is incidentally reinforced by the introduction of a fifth science; stereometry is inserted between geometry and astronomy, obscuring the significant symmetry of the fourfold Pythagorean scheme in favor of a different systematic concept. Of each of the disciplines Plato stresses the abstract and ideal character; they are not concerned with practical use, nor with experienced objects at all. In the case of music, it is not only a concern with actual tones that Plato discards, but also what he takes as the interest of the Pythagoreans – the study of harmonic numbers and proportions. Harmonics is to deal instead with the problem of why certain numbers are harmonic, the problem of the nature of harmony. Music becomes the most typical representative of the *mathemata*, the last and most general science.

Numbers are succeeded by plane figures, plane figures by solids, solids by the motion of solids, and this motion by the motion of sounds. The Pythagorean classification – although it may originally have been connected with a notion of cosmogonical succession – is in fact a static analysis of being; but this is transformed by the introduction of stereometry and by the pedagogical and propaedeutic function of the Platonic system. At each step, abstraction is made from sensory phenomena to principles. Then, after a study of the interrelationships of the principles of all the disciplines, which is an investigation itself harmonic in nature, the ascent of dialectic begins.

But dialectic too, if we treat the *Republic* as an example, is largely the study of harmony, in man and state and world. And when we are told that the preliminary sciences are the handmaids and helpers of dialectic, the intention seems to be not only that their help is preparatory, but also that they are continuous adjuncts. Again the *Republic* provides its own confirmation: much more than the proposal of a curriculum, it is an actual instance of the philosophical use of the principles of the preparatory disciplines.

The *Timaeus* also reveals the cooperative function of the quadrivial sciences, but as adjuncts to the study of being and the cosmos; the *mathemata* are at once ontological and scientific in importance, and the unity of mathematics derives from the nature of the world and of thought. Still more strongly here, however, the interrelation of the component disciplines is shown to be grounded in harmonics; the arithmetic, geometric, and astronomical structure of the cosmos is harmonic in nature throughout, and harmony is again associated with ethical value, but in a cosmic sense rather than a human or social one. Commentaries on the *Timaeus* understandably become compendiums of the quadrivial studies, with harmonics in the commanding role. But the concept of cosmic harmony, which ensures the relevance of music to astronomy, is kept alive not only by the tradition of the *Timaeus* but also by that of the *Republic*. In this regard, Cicero's *Somnium Scipionis* and the commentary on it by Macrobius are of outstanding importance. With the commentary of Macrobius, Plato's myth of Er is transformed into a new focal point of mathematical knowledge, and the cosmic harmony of the *Republic* – originally quite different in its concept – comes to resemble that of the *Timaeus*.

Standing at the head of the quadrivial studies, the arithmetic treatise more than any of the others may be expected to furnish evidence concerning the role of music in mathematics. In his important *Introduction to Arithmetic,*[5] which is carried over into Latin as the *Arithmetic* of Boethius, Nicomachus discusses the nature of the quadrivium in detail. Science is characterized as dealing with limited multitude and limited magnitude, or with quantity and size. Arithmetic treats of absolute quantity and music of relative quantity, while geometry treats of size at rest and astronomy of size in motion and revolution. Arithmetic is the source of all the studies, and the only one that can exist alone; music depends upon it because the absolute is prior to the relative and the harmonies are named after numbers. But astronomy in turn is dependent upon music, for the motions of the stars proceed in perfect harmony. Logically, then, music should follow arithmetic and precede astronomy, thus occupying either the second or third position in the mathematical series. But in fact, music would seem to be entitled also to the first place, for Nicomachus's treatise reveals that arithmetic is thoroughly harmonic in nature. Number is formed from the harmony of the limited and the boundless, and odd and even thus become a harmony extending throughout the numerical domain. Harmonic conceptions enter again in the consideration of perfect numbers, those which are "equal to their own parts," like 6, the sum of 1, 2, and 3. Compared to superabundant and deficient numbers, not equal to their own parts, the perfect number appears as a mean. "For the equal," Nicomachus tells us, "is always conceived of as in the mid-ground between greater and less, and is, as it were, moderation between excess and deficiency, and that which is in tune, between pitches too high and too low." Finally the study of ratio and proportion – the subject matter of music in its most general sense – takes up a surprisingly large part of the treatise and is found most suitable to bring it to a close. Proportions are held to be most essential "for the propositions of music, astronomy, and geometry." The three basic types of proportion – arithmetic, geometric, and harmonic – are actually illustrated in terms of music. They can be produced in the division of the canon, Nicomachus says, "when a single string is stretched or one length of a pipe is used, with immovable ends, and the mid-point shifts in the pipe by means of the finger-holes, or in the string by means of the bridge." As the concluding topic of the *Arithmetic* the proportion 12, 9, 8, 6 is introduced: "It remains for me to discuss briefly the most perfect proportion, that which is three dimensional and embraces them all, and which is most useful for all progress in music and in the theory of the nature of the universe. This alone would properly and truly be called harmony rather than the others."

Since Plato's *Timaeus* is the *locus classicus* not only for the philosophical role of the quadrivium but also for the interrelation of its component disciplines, it is not surprising that the clearest explanation of the varying place of music can be found in a work based on this dialogue – the pedagogical treatise of Theon of Smyrna,[6] which seeks to prepare the student mathematically for the reading of Plato. We have no need of instrumental music, Theon says at the outset in close dependence on Plato; what we desire is to comprehend harmony and celestial music. We cannot examine this harmony, however, until we have studied the numerical laws of sound. Thus when Plato remarks that music occupies the fifth position in the study of mathematics, he is speaking of celestial music, which results from the movement, the order, and the concert of the stars moving in space. But to harmonics, Theon continues, we must assign the second place, setting it after arithmetic, as Plato wished, since we can understand nothing of celestial music if we do not know its foundation in numbers and in reason, and the numerical principles of music are attached to the theory of abstract numbers. Here we have come upon the chief cause of the variable place of music in mathematics; in addition to its general diffusion throughout the quadrivial sciences, it has especially powerful ties to both arithmetic and astronomy; thus as a distinct discipline, music has a legitimate claim to two well-defined positions in the quadrivium. In compendiums of the liberal arts it appears variously in either the second or the last place, but when separate treatises are written the Pythagorean rather than the Platonic tradition is decisive. For the history of musical thought this becomes on occasion a fortunate circumstance accounting for the existence of arithmetical and musical tracts where geometrical and astronomical ones are absent, since the writers in question did not succeed in realizing the projected cycle in its entirety. Thus we possess only an *Arithmetic* and a *Music* of Nicomachus, works on the same two subjects by Boethius, only an *Arithmetic* of Iamblichus, and only a *Music* of Augustine.

To understand fully the place of music in the liberal arts we must also examine the trivium, which consists of grammar, dialectic, and rhetoric. Here music as a mathematical study clearly has no place; but curiously enough, the origins of the trivium in ancient Greek education are closely connected with music in another sense – with musical practice and the theory of performance, and traces of this connection can still be found in the medieval trivium. Liberal education was originally not a process of imparting knowledge but of fashioning and cultivating the character; thus the trivium, frankly ethical in nature throughout its history, is actually the older of the two divisions of the liberal arts. But education was initially centered in music, in the leisured musical pursuits of an aristocracy to which was added the civic ceremonial of the polis; preparation for participation in symposium and choral dance was the basic motivation. And this concern with sonorous music, which has already become evident in the Homeric world, is in effect a group of studies rather than one, for musical composition and performance meant ability in dance, song, and lyre playing. Although it was connected with dance, gymnastics stood somewhat apart because of its connection with military prowess and later increasingly with athletics and sport. Grammar was more completely a part of the musical complex, which consequently can be thought of as dealing with a linguistic composite of meaning, melody, and rhythm, plus the additional manifestation of rhythm in dance. Evidently the traditional compact description of the lower education as consisting of music and gymnastics is an accurate representation of its content. It was also conceived of as an *enkyklios paideia,*[7] a cultivation that would seem to pertain to the *kyklios,* or circle, of the choral dance, and the meaning of the term may have been reinforced by the coincidence that the skolion, too, involved a circle as the singing passed around the table to each guest in turn. Thus the *enkyklios paideia* had an aristocratic and specifically ethical connotation, designating education for a cultivated and urbane way of life and in particular for the chief manifestation of this life in music. But the *enkyklios paideia* is certainly not the trivium; the historical course of events subjected it to radical changes in which its musical nature was largely lost. With the decline of the ancient musical institutions and their society, philosophy and rhetoric fought over the right of succession. We can see in Plato's *Theaetetus*[8] how the whole musical conception with its class prerogative of leisure and its scorn for the servitude of practical occupations is taken over by philosophy. Rhetoric becomes the antithesis, representing illiberal employment for gain. A specific terminology based on music embodies the contrast of the two social classes, and this is also adopted by philosophy. Conscious of its role as a successor of music, philosophy even invades the symposium and supplants song, while the Platonic Academy similarly replaces the music of the poetic school with discussion. But in terms of educational trends and the whole temper of society, it is rhetoric that conquers; grammar grows in importance and becomes the cornerstone of education, and eventually the *enkyklios paideia* is transformed into the trivium of the encyclical studies, dialectic and rhetoric joining grammar in the service of oratory. Gymnastics and music, almost invisible but still present, make a modest contribution to the same end. This process begins during the course of the fifth century B.C.; the disintegration of the composite art of music, accompanied by political ferment and the growth of a rhetorically minded culture, brings about the demusicalization of education. With these changes, the *enkyklios paideia* begins to expand its scope, and the term itself is used in a more general and preparatory sense, as we can find it in Aristotle, to mean usual or customary; the ethical significance also fades. The quadrivial studies as well, to which rhetoric already had laid claim even in the time of Socrates, come to be included in the Hellenistic concept of encyclical education. At the same time, the Roman interpretation of *enkyklios paideia* as a "circle," or group, of studies (*orbis doctrinae*) left the limited and specific selection of the subjects unaccounted for; new ethical aims could easily be set for the whole, and the most prominent of these, apart from rhetoric, was supplied by theology. Ultimately the term became "encyclopedia"; the "circle" was gradually widened to comprise the universality of encyclopedic knowledge. But that the term and the concept absorbed the *mathemata* and not vice versa, and indeed eventually absorbed all of knowledge, confirms the essentially ethical nature of sonorous music and education. Science extended and deepened the ethical goals by adding new ones of a metaphysical nature, but neither science nor education as a whole was ever concerned in ancient and medieval times with knowledge for its own sake.

If the departments of the *enkyklios paideia*, like those of the *mathemata*, are tied together by musical factors, the possibility suggests itself that the two large divisions of the liberal arts may be importantly interconnected, perhaps by some bond of a musical nature. The higher education might even turn out to contain the theory of the lower. If this were so, the Greek concept of the identity of doing and knowing would find confirmation, and education as a whole would have the strongest possible unity, even if that unity – as Plato believed – could be fully real-ized only by a few superior people. Now the theoretical study of music and dance can be fairly represented by grammar, harmonics, and rhyth-mics; metrics and orchestics might even have existed as distinct divi-sions of rhythmics. Other musical studies must have been known also, such as those of composition and performance and of the function and utility of music. The theory of composition and performance would re-main closely united to practice even if it was formalized, and its rudi-ments would doubtless have been taken up as part of the *enkyklios paideia,* along with the fundamentals of grammar, harmonics, and rhythmics. Theories of the ethical value of music might also have been touched upon, although properly speaking, since Plato places them in philosophy, they were above liberal education rather than within it. But the detailed study of composition and performance, and of ethics in its relation to music, clearly belongs to the sphere of professional educa-tion. The same would seem to be true of the basic disciplines of gram-mar, harmonics, and rhythmics: their rudiments would belong to the *enkyklios paideia,* their full and adequate treatment to the field of pro-fessional or technical training. They are certainly not the sciences con-stituting the *mathemata,* which apparently have a different source and grow out of the conception of harmony rather than out of practical music, so that they have from the start a metaphysical and cosmological interest. But harmonics has a double attachment: it is the theory of melos but it is also part of the quadrivium; its equivocal position is of particular interest in pointing to the existence of various types of the-ory, differing in degree of practicality. Thus there may very well have been two harmonic disciplines, one more practical in orientation and one more speculative; it is too much to expect that these interests will coincide, so that the details of musical structure, for example, will be of purely theoretic value in mathematics or philosophy; the theories of Plato undoubtedly represent a remarkable rapprochement in this re-spect. To some extent the same considerations apply to rhythmics, for this study too has some claim to membership in the quadrivial sciences; the mathematical discipline of harmonics is so general and so abstract that it can be taken to include a theoretical form of rhythmics implic-itly. In any event, it has become apparent that the larger relationship be-tween practical and theoretical education cannot be described as a sim-ple correspondence. An additional factor of importance is that studies may arise not only through the reflective examination of practice, but also through the application of theory. It is in this sense that Aristotle treats harmonics as an instance of applied mathematics rather than as a department of mathematics itself, and he places it between mathematics and physical science. The harmonics of Aristoxenus, on the other hand, seems to conform to our picture of the theoretical studies derived from musical practice. Finally there is also a mystic pseudoscience of harmonics that comes into prominence in Neopythagorean times. Descended from an ancient and universal sphere of harmonic thought, speculative notions about harmony in man and the world found themselves unrepresented in the era of specialized and defined sciences. Their persistence helps to explain the wide variety of subject matter found in the harmonic treatises of late antiquity as well as the innumerable links between harmonics and other studies.

To help elucidate the ambivalence of harmonics we can turn briefly to the somewhat similar situation of astronomy, for this is not only one of the *mathemata,* or in Aristotle's view a branch of physical mathematics, but is also one of the Muses. In the developed classical system of the nine Muses, there are comprised the various forms of *mousike,* including epic and lyric poetry, drama, history, dance, and astronomy. Evidently the classification represents a sophisticated point of view in which the original *mousike* has been elaborated and in part dissected into component arts. The presence of astronomy can be explained by the mathematical and synesthetic connections between the cosmos and music; it is present where arithmetic and geometry are absent because it deals with time and motion even more essentially than harmonics does. The heavens are a complete work of art, even though they can be subjected to scientific analysis. Astronomy can become a Muse, which is to say it can become sonorous, because motion connects it with sonority; just as harmony – not harmonics – can be the Mother of the Muses because its broad domain comprises temporal manifestations as well as static. Like the *enkyklios paideia,* the Muses testify to a musical conception of culture, and they represent the sphere of artistic practice, in contrast to that of mathematical cosmology and scientific theory.

That grammar, harmonics, and rhythmics were indeed associated with the *enkyklios paideia* as rationalizations of musical practice is strongly suggested by certain passages in Plato's *Cratylus, Theaetetus,* and *Philebus.*[9] Socrates compares the letters, syllables, words, and articulate speech of grammar to the tones, intervals, systems, and melody of harmonics, and also to the durations, feet, meters, and poetic form of rhythmics. Here we have exactly the divisions of an empirically oriented harmonics and rhythmics, as these studies are known in the writings of Aristoxenus. But in the very element of the comparison – the letter, tone, and basic duration – there is contained something more than a simple correspondence; the relationship is closer than one resulting from a single system of analysis applied to three different fields. The element of grammar was not the *gramma*, or letter, but the *stoicheion*,[10] a sonorous entity, a vowel sound; speech and melody both involved the organization of tone, one according to verbal reason and the other according to pitch. Rhythm was the organization of durational form and also followed harmonic principles. The identity of vowel sound and tone is clearly shown by solmization; the vowel was the only way to realize the vocal tone, but still more, it revealed the serial position of the tone in the tetrachord and was thus directly coordinated with pitch. Thus the grammatical *stoicheia* were measured tones capable of serial arrangement, and not simply elemental constituents indifferent in nature. This new concept of element can have originated only in music, although it soon developed into a general word for elements of any type. If in their search for first principles the Pythagoreans turned from the notion of primitive material constituents to formal ones, if they found their *arche*, as Aristotle reports, in number, then the concept of *stoicheion* can with some probability be attributed to them, especially since such serial constituents were both numerical and harmonic and could very well have been durational also. The numbers they found in all things would here have been concrete tones of defined pitch and duration, possibly thought of in addition as the bearers of conceptual meaning. Again it is in the fifth century, shortly after the term *stoicheion* itself appears, that the *stoicheion* of grammar begins to change into the *gramma*; the sonorous and tonal "element" becomes identified with its symbol, a visual and purely linguistic "letter." But its original significance argues persuasively that grammar, harmonics, and rhythmics all arose from the unity of music. The parallel of grammar and harmonics persists for centuries within the sphere of Neoplatonic thought; it is found in the commentary of Calcidius on Plato's *Timaeus* (4th century A.D.) and in various musical treatises starting in the ninth century.[11] From a purely structural point of view, the detailed correspondences between various disciplines are produced by an analytical method that has a numerical basis. The *Philebus* emphasizes the role of number in grammar, harmonics, and rhythmics, and Socrates observes humorously that "he who never looks for number in anything will not himself be looked for in the number of famous men." In the *Theaetetus* also, where the same method of division is illustrated, grammar is used in conjunction with arithmetic, and letters are expressly coupled with the elements of all things. Indeed all the relevant Platonic passages point to a Pythagorean origin for this analytical conception. The generality of the method and its metaphysical significance again can be found in the Middle Ages, in the *De divisione naturae* of John Scotus (ninth century), where all the sciences are conceived as proceeding from unity, and the tonus of music is expressly compared with the monas, signum, and atom of arithmetic, geometry, and astronomy.[12] If the application of quantitative thought to the external world and to being in general gave rise to the quadrivial sciences, a similar process applied to musical practice created the formal subjects of the *enkyklios paideia*. The coincidence that music was the major determinant of both spheres of knowledge produced a confusing overlap of subject matter, our chief source of difficulty in attempting to understand the system of liberal arts.

As the arts of the Muses drew apart, the specifically verbal aspect of music became an object of study in its own right. But it was only natural that the trivium should preserve remnants of the earlier comprehensive art. We have seen that the fundamental divisions of grammar – vowel sounds, syllables, words, and so on – mirror the fundamental divisions of harmonics and rhythmics. But this basic science of the trivium also literally includes the musical disciplines of rhythmics and metrics, elaborate discussions of which are to be found in the treatise of Donatus, perhaps the most important grammatical source for compendiums of the liberal arts. Isidore describes 124 kinds of rhythmical feet, as well as various meters and types of poetry such as bucolic, elegiac, and so forth – all within the scope of his discourse on grammar. He tells us, for example, that the hexameter "excels the rest of the meters in authority, being alone fitted as well to the greatest tasks as to the small, and with an equal capacity for sweetness and delight," and that David the prophet "was the first to compose and sing hymns in praise of God," while Timotheus "wrote the first hymns in honor of Apollo and the Muses."[13]

But it is not only grammar that contains musical material. In a more impressive fashion, rhetoric appears to have taken up every feature of music into its province; and although the literally musical character of oratory is often inconspicuous in manuals of the liberal arts, the specialized treatises from which these are derived – most importantly, the writings of Cicero and Quintilian – reveal the true importance of music in rhetorical practice and theory. The delivery of a speech demands attention to the quality and pitch of the voice, to bodily movements of all kinds, and to emotional expression, while rhythmics and metrics assume considerable importance in the discussion of rhetorical style, especially in connection with clausulae. Indeed the study of prose style in general, which grew out of oratory, is centrally concerned with euphony and rhythm; composition and its musical properties are its main themes. The orator of late antiquity can with justice be called the leading practitioner of music, even in respect of his ethical mission, his social role, and his powerful influence on the feelings of the audience; he was the positive counterpart of the musical virtuoso of the theater.

Important as they are, the musical components of grammar and rhetoric are by no means the only musical constituents of lower education, for with the change from rhetorical motivation to religious utility, the conventional trivium was replaced by a new group of studies: music, grammar, and computational arithmetic. In this "Carolingian trivium," music once again became the controlling interest, just at it had been in earliest antiquity. Education was transformed by the inherent powers of music, now manifested in the vital musical practice of liturgical singing. Whether attached to a cathedral, a church, or a cloister, the medieval lower school was concerned primarily with the *cantus ecclesiasticus*. The pupils were essentially singing students; they studied musical notation along with their letters, and even grammar and the computation of the church calendar were approached through song. The obvious values of the curriculum stood in contrast to the older justification of the classical liberal arts, which had been admitted by Augustine and Cassiodorus only insofar as they served the understanding of scripture. Thus the *ars musica* had been an adjunct, while the *cantus ecclesiasticus* was an integral part of the Christian world. In a process reminiscent of the ancient evolution of the *enkyklios paideia*, a new body of theory was gradually derived from medieval musical practice, but the development was complicated by the necessity of harmonizing the novel science with the traditional one.[14] The tracts of the Carolingian era were in part devoted to the elementary pedagogy of the *schola cantorum,* but they were also concerned with a more elaborate theoretical elucidation of contemporary music, a speculative interest that was doubtless of value in the professional training of the cantor. A knowledge of the heritage of Greek theory was decisive in this connection, and while the liberal ideal of Cassiodorus had been counteracted first by asceticism and then by an exclusive concentration on liturgical song, the secular learning of Irish monks was transported to the continent as early as the seventh century and gradually brought the liberal arts into prominence, achieving its greatest influence and diffusion through the work of Alcuin and his pupils. In the larger monastic schools before the Cluniac and Cistercian reforms, in the episcopal schools, and later in the *studium generale* and the university, medieval scholars and professors accomplished an impressive rationalization of musical practice. The science they created was specifically medieval, and it successively examined every current technical problem of polyphony and rhythm in systematic detail; but it had its basis in the reinterpretation of Greek concepts and its procedure was characteristically mathematical. Tracts would often open with a series of traditional topics borrowed from the hortative or introductory vein of the quadrivial science of music, and the spirit that informed the musical speculum or summa belonged more to the quadrivium than to the trivium. Indeed the scientific dignity of practice had its reflection in the very style of Gothic polyphony and its corollary in the fact that composer and theorist were often one and the same person.

But if treatises on practical music were shaped by the rational attitude of the quadrivium and even found their way into the university curriculum, an opposite change had taken place long before in the earlier quadrivial study of music, for this had assimilated many of the conceptions that arose in the sphere of practice. The subject explicitly designated as "music" (or "harmony") in the system of liberal arts was by no means a strictly mathematical study of ratios and scales but to a considerable degree was also humanistic and historical. The duality of the sources of the medieval notion of *ars musica* is clearly reflected in the diverse definitions found in the treatises; the two main traditions can even be represented side by side in the same compendium. The science of music is defined variously as treating of proper movement, of relative quantity, or of measurement in relation to sound; by way of contrast, practice rather than theory accounts for the definition of music as the science of poems and songs, or as the science of melody and singing. The former group of definitions closely parallels those of the other divisions of the quadrivium, while the latter group duplicates the form and phraseology of the definitions of grammar and rhetoric.

The contents of the scientific musical tract were initially liberalized by Aristotle, who freed harmonics from its subservience to philosophy and gave it a new relationship to sense; this process was continued by his pupils and given its final impetus by rhetoric, which discovered important expressive values in musical sonority. Music in the quadrivium of the liberal arts combines Aristoxenian and Pythagorean theory; harmonics can be based almost entirely on Aristoxenus or the first book of Aristides Quintilianus. And rhythmics is also included, again in a form combining empiricism and mathematics. But throughout the Middle Ages the mathematical conception, nourished by the constant influence of Neoplatonism, remained the dominant one; while the contrition of the laity was appropriately fostered by the concrete moral force of song, theology was better served by the transcendent tendency of mathematical speculation.

A final constituent of the *ars musica* was a traditional stock of ethical material, legends of the effects of music and theories of its value, all obviously associated with musical practice rather than mathematics. To be sure, Pythagorean harmonics itself represented a final and general stage in the process of purifying the soul from the world of sense; but the more conspicuous ethical values of sonorous music reinforce this superiority and become responsible for a continuing emphasis on the worth of music. "Of the four mathematical disciplines," Boethius says, "the others are concerned with the pursuit of truth, while music is related not only to speculation but also to morality."[15] Music is preferred for a property the other quadrivial sciences obviously cannot claim to possess, for their sensible and applied forms have a purely utilitarian character.

NOTES

From *Aspects of Medieval and Renaissance Music: A Birthday Offering to Gustave Reese* (New York: W. W. Norton, 1966), pp.545–59.

1. The different arrangements of the liberal arts are examined in Karl Wilhelm Schmidt, *Quaestiones de musicis scriptoribus romanis inprimis de Cassiodoro et Isidoro* (Darmstadt 1899).

2. The Archytas fragments can be found in Hermann Diels and Walther Kranz, *Die Fragmente der Vorsokratiker,* 1 (5th ed., Berlin 1934–37), ch.47.

3. *Laws* 967e. The translation is by Jowett.

4. *Republic* 521c–32a.

5. The passages cited are given in the translation by M. L. D'Ooge.

6. *Expositio rerum mathematicorum ad legendum Platonem utilium,* edited by E. Hiller (Leipzig 1878).

7. See the study by Hermann Koller, "Enkyklios Paideia," *Glotta* 34 (1955).

8. *Theaetetus* 172c–77c.

9. *Cratylus* 424b–25b; *Theaetetus* 201e–6c; *Philebus* 16c–18d.

10. See the study by Hermann Koller, "Stoicheion," *Glotta* 34 (1955).

11. *Timaeus a Calcidio translatus commentario que instructus,* edited by J. H. Waszink (London 1962), pp.92–93. The examples in musical treatises can be found conveniently in Martin Gerbert, ed., *Scriptores ecclesiastici de musica* (St. Blasien 1784), 1:152, 275–76; 2:14–15.

12. *Patrologiae cursus completus, Series latina,* edited by J. P. Migne (Paris 1865), 122:869.

13. *Etym.* 1:39.

14. See the article by Joseph Smits van Waesberghe, "La place exceptionelle de l'*Ars musica* dans le développement des sciences au siècle des carolingiens," *Revue grégorienne* 31 (1952).

15. *De inst. mus.* 1:1.

6

The Place of Aesthetics in Theoretical Treatises on Music

THE DISTINCTION between music aesthetics and music theory, which seems today to be unproblematic, is nevertheless fundamentally dependent on historical contexts of thought. The relationship between aesthetics and theory will clearly vary with the nature of the ideas considered to belong to each of the two areas of thought, with the prevailing conception of what each field is properly devoted to, and with the genre of theoretical treatise that is studied. Indeed we cannot even assume that the two fields have always existed or that they have always had a defined subject matter. Thus the problem we have posed can be answered only within a historical framework that takes into account the character of each field at a given time and the various types of writing found in each. Since these preliminary questions have not yet received definitive answers, however, our study cannot go beyond a number of examples that seem to permit generalizations within certain areas of theory. One basic consideration that can nevertheless be treated at the outset is the ambiguity that attaches to the term *aesthetics.* For the field of aesthetics, which deals with beauty and art and the expressiveness of art, ultimately concerns epistemology and metaphysics or, in a word, philosophy as a whole; *but only insofar as these matters bear on art* – on the experience of art and the nature of beauty. In treatises on music theory, on the other hand, we meet with discussions of cosmic harmony, ethics, mathematics, science (acoustics, physiology, psychology), ontology, theology, and still other matters, most of which are clearly philosophical, but from our present-day viewpoint, hardly involved in the experience of art. As a result, the concept of "the philosophy and aesthetics" of music, or of art, has gained currency, and I have had recourse in this essay to the term *philosophic-aesthetic.*

These introductory considerations immediately and inevitably come to the fore when we turn to the extant treatises of antiquity. As a quadrivial treatise, for example, Euclid's *Sectio canonis* (ca. 300 B.C.) deals with a branch of mathematics that has its basis in aesthetic and philosophical principles. Little space is given to these, yet they are an intrinsic part of the subject. The bulk of the treatise is devoted to demonstrating a series of theorems in mathematics and acoustics. But the preliminary considerations have a different status and belong to the presuppositions of the science. If anything is to be heard, Euclid asserts, pulsation and motion must exist.[1] Motions, however, are greater, or more frequent – producing higher notes – and lesser, or less frequent ("more intermittent") – producing lower notes. It follows, then, since motions are made up of parts, that notes are made up of parts. But all things made up of parts, and therefore notes in particular, are related to one another in numerical ratios. Whereupon Euclid proceeds to a consideration of the nature of consonance and dissonance. In this treatise, clearly, philosophic-aesthetic considerations are an essential foundational component of the whole.

This is still more the case in the *Harmonic Elements* of Aristoxenus (ca. 350 B.C.), even though this treatise is not quadrivial, but technical. In undertaking to ground the science of harmonics, Aristoxenus seeks to determine – in Aristotelian fashion – the laws that are intrinsic to melody. He rejects any derivation of principles from sources that lie outside melodic experience per se. Here is an expression of his powerful new approach:

Continuity in melody seems in its nature to correspond to that continuity in speech which is observable in the collocation of the letters. In speaking, the voice by a natural law places one letter first in each syllable, another second, another third, another fourth, and so on. This is done in no random order: rather, the growth of the whole from the parts follows a natural law. Similarly in singing, the voice seems to arrange its intervals and notes on a principle of continuity, observing a natural law of collocation, and not placing any interval at random after any other, whether equal or unequal. In inquiring into continuity we must avoid the example set by the Harmonists in their condensed diagrams, where they mark as consecutive notes those that are separated from one another by the smallest interval. For so far is the voice from being able to produce twenty-eight consecutive dieses, that it can by no effort produce three dieses in succession. . . . It is not, then, in the mere equality or inequality of successive intervals that we must seek the clue to the principle of continuity. We must direct our eyes to the natural laws of melody and endeavor to discover what intervals the voice is by nature capable of placing in succession in a melodic series.[2]

In Ptolemy's *Harmonics* (second century A.D.),[3] a large technical work that modifies and in many ways exceeds the scope of the traditional quadrivial conception from which it seems to have developed, philosophic-aesthetic concerns of various kinds are a prominent feature. Some of these are foundational and clearly intrinsic, such as those to which the first four chapters of the first book are devoted: criteria in harmonics, the task of the music theorist, the highness and lowness of sounds, and tones and their differences.

Chapter 1, for example, is based on the following consideration, which applies equally to hearing and vision:

The criteria in harmonics are hearing and reason, but they judge different things: hearing, the material and the condition, reason, the form and the cause. For it is generally characteristic of sense perceptions that they produce only a coarse impression, taking an exact understanding from the other criterion. Reason, on the other hand, though it takes over from outside of itself a coarse notion, itself achieves an exact understanding. For since the material is limited and defined by the form, and the conditions by the causes of the motions, and of these concepts, the first of each pair belongs to sense perception and the second to reason, it follows obviously that the perceptions of the senses are limited and defined by the judgment of reason. Namely, sense perceptions at first present reason with their approximate impressions – insofar as these are in fact perceptible by the senses – but are led by reason to exact and recognized conclusions.

In addition to such foundational and methodological concerns at the beginning of the treatise, most of the third and last book is devoted to the human soul and the movements of the stars – to ethics and astronomy – in particular to the relationship these studies bear to the tonal system. The discussion is opened by chapter 3: "In What Context Should We Place Harmonic Power and the Theories Pertaining to It?"

These are philosophical matters that are obviously of a very different nature than what we have come upon so far; they are part of music theory only if "music theory" extends its range well beyond the technical structure peculiar to music. But how can we define such a larger scope of the field? The relationships that the soul and the stars bear to the musical system are relationships of structure; they have this much in common with music theory as ordinarily conceived. But if they are taken to be musical in themselves, if "music" is understood to encompass, along with tonal phenomena, both the soul and the stars, even though these are not literally manifested in tone, then it is clearly the breadth of the ancient conception of music that is responsible for a correspondingly broad conception of music theory.

Alongside this cosmic and metaphysical conception of music in antiquity, there was a comparably large view of music as an art of dance, poetry, and melody, which gave rise – in the field of music theory – to the disciplines of rhythmics, metrics, and harmonics. It is clearly the wide significance possessed by music that is responsible for the diversified contents and almost universal scope of musical treatises. Perhaps the single most striking example of this is the treatise *On Music* (second century A.D.) of Aristides Quintilianus, which belongs to the Aristoxenian tradition. This work, roughly contemporaneous with that of Ptolemy, has in fact been considered to represent the philosophy and aesthetics of music, or music ethics, rather than music theory. There is support for this view in the suggestion of dialogue form at the opening of the work and in the absence, or at least the subordination, of the discussion and elucidation of musical structure. Aristides marvels at the effort of the ancient philosophers, he tells his friends at the outset:

I most especially admire the elevation of thought of these men whenever – as is our custom – we have a dialogue about music. For with them, this was not the pursuit of common men – as many of those ignorant of the subject, and especially our contemporaries, conjectured – but rather it was valuable in itself; and as it was useful in relation to the remaining sciences, presenting – so to speak – an expression of the beginning and the end, it was marveled at exceedingly. To me, there is especially apparent a specific good in the art, for its utility is considered not like the rest of the subjects that respect one matter or a small interval of time, but every age and the whole of life, every action should at last be set in order by music alone.[4]

After disposing of other individual liberal arts he turns again to music:

Only the aforesaid, music, is extended through all matter – so to speak – and reaches through all time, adorning the soul with the beauties of harmonia and composing the body with proper rhythms, suitable for children because of the good things deriving from melody and for those advancing in age because it transmits the beauties of measured diction and, simply, of discourse as a whole. But for those still older, it explains both the nature of numbers and the variety of proportions; it gradually reveals the harmoniai that are, through these, in all bodies; and most important and most perfect and concerning a thing difficult for all men to comprehend, it is able to supply the ratios of the soul – the soul of each person separately and, as well, even the soul of the universe.[5]

Here we have reached an instance, we might well maintain, not of the place of aesthetics in music theory, but of the place of music theory in aesthetics – and conspicuously also in metaphysics and in ethics and education.

What is true of Ptolemy and Aristides is also true of Boethius and Martianus Capella, who have conveyed the substance of the Greek authors into Latin. Saint Augustine represents a special case, for the combination of music theory (rhythmics) with aesthetics – or really theological aesthetics – in his *De musica* (ca.400) is a special circumstance connected with his conversion to Christianity.

An examination of medieval theory will reveal a number of different ways in which philosophy and aesthetics find a place in works on music. Polyphony, for one thing, which seems to show an intrinsic tendency to invite speculation, is naturally receptive to philosophical excursus. In the *Scholia enchiriadis* (ca.900), for example, it seems entirely natural when an exchange takes place concerning the nature of consonance. The Disciple asks, "But will you give now the reason why at some levels sounds are thus consonant, while at others they are either discrepant or not so much in agreement?" Whereupon the Master answers:

Certainly one is at liberty to consider what reasons God has assigned, and thus in a delightful way we perceive a little the causes of the agreement and discrepancy of sounds, as well as the nature of the different tropes and why in transposing they pass over into other species or revert again to their own. For just as in counting absolutely the numerical series used (that is, 1, 2, 3, 4, and so forth) is simple and by reason of its simplicity easily grasped, even by boys, but when one thing is compared unequally with another it falls under various species of inequality; so in Music, the daughter of Arithmetic (that is, the science of number), sounds are enumerated by a simple order, but when sounded in relation to others they yield not only the various species of the delightful harmonies, but also the most delightful reasons for them.[6]

And in considering the subject matter of mathematics, the Disciple asks what abstract quantities are. The Master answers:

Those which being without material, that is, without corporeal admixture, are treated by the intellect alone. In quantities, moreover, multitudes, magnitudes, their opposites, forms, equalities, relationships, and many other things which, to speak with Boethius, are by nature incorporeal and immutable, prevailing by reason, are changed by the participation of the corporeal and through the operation of variable matter become mutable and inconstant. These quantities, further, are variously considered in Arithmetic, in Music, in Geometry, and in Astronomy. For these four disciplines are not arts of human invention, but considerable investigations of divine works; and by most marvelous reasons they lead ingenious minds to understand the creatures of the world; so that those who through these things know God and His eternal divinity are inexcusable if they do not glorify Him and give thanks.[7]

The *Micrologus* (ca.1027) of Guido d'Arezzo is particularly rich in aesthetic discussion. One has the feeling in this case that the reason can be ascribed to his unusual intelligence and his personal interest in general ideas. There is a characteristic discussion of the ending of melodies that testifies to Guido's understanding of the importance of an ending and his insight into the mysterious way in which it informs the melody with meaning retroactively:

Though any chant is made up of all the notes and intervals, the note that ends it holds the chief place, for it sounds both longer and more lasting. The previous notes, as is evident to trained musicians only, are so adjusted to the last one that in an amazing way they seem to draw a certain semblance of color from it.[8]

Guido continues with the principles of this melodic adjustment:

The other notes should have a harmonious relationship with the note that ends a neume by means of the aforesaid six melodic intervals. The beginning of a chant and the end of all its phrases and even their beginnings need to cling close to the note that ends the chant.[9]

He then concludes his discussion with additional explanations and justifications of the unique importance of the ending:

Furthermore, when we hear someone sing, we do not know what mode his first note is in, since we do not know whether tones, semitones, or other intervals will follow. But when the chant has ended, we know clearly from

*the preceding notes the mode of the last one. For at the start of a chant you
do not know what will follow, but at its end you realize what has gone before. Thus the last note is the one we are better aware of. So if you wish to
add to your chant either a verse of a psalm or anything else, you should ad-
just it most of all to the final note of the former, not go back and consider
the first note or any of the others. This too we may add, that carefully composed chants end their phrases chiefly on the final note of the chant.*

*It is no wonder that music bases its rules on the last note, since in the el-
ements of language, too, we almost everywhere see the real force of the
meaning in the final letters or syllables, in regard to cases, numbers, persons, and tenses. Therefore, since all praise, too, is sung at the end, we
rightly say that every chant is subject to, and takes its rules from, that
mode which it sounds last.*[10]

In the *De musica* (ca.1300) of Johannes de Grocheo, so interesting for
its comprehensive picture of musical genre, philosophical considerations are situated, more traditionally, among the introductory material, notably in a discussion of the source of consonance and of how the
consonances are related. About these "difficult" matters Grocheo can
only "attempt to say something that is probable":

*There is a basic harmony like a mother, which has been called a diapason
by our ancestors, and another like a daughter contained within it, called a
diapente, and a third derived from these, which is named a diatesseron.
And these three sounded at the same time give the most perfect consonance. Perhaps certain followers of Pythagoras, influenced by a natural inclination, sensed this, not having dared to admit it in these very words, but
spoke of it in numbers in a metaphorical way. Let us say therefore that the
human soul immediately created from its principle retains the type or image of its Creator. This image is called by John of Damascus the image of
the Trinity, by whose means natural awareness is innate within it. And
perhaps by this natural awareness it perceives a triple perfection in sounds,
something not possible to the soul of brutes because of its imperfection.*[11]

In its location and its invocation of the Trinity, this suggests a traditional introductory *topos,* but it is notable in its concern with perception, reflecting, incidentally, the tonal ideal of its time rather than the
later sensuous ideals attached to the triad – of harmony, blending, and
fusion.

Like the medieval concern with polyphony, the new examination of

rhythm in the fourteenth century also provoked its own type of philosophical speculation, most conspicuously in the treatises of Marchetto
da Padova and Jean de Muris. In the discussion of imperfect time in the
second book of his *Pomerium* (1318), Marchetto is almost obsessively
concerned with the secure grounding of the new species of rhythm. He
tries to construct an absolutely conclusive argument, using principles
and distinctions derived from Aristotle, in which a central purpose is to
define the difference between perfect and imperfect time. The following
discussion, for example, appears at the outset:

*In the first place we say that imperfect musical mensurable time is that
which is a minimum, not in fullness, but in semi-fullness of voice. This
definition we demonstrate as follows. It is certain that just as the perfect is
that which lacks nothing, so the imperfect is that which lacks something.
But it is also certain, by the definition of perfect time already demonstrated, that perfect time is that which is a minimum in entire fullness of
voice, formed in the manner there expounded. It follows, therefore, that
imperfect time, since it falls short of perfect, is not formed in entire fullness
of voice.*

*But someone may say: You ought to derive the deficiency of imperfect
time with respect to perfect, not from fullness of voice, but from lessness of
time. Whence you ought to say that both times, perfect as well as imperfect, are formed in fullness of voice, but that fullness of voice is formed in
less time when it is formed in imperfect time than when it is formed in perfect. Whence (our opponents say) that minimum which is formed in fullness of voice is imperfect time, not perfect.*

*But to this we reply that to be in fullness of voice and to be a minimum
is necessarily perfect time, for perfect musical time is the first measure of
all, for which reason also the measure of imperfect time is derived from it
by subtracting a part, as will presently be explained. Therefore, since the
minimum in any genus is the measure of all other things in it, as previously observed, we conclude that minimum time is always perfect of itself, provided it be formed in fullness of voice, for as soon as we subtract
from the quantity of perfect time we constitute imperfect.*[12]

The mathematician Jean de Muris discusses musical rhythm in the
second book (the *musica practica*) of his *Ars novae musicae* (1319). Although certain foundations of rhythm are treated in the first book of
the treatise, the "practical theory" of rhythm is highly philosophical,

concerned conspicuously both with the basis of the rhythmic system and with its coherence and completeness. After considering the difference between ternary and binary number, Muris continues:

Seeing, on the other hand, that sound measured by time consists in the union of two forms, namely the natural and the mathematical, it follows that because of the one its division never ceases while because of the other its division must necessarily stop somewhere; for just as nature limits the magnitude and increase of all material things, so it also limits their minuteness and decrease. For it is demonstrated naturally that nature is limited by a maximum and a minimum; sound, moreover, is in itself a natural form to which quantity is artificially attributed; it is necessary, therefore, for there to be limits of division beyond which no sound however fleeting may go. These limits we wish to apprehend by reason.[13]

Muris then proceeds to deduce the whole elaborate system of musical rhythm from the principles of perfection and the properties of number. His discussion, however remarkable in its fusion of abstract thought and musical practice, is anything but unique in the history of music theory; rather, it is an instance of a pervasive feature of the field.

Something similar is found again in the theory of polyphony, for in the fourteenth and fifteenth centuries the rules for the contrapuntal succession of intervals rest at times on aesthetic value as well as on reason. The role of beauty was acknowledged for *musica ficta* in general, and it can be found in a polyphonic context in the rules for the motion of an imperfect to a perfect consonance, when the imperfect consonance must be inflected as major or minor to bring it as close as possible to the consonance that follows. Prosdocimo de' Beldomandi, for example, offers the following explanation in his *Contrapunctus* (1412):

There is no other reason for this than a sweeter-sounding harmony. Why the sweeter-sounding harmony results from this can be ascribed to the sufficiently persuasive reason that the property of the imperfect thing is to seek the perfect, which it cannot do except through approximating itself to the perfect. This is because the closer the imperfect consonance approaches the perfect one it intends to reach, the more perfect it becomes, and the sweeter the resulting harmony.[14]

Marchetto and Ugolino also explain this principle, although in their account perfection is a more prominent consideration than beauty.[15]

In spite of Tinctoris's concern with the new sensuous properties of the music of his time and of the decades immediately preceding him, most of his theoretical treatises (all of which seem to date from the decade 1474–84) adhere closely to their technical subject matter. They include, however, aside from his dictionary of musical terms (*Terminorum musicae diffinitorium*), two works concerned not with structural theory but with matters more or less aesthetic in nature, namely with the effects of music (*Complexus effectuum musices*) and with the invention and practice of music (*De inventione et usu musicae*). His works as a whole, then, seem to represent a piecemeal version of the all-encompassing medieval *summa*, although his rejection of the larger, nonsonorous conception of music excludes any adequate treatment of metaphysical ideas.

While a variety of philosophical and aesthetic considerations is understandably always present in *musica theorica, musica practica* also often contains aesthetic ideas. Indeed, in the sixteenth century these are sufficiently frequent and striking to point to the eventual development of aesthetics as an independent concern, although the Renaissance ideas are still not characteristically directed to a middle-class audience that is concerned specifically with the experience of listening and that is largely untrained musically. Rather, aesthetic values appear in intimate conjunction with mathematical and structural interests, and it is only in writings on monody and the later madrigal that this Renaissance tradition is broken by a more exclusively aesthetic purpose.

A well-known Renaissance passage dealing with aesthetic matters appears in Heinrich Glarean's *Dodecachordon* (1547):

No one has more effectively expressed the passions of the soul in music than this symphonist, no one has more felicitously begun, no one has been able to compete in grace and facility on an equal footing with him, just as there is no Latin poet superior in the epic to Maro. For just as Maro, with his natural facility, was accustomed to adapt his poem to his subject so as to set weighty matters before the eyes of his readers with close-packed spondees, fleeting ones with unmixed dactyls, to use words suited to his every subject, in short, to undertake nothing inappropriately, as Flaccus says of Homer, so our Josquin, where his matter requires it, now advances with impetuous and precipitate notes, now intones his subject in long-drawn tones, and, to sum up, has brought forth nothing that was not delightful to the ear and approved as ingenious by the learned, nothing, in short, that was not ac-

*ceptable and pleasing, even when it seemed less erudite, to those who lis-
tened to it with judgment.*[16]

Glarean's obvious sensitivity to the expression of the passions, to individual genius, and to the aesthetic equivalence of the arts is combined
in this passage and in this chapter of the treatise (book 3, chapter 24)
with a discussion of the combination of the modes and thus set into a
technical context.

Much the same characteristics are found in the "practical division"
(parts 3 and 4) of Gioseffo Zarlino's *Le istitutioni harmoniche* (1558):

*For just as the builder, in all his operations, looks always toward the end
and founds his work upon some matter which he calls the subject, so the
musician in his operations, looking toward the end which prompts him to
work, discovers the matter or subject upon which he founds his composition. Thus he perfects his work in conformity with his chosen end. Or
again, just as the poet, prompted by such an end to improve or to delight
(as Horace shows so clearly in his* Art of Poetry, *when he says:*

> *Aut prodesse volunt, aut delectare poetae
> Aut simul et iucunda et idonea dicere vitae),*

*takes as the subject of his poem some history or fable, discovered by himself
or borrowed from others, which he adorns and polishes with various man-
ners, as he may prefer, leaving out nothing that might be fit or worthy to
delight the minds of his hearers, in such a way that he takes on something
of the magnificent and marvelous; so the musician, apart from being
prompted by the same end to improve or to delight the minds of his listeners with harmonious accents, takes the subject and founds upon it his
composition, which he adorns with various modulations and various harmonies in such a way that he offers welcome pleasure to his hearers.*[17]

Here rhetorical conceptions dominate, but the passage is followed immediately by structural rules and an appeal to mathematics, which of
course preponderate in part 3 as a whole.

Chapter 71 of part 3 devotes substantial attention to principles of
perception and emphasizes the importance of specifically auditory
values. In the elaboration of this point moral values are joined to aesthetic ones, evoking the tradition of which Horace became the classic
instance:

*For since music was indeed discovered to improve and to delight, as we
have said at other times, nothing in music has validity except the voices
and the sounds which arise from the strings. These, as Aurelius Cassiodorus imagines, are so named because they move our hearts, a thing he
shows most elegantly with the two Latin words* chordae *and* corda. *Thus it
is by this path that we perceive the improvement and delight that we derive from hearing harmonies and melodies.[18]*

Aesthetic matters continue to be prominent in part 4 of the treatise, especially in connection with the appropriateness of melody, harmony,
and rhythm to the text of a composition (chapter 32).[19] Zarlino's discussion here, while exemplifying the rhetorical conception of appropriateness, is grounded in the theories of Plato and also adumbrates major
concerns of aesthetics in coming centuries, notably the nature of musical imitation and the ideal of the unity of the musical work.

     Philosophical or, more properly, theological conceptions are con-
spicuous in German triadic theory of the early seventeenth century in
the work of Johannes Lippius. His *Synopsis musicae novae* (1612) deals
extensively with the triad, defining its properties exhaustively and extol-
ling it as the fundamental source of both music and universal harmony.
The ethical and religious aspect of Lippius's thought easily suggests the
luminous aura of mystery and revelation that surrounds the triad in
Bruckner and in post-Romanticism, creating a bond that seems to span
the three centuries of the "modern" era:

*The harmonic, simple, and direct triad is the true and unitrisonic root of
all the most perfect and most complete harmonies that can exist in the
world. It is the root of even thousands and millions of sounds, because each
of them should ultimately be reducible to the image of that great mystery,
the divine and solely adorable Unitrinity (I cannot think of a semblance
more lucid). All the more, therefore, should theologians and philosophers
direct their attention to it, since at present they know fundamentally little,
and in the past they knew practically nothing about it. Recently some have
had intimations of it in a somewhat confused manner, although (very
strangely) it is much employed in practice and, as will soon be seen, stands
as the greatest, sweetest, and clearest compendium of musical composition.
It draws a happy limit to other musicians' infinite and loosely scattered
considerations regarding complete harmony.[20]*

As Lippius's writings reveal, his notion of the triad as the foundation of music is more than an automatic ingredient of a universal eulogy; for the triad at that time was the center of both the music and the music theory of Germany, a position that it continued to occupy in western Europe until about 1900.

Both philosophical and aesthetic conceptions are integrally bound up with music theory in the treatises of Jean-Philippe Rameau. The interpretation of these three areas of thought is especially evident in his *Observations sur notre instinct pour la musique, et sur son principe* of 1754. "The full enjoyment of the effects of music," Rameau maintains,

calls for a sheer abandonment of oneself, and the judgment of it calls for a reference to the principle by which one is affected. That principle is Nature itself; it is through Nature that we possess that feeling which stirs us in all our musical instinct.[21]

Thus our instinctual feeling in response to music will guide us to the principle on which it rests, which is grounded in nature. This principle is one of broad applicability. Indeed, in a type of Pythagoreanism, Rameau eventually finds that music gives the law to every manifestation of human thought and creativity. And as we can see in the following passage, the structure of music is indissolubly connected with its expressiveness: its technical theory, that is, with its aesthetics, but also with its metaphysical foundation.

It is necessary first to sing this music with the motion the words require, without adding to them and without concerning oneself with any other feeling but that which the melody is able to give rise to of itself, while re-marking in it the aspect towards which one will feel more inclination to softness or to pride: and then, all bias aside, the new flat *that derives from the sphere of the subdominant, either in descending or in ascending, will be inclined naturally towards softness: whereas the new* sharp, *given by the resources of harmony from the sphere of the dominant, will demand the animation of the melody, and render it susceptible of all the pride with which one would wish to accompany it.*[22]

During the course of the eighteenth century an independent aesthetics arose with its own circle of problems, directed to an audience that was to a considerable extent unversed in music. Theory limited to technical matters seems to have become more common as a result.

Speculative theory – *musica theorica* – did not disappear, although it became relatively uncommon. It continued also to contain a variety of philosophical matters concerned mostly with mathematics, cosmic harmony, and ethics, and often with music history as well, which had long since outgrown its mythic and legendary character. But philosophy and aesthetics were by no means drained even from practical theory and from *musica poetica.* They play a role of one kind or another with a persistence that argues their intrinsic relevance to music theory as it is normally understood: to the study of harmony, counterpoint, and form, that is, to treatises on musical structure and on composition.

In addition, since scientific ideas of various kinds enter into theoretical works – ideas belonging to acoustics, physiology, and psychology – the fields that are found relevant by music theorists are numerous as well as diverse. But music theory as a modern discipline, entirely apart from the technically oriented treatises in the tradition of *musica practica* and *poetica,* has also laid claim to music philosophy and aesthetics as such, and essays and studies belonging to this area of thought are now often considered to belong to theory instead. Articles purely philosophical or aesthetic, for example, are frequently published in American periodicals that are designated as journals of music theory. They have come to be "music theory" rather than "musicology" or "music aesthetics," in part for cultural and sociopolitical reasons – music theory is an expanding field with a huge appetite for material of all kinds – and in part because American musicology has not developed organs of publication for essays devoted to aesthetics.

But yet another reason would be that there is a new conception of music theory that has come to exist alongside its traditional definition as a field dealing essentially with musical structure in all its forms. This new conception, however, has an old ancestry, for it goes back to the Greek meaning of theory as intellectual contemplation, a broad category that Aristotle contrasts with doing and with making. In this sense, music theory would encompass all ideas that deal with music and would stand opposed, being philosophical, to performance and to composition as activities, but not to the theory of these activities. We may speak, then, of a circle that has closed in the history of music theory and left behind the traditional divisions of music study that belonged to the general and still evolving fractionation of the intellectual world.

A factor, finally, that brings the two conceptions of theory together to some extent is derived from the efflorescence in this century of the idea of "analysis," an idea, as is known, that has permeated Anglo-American intellectual culture in general and given rise to an endless succession of analytical techniques. Thus not only formal dissection and the interrelating of formal constituents is music analysis, but also the uncovering of encompassing linear features of a musical composition, and – what is of peculiar interest – the careful characterization of musical experience and perception. But "phenomenological analysis," which has appeared in recent years, is hardly analysis in a literal sense, just as Schenkerian analysis is less analysis than a type of subterranean synthesis. The notion of analysis, nevertheless, effects a certain appearance of unity in the motley makeup of present-day "music theory."

NOTES

From *Music Theory and the Exploration of the Past* (Chicago: University of Chicago Press, 1993), 217–32. © 1993 by The University of Chicago.

1. For the translation on which my discussion of the *Sectio canonis* is based I am indebted to Professor André Barbera of St. John's College, Annapolis. There is a conveniently available English translation by Thomas J. Mathiesen in the *Journal of Music Theory* 19 (1975): 236–58.

2. *The Harmonics of Aristoxenus*, ed. Henry Macran (Oxford 1902), 184–85.

3. I am indebted to Thomas W. Baker for the English version of Ptolemy on which this discussion is based. There is a published German translation of the treatise by Ingemar Düring in "Ptolemaios und Porphyrios über die Musik," *Göteborgs Högskolas Årsskrift* 40 (1934).

4. Aristides Quintilianus, *On Music*, trans. Thomas J. Mathiesen (New Haven 1983), 71.

5. Ibid., 72

6. Oliver Strunk, ed., *Source Readings in Music History* (New York 1950), 134.

7. Ibid., 134–35.

8. *Hucbald, Guido, and John on Music*, trans. Warren Babb, ed. Claude V. Palisca (New Haven 1978), 6.

9. Ibid.

10. Ibid., 67.

11. Johannes de Grocheo, *Concerning Music*, trans. Albert Seay (Colorado Springs 1967), 6.

12. Strunk, *Source Readings*, 161.

13. Ibid., 174.

14. Prosdocimo de' Beldomandi, *Contrapunctus*, trans. Jan W. Herlinger (Lincoln, Nebr., 1984), 83 and 85.

15. Ibid., n.13 on 85 and 87.

16. Strunk, *Source Readings*, 220–21.

17. Ibid., 229.

18. Ibid., 250.

19. Ibid., 255–59.

20. Johannes Lippius, *Synopsis of New Music,* trans. Benito V. Rivera (Colorado Springs 1977), 41.

21. Edward A. Lippman, ed., *Musical Aesthetics: A Historical Reader,* vol.1 (New York 1986), 339.

22. Ibid., 355.

7

An Interpretation of Bach's "Ich folge dir gleichfalls"

S INCE a musical work is written in a social and cultural setting and is intended for an audience and for some particular occasion, it is generally able to fill its role in the world without explication or aid. Yet the necessity for interpretation or explanation repeatedly arises, either because the composer is following a train of thought that is not completely understandable to his contemporaries or because the lapse of time has transformed obvious meanings into obscure ones.

What interpretation seeks to make clear is the complex of feelings, associations, and ideas that were initially formulated in tone by the composer and produced by an adequate performance at the time the work was composed. The conceptions and feelings that are embodied in a composition are in large measure specific to music itself; they are essentially unknown in any other way. Meaning of this type nevertheless resides in a community of understanding and ways of feeling and in subtle departures from tradition; it is by no means inevitably attached to given acoustic patterns. The opening motif of "Ich folge dir gleichfalls," for example, reappears literally in *Don Giovanni* as an accompaniment to the serenade "Deh, vieni alla finestra," but the stylistic context gives it a meaning that is almost completely unrelated to its meaning in Bach's aria. Yet the social and cultural foundation of musical significance often escapes our notice, for we become familiar with style by an intuitive rather than a conscious process; we understand a particular repertory of tonal phrases and forms in an immediate way from the hearing of only a few representative works of the same idiom, provided these are not too distant from us in time. Indeed the spontaneous appreciation of musical expressiveness is possibly the best example of historical insight that can be found in any field of human activity. It is in spite of this susceptible of error, and we can readily discover instances of the flagrant misconception of older music. Interpretation undertakes to prevent or correct such errors in apprehension, to make the various symbols of past music, and the peculiar responses provoked by motifs and progressions again familiar.

In this process of reconstruction, performance and verbal explication are equally indispensable. Language can point to meanings that cannot be revealed at all in performance: it can explain the significance of individual symbols and elucidate the import of the composition as a whole, defining whether it is subjective, spontaneous, liturgical, or pedagogical. But a third problem, putting us in intimate touch with the precise quality and the temporal course of musical experience, remains intractable to verbal description and is best approached through performance. Yet even this problem has seen solutions in language, first in the poetic criticism of the Romantic era, then in the hermeneutics of Kretzschmar, which was inspired by Dilthey, and again in the writings of Ernst Kurth. What words and images can claim in respect of capturing the actual flow of musical experience, however, is doubtless no more than a limited pedagogical value which will be more instructive than a fine performance only for those who are musically insensitive.

In the case of Bach, explication in language has assumed an increasingly large share of the task of interpretation, for the twentieth century has emphasized more and more the extramusical meanings of his art. The almost graphic precision of his music has been shown to depend upon a remarkable synthesis of tonal imagination and external stimulus. This discovery started with the work of Schweitzer and Pirro and achieved its greatest value with the articles of Schering in the 1920s, just when – in a curious paradox – the abstract properties of Bach's music became a major determinant of twentieth-century style. Schering revealed the true nature and full extent of the external meanings of Bach's music, and demonstrated in particular that its significance is based on a rhetorical conception of music and on the use of rhetorical principles to produce effectiveness and specificity.

The most prominent symbolic device in the aria under discussion is doubtless canonic technique, or fuga, which is used as a musical simile of following. This rhetorical application of canon has a close parallel in Bach's Cantata no.159, *Sehet, wir geh'n hinauf,* where the text is "Ich folge dir nach" (BG 32:160), and in his Cantata no.12, *Weinen, klagen,* where the text is "Ich folge Christo nach" (BG 2:73). In all these representations of *folgen,* the imitation is at the unison or the octave, as it usually is also in the canons that symbolize adherence to law. Other metaphorical canons, however, that represent fetters or bonds, are at different intervals; the aria preceding "Ich folge dir gleichfalls" in the *St. John Passion* provides a striking contrast in canonic style: the text is

"Von den Stricken meiner Sünden mich zu entbinden," and the imitation is at the minor second, with considerable friction created by dissonance and suspension.

In Handel's setting of the *Brockes Passion,* which like his *St. John Passion* was well known to Bach, canon at the octave is used at the very same point of the narrative that Bach selected for "Ich folge dir gleichfalls." The text Handel illustrates in this way is "Nehmt mich mit," which is sung by Peter. Presenting the individual protagonists of the story in scriptural words and in recitative, Bach could expand the idea of following neither for Peter nor for the other disciple who joins Peter in following Jesus, but assigned it in his regular fashion to an ideal representative of the Christian congregation of his own time. Unlike that of Handel, however, the canonic imitation of Bach's aria is a double one, since the word *gleichfalls* makes reference to Peter, who has similarly followed Jesus, and if we wish, to the other disciple as well. Directly after the vocal imitation of the continuo at the distance of a measure, the close following of the voice by the flutes is particularly graphic; it seizes our attention also because it entails a rhythmic displacement of the motif, which at the same time evokes the impression of eagerness.

Canons at the unison or octave with a triadic basis and in triple rhythm may have been conceived by Bach as containing a metaphorical reference to divinity, but in the present case there is much less speculation involved in tracing the individual musical features to the representation of joy and of footsteps, both of which are associated in the text with the activity of following. It is characteristic of Bach to connect an affection with a physical action and also to prefer highly specific images of motion. Thus step motifs inevitably accompany the depiction of following even when the text does not call for them explicitly. Scalar progressions that represent purposeful stepping are found throughout "Ich folge dir gleichfalls," not only in the canonic motif itself but in the measure-by-measure progress of the bass and the flute figuration. The rising and falling sequences of the flutes that first appear in the ritornello are in fact a development of the important melodic step to which the word *Schritten* is set, and in the earlier version of the aria, this step was provided with the same ornamental treatment that is employed throughout its sequential development.

Bach's representation of joy consistently makes use of rapid scalar passages, and also of a triadic pattern or framework, perhaps in part derived from fanfare motifs. Scalar triadic runs are regularly connected with the word *Freude* in his secular cantatas, and the text "Freut euch" in a movement intended for the *Magnificat* even involves a triadic canon in the same key as "Ich folge dir gleichfalls." The affections of the Baroque were associated in general with the rhythms and melodic characteristics of various dances, and the reference to joy is undoubtedly responsible for the triple rhythm and the dancelike character of the aria we are examining. Frequent omission of the strong beat of the measure in the bass produces an appropriate lightness of rhythm, while at the same time, the change of chord on the second beat emphasizes the action of stepping and its purposefulness. The affection of joy is also conveyed by the choice of the soprano voice and especially of the concerting instrument, for the contemporary rhetorical analysis of joy found it to be expressed in a soft and light quality of voice; to this the flute is a peculiarly suitable complement, especially when it displays its characteristic agility, which adds, by means of the ceaseless sixteenth-note motion, an attractive feeling of effervescence to the affection. Finally the key of B♭ major had a character in Bach's time that made it appropriate for affections that were joyous but at the same time not frivolous; it is described by Mattheson in his *Neu-Eröffnete Orchester* of 1713 (part 3, ch.2) as "sehr divertissant und prächtig; behält dabei gerne etwas modestes, und kan zugleich vor magnific und mignon passiren." Something of the character and the sixteenth-note figuration of "Ich folge dir gleichfalls" is also manifest in the B♭-major aria "Mache dich, mein Herze, rein" of the *St. Matthew Passion.*

The repetition that is so typical of the aria we are discussing is due primarily to the word *gleichfalls* rather than *folgen*. Right at the opening of the ritornello there is an exact and immediate repetition of the first measure at the same pitch, and the vocal version of this phrase still more pointedly employs the repetition of a tone in the setting of *gleichfalls*. Tonal repetition is again used to capture the meaning of "Und lasse dich nicht," but its most general occurrence is really in the nature of a pedal point against which the progress of the stepping is measured and set off. The fact that such pedal points occur typically on the tonic reinforces the impression of simplicity that is associated with the basic affection of the aria.

The melodic treatment of the first line of text conveys the natural declamation flawlessly and clearly defines the significance of the various motifs. *Folgen* is associated with the opening triadic passage, *gleichfalls* with tonal repetition, *freudig* with the brightness of the high point of the melodic line and with the scalar sixteenth-note motion in general, and *Schritten* with the eighth-note step figure. The second line of text, "Und lasse dich nicht, mein Leben, mein Licht," is appropriately conveyed by another and more persistent repetition pattern. In the middle section of the aria, "Befördre den Lauf" is illustrated by the retention of the initial *folgen* motif, which becomes especially prominent during the second statement of this text, when the motif is ceaselessly carried to different pitches in its characteristic repeated form as heard at the opening of the ritornello. The next phrase of the text, "und höre nicht auf," is also repeated again and again, with the verbal repetition reflected in the use of the same melodic pattern although in different forms and at different pitches, a figure that obviously vivifies the sense of the words as well as enhancing the whole representation of persistence. The final phrase, "An mir zu ziehen, zu schieben, zu bitten," is fittingly presented in modified and more urgent step motifs, the more important of which conveys a sense of pressure by sixteenth-note motion, anticipations, and a startling change from diatonic to chromatic succession on *schieben*. Other deft touches also come to our attention. At one point *schieben* is vividly depicted by the introduction of a suspension that thrusts the regular stress forward from the first to the second beat of the measure (m.100*f.*). And in both statements of the text of the middle section, the rising sequence at the close comes to a halt with *schieben*, and a rest effectively sets off the more feelingful declamation of *zu bitten* (m.65*f.*, 111*f.*).

The middle section of a da capo aria can best be considered in general as revealing another facet of the single affection of the composition, since the Baroque affection was a general concept that comprised innumerable particular variants; but in the aria under discussion, the middle section really presents a distinct change of conception. The singer becomes troubled instead of joyful, and he appeals to Jesus to draw near and to urge him onward ceaselessly. Where the main section is set in B♭ major and modulates to the dominant, the middle section moves rapidly to G minor and then to C minor, mirroring major with minor and the dominant with the subdominant. The symbolic problem is to project the continuance of the following but under changed conditions, and the solution of this problem turns the section into what is essentially a development of the original material. In addition to freer motivic treatment of the patterns of the main section, the last three-quarters of the ritornello appears intact at the end of the G-minor passage, and the whole ritornello becomes the background of the C-minor passage. But the path is now difficult; it seems long and tortuous; sequences carry us restlessly through a variety of keys, and the step motif reaches its maximum extension in the bass, now – as in the inversion of mode and key relationship – moving downward instead of upward, and over a span so great that if it were not transposed upward in the middle of its journey it would cover nearly three octaves. A point of additional interest is the elimination of the first part of the ritornello in the G-minor passage, so that the characteristic first line of the text is not represented; it is only with the repetition of the appeal to Jesus that the *folgen* motif is reinstated, as though in answer to the singer's request.

Although the rhetorical cast of eighteenth-century music has for some time provided an indispensable foundation for the interpretation of the particular symbols of Bach's music, it has been relatively neglected in respect of certain larger problems of significance. Yet rhetoric seems to have been responsible for transforming the individual musical composition altogether into a kind of oration, and we can often profitably interpret the da capo aria from this point of view, and perhaps ultimately the development section of the classical sonata as well. Thus the opening ritornello of "Ich folge dir gleichfalls" will take on the character of an exordium. The topic awaits verbal statement, but it is foreshadowed, even with its insistence upon the step motif; the mood is set and the proper frame of mind evoked. Then the voice continues with the propositio by announcing the theme in the devise, and subsequently this is restated and the argument advanced. Confirmatio is followed by confutatio, as alternatives are set forth and examined in the light of the main theme. That the middle section will take on the character of a development under the influence of such an outlook is almost a necessary consequence. The final section can be construed as a peroration rather than a literal return to the beginning, a conception that is supported by the abridged but intensified character of the music and its free departures from the previous forms of the material. The key word *folgen* in particular receives a new and striking melismatic shape, set to a typical figuration derived from the step motif, and again canonically.

In the middle of the eighteenth century Krause urges his contemporaries not to assign music too quickly to a place lower than poetry and rhetoric, for "a well composed and well performed musical work," he writes, "even a purely instrumental one, makes the same kind of impression as many an oration and many a poem, if not even stronger ones. . . . Often the most important effect of a speech as far as most of the audience is concerned consists not in an actual improvement of their knowledge but solely in forming their feelings and impelling them to a particular course of action, without their memory clearly retaining much of the substance that has been adduced" (*Von der musikalischen Poesie,* p.107f.). Such an outlook reasonably entitles us to regard the arias of Bach's Passions as protreptic or homiletic orations, with a hermeneutic intention that is directed toward the scriptural portions of the music, very much like the actual sermon that separated the two large divisions of the Passion. Indeed this rhetorical purpose becomes explicit in the very theme of "Ich folge dir gleichfalls," for the melody of the aria is clearly based on the preceding recitative; it faithfully follows and expands the musical phrase of the Evangelist that is heard immediately before, to the words "Simon Petrus aber folgete Jesu nach." Rhetorical motivation may also lie behind the change of attitude in the middle section of the aria; the feelings and reflections of the singer always act as an ethical model for the congregation, and serve the purpose of instruction and edification for the churchgoer, but the appeal to Jesus superimposes on this general function the more obviously rhetorical task of direct persuasion.

"Ich folge dir gleichfalls" has been judged by Kretzschmar and others to be a poor piece, an opinion we may find supported mostly by the middle section, for the shift in attitude, based as it is on a continuity of the tempo and musical material devised for the expression of joy, is necessarily something less than convincing or well defined; in the chromatic symbolization of *schieben,* to cite a particular feature, logic easily seems to outweigh musical feasibility and expressive value. A still more fundamental consideration is that the aria grows out of an apparently unimportant turn of events in the Passion narrative or, in any case, an unemotional one. Indeed Smend has justified the existence of the piece purely on the basis of the formal symmetry of the whole Passion, which he explains by the theory that Bach was transferring the prevalent arch form of his Cöthen instrumental works to the new area of large-scale vocal works. On the other hand, the symmetry of the *St. John Passion* also provides an explanation for the key of B♭ major, but that does not prevent the key from being appropriate musically at the same time, and we know in general that formal considerations need not override or vitiate expressive ones. It is obviously pertinent also that an aria occurs at just this point in Handel's *Brockes Passion;* formal symmetry could hardly have been the only basis of Bach's decision. As a matter of fact, he retained and adjusted details in "Ich folge dir gleichfalls" even when he substantially revised the *St. John Passion,* which argues that he thought well of the aria, although the changes he introduced in the text indicate that he was dissatisfied with the middle section.

But when Bach made these changes in the text toward the end of his life – possibly because the Passion arias were closely connected with his personal religious experience – there can be no doubt that much more was lost than gained. The substitution of "mein Heiland mit Freuden" for "mit freudigen Schritten" transformed the step motif on *Schritten* from a kind of simile to a metaphor which illustrated *Freuden* by purely musical steps that had no explicit counterpart. The symbolic value of the motif might then easily go unrecognized, with a serious loss to its changing significance throughout the aria. In the middle section the new text no longer appeals to Jesus to urge the singer onward, but in- stead describes the path as one of ceaseless longing until Jesus shall have taught patient suffering: "Mein sehnlicher Lauf hört eher nicht auf, bis dass du mich lehrest geduldig zu leiden." The musical setting of *befördre* is thus inappropriately applied to *sehnlicher,* while *geduldig* is never ade- quately treated and sounds impatient rather than patient, especially when it takes the place of *schieben.* Equally unfortunate is the initial oc- currence of *leiden,* which coincides with *ziehen* and *schieben* and is thus projected in a hurried rising passage where we would reasonably expect a slow falling one. The unceasing idea remains common to both texts, but the replacement of urgency with longing and patient suffering could only have been accomplished with partial success. The adaptation is useful for our present purpose, however, for it furnishes a modest demonstration of the specificity of Bach's music and thus of the impor- tance of determining its meaning accurately.

From *College Music Symposium* 5 (1965): 88–96.

8

The Tonal Ideal of Romanticism

THE ROMANTIC ideal of tone can be compactly characterized by means of two related properties: vagueness, or lack of definition, and fusion, or blending. The first of these is applicable to individual tones as well as to tonal simultaneity, while blending is less a separate property than the polyphonic result of a lack of definition of the constituent tones. There is a certain elementalism in these preferences, an enjoyment of sensuousness as opposed to structure and articulation. During the Enlightenment, imitation served as the appropriate principle common to all the arts, and music accordingly strove to resemble speech or simple song. Such an outlook left little room for purely musical delight, but later in the eighteenth century a more adequate appreciation develops of harmonic and melodic factors that cannot be explained in terms of imitation. There is a new interest in sound qualities also. The Mannheim symphonists in particular often treat the orchestra as a sonorous entity rather than an ensemble of individuals; unison passages, nonthematic fortissimo sections for full orchestra, and transitional dynamics – all realized with impressive precision in performance – help to produce a style that is peculiar to the medium and that rests to a large extent on tonal effects of unprecedented emotional potency. High Classicism combines this dynamic subjectivity with the defined spatial interplay descended from the Baroque concerto, but by the end of the century the balance is irreversibly upset by tonal forces of a more specifically Romantic kind. The realm of music seems to take on a mysterious and self-contained character that stands in opposition to the world of everyday experience. Musical themes are at times set off by an introductory gesture that is somewhat like the unveiling of a secret domain. Outstanding instances are the opening of Mozart's Symphony in G Minor (KV 550) and of Beethoven's Ninth Symphony and the initial rising third that was prefixed to the slow movement of the *Hammerklavier* Sonata (Wagner uses the same mystic motif in his early C-Major Symphony). Outside the mainstream of music, instruments with delectable but elusive tonal qualities, such as the glass harmonica and the aeolian harp, find an enthusiastic response with a wide public. But the enjoyment of sensuous vagueness is not restricted to the peripheries of the serious musical world; it is found also – to cite a central example – in the novel effects achieved with French horns (the most famous early passages occur in the Scherzo of Beethoven's *Eroica*, in Weber's later operas, and in Mendelssohn's *Sommernachtstraum*).

A similar concern with blending and lack of definition is an important factor in the adoption of the piano and its gradual improvement, while starting with Mozart and Schubert, there is a corollary development of novel harmonic effects and soft lyricism. The piano soon becomes capable of neglecting melody entirely in order to indulge at length in purely sensuous qualities and in the effects of fusion made possible by the pedal. In the piano works of Chopin and Schumann, the tonal ideal of Romanticism reaches early maturity. Again with Schubert as an important predecessor, similar qualities are contained in the orchestral music of Berlioz and Mendelssohn. Blending and lack of definition celebrate their triumph in the preludes of *Lohengrin* and *Rheingold* and in the grail scenes and the distant bells of *Parsifal*. The very appearance of the conductor upon the scene meant that the orchestra was no longer a collection of individual performers, but a single tonal source, extensive and fused, and now capable of those inner effects that would seem to have the personality of a single executant as their prerequisite. With inexhaustible inventiveness, Romantic instrumentation ceaselessly mixes and blends tone-colors. An oboe will overlap with a clarinet and then succeed it during the course of a melody, or the two will sound a phrase in unison. The overriding aim of the scoring of Schumann and Brahms and Wagner is a versatile but unified color, while Bruckner takes as a model the diffused and collective unity of the organ.

All these changes in the tonal constitution of music have their complement in the musical descriptions of Romantic literature, where the new ideals of sonority seem to find a much more striking expression than in music itself. Both the vagueness and the elemental qualities of tone are illustrated by the frequent association of music with water or air, and the vagueness is emphasized still more by distance, echo, and reverberation. Night and darkness, regarded as the ideal setting of musical performance, provide a final enhancement of tonal indefiniteness. Of the numerous musical passages in the writings of Jean Paul, we may take as an example a description from his *Hesperus* (1795):

Ach in solchen Tönen schlagen die zerlaufenden Wellen des Meeres der Ewigkeit an das Herz der dunklen Menschen, die am Ufer stehen und sich hinübersehnen! – Jetzo wirst du, Horion, von einem tönenden Wehen aus dem Regendunst des Lebens hinübergehoben in die lichte Ewigkeit! – Höre, welche Töne umlaufen die weiten Gefilde von Eden! Schlagen nicht die Laute, in Hauche verflogen, an fernen Blumen zurück und umfließen, vom Echo geschwollen, den Schwanen-Busen, der seligzergehend auf Flügel schwimmt, und ziehen ihn von melodischen Fluten in Fluten und sinken mit ihm in die fernen Blumen ein, die ein Nebel aus Düften füllt, und im dunkeln Dufte glimmt die Seele wieder an wie Abendrot, eh' sie selig untergeht?

Ach Horion, ruht die Erde noch unter uns, die ihre Todeshügel um das weite Leben trägt? Zittern diese Töne in einer irdischen Luft? O! Tonkunst, die du die Vergangenheit und die Zukunft mit ihren fliegenden Flammen so nahe an unsre Wunden bringst, bist du das Abendwehen aus diesem Leben oder die Morgenluft aus jenem? – Ja, deine Laute sind Echo, welche Engel den Freudentönen der zweiten Welt abnehmen, um in unser stummes Herz, um in unsre öde Nacht das verwehte Lenzgetön fern von uns fliegender Himmel zu senken! Und du, verklingender Harmonikaton! du kömmst ja aus einem Jauchzen zu uns, das, von Himmel in Himmel verschlagen, endlich in dem fernsten stummen Himmel stirbt, der aus nichts besteht als aus einer tiefen, weiten, ewig stillen Wonne.[1]

Literary descriptions provide information not only about the physical features of music, but also about a group of conceptual factors – aesthetic, magical, religious, and metaphysical – which are all interrelated and which can be regarded as motivations of the tonal changes. Such conceptions appear again in the subject matter of opera, song, and program music, and their most adequate treatment is of course to be found in aesthetic and philosophical writings. We cannot consider them in detail, but we may note the interesting tendency, in the passage given above, to identify the fluid properties of air, taken as analogous to tonal properties, with the actual medium of tonal transmission, and then to extend this, more importantly, to an impalpable substance diffused throughout the cosmos. Thus the listener is often described as carried aloft by music, in a conception that, having shifted imperceptibly from physics to metaphysics, now moves just as easily into religion. We can view the process as exemplified in Wackenroder's *Herzensergießungen* (1797):

*Erwartungsvoll harrte er auf den ersten Ton der Instrumente; – und indem
er nun aus der dumpfen Stille, mächtig und langgezogen, gleich dem
Wehen eines Windes vom Himmel hervorbrach und die ganze Gewalt der
Töne über seinem Haupte daherzog, – da war es ihm, als wenn auf einmal
seiner Seele große Flügel ausgespannt, als wenn er von einer dürrren Heide
aufgehoben würde, der trübe Wolkenvorhang vor den sterblichen Augen
verschwände, und er zum lichten Himmel emporschwebte.²*

It is important to realize that the religious effect is not confined to
church music but belongs to music of all types, for music in general is
conceived in the Romantic era as somehow religious, as exerting a ca-
thartic and moral influence by its very nature. Thus Herder tells us that
it was Andacht that raised music above vision, dance, gesture, and poetry, and made it independent;³ and it is Andacht again that Joseph
Berglinger brings to music in the *Herzensergießungen*.⁴ Wackenroder
first describes the effect of church music on Berglinger, but shortly afterward he applies the very language of the passage we have excerpted to
Berglinger's experience at a concert; there is the same release from
earthly cares, the same sensation that soul and body are soaring and
being carried aloft, the same visions – and all this occurs again with the
body motionless and the gaze fixed: Berglinger's eyes are turned to the
floor, and he sees nothing.

The religious nature of music is made just as explicit in the *Phanta-
sien über die Kunst,* where Wackenroder writes, "so schliess' ich mein
Auge zu vor all dem Kriege der Welt – und ziehe mich still in das Land
der Musik, als in das Land des Glaubens, zurück, wo alle unsre Zweifel
und unsre Leiden sich in ein tönendes Meer verlieren ——."⁵ It is evident,
then, that not only the vague celestial origin and destination of tone,
but also the other properties of reverberation, luminosity, and fusion
that were connected with the a cappella religious ideal and with the
organ, could logically become tonal characteristics of all music. The
process seems to be exemplified especially well in the works of
Bruckner.

We need not wait for Schelling or Schopenhauer to discover the
metaphysical status of music, for Romantic literature clearly depicts it
as an instrument of philosophy that provides insight into the reaches of
time as well as those of space. Time enters into the passage we have already considered from the *Hesperus,* and additional examples are read-

ily furnished by the same work: "Rinnen nicht diese Laute, Horion, wie Menschentage ineinander?"[6] Or in greater elaboration:

O wenn noch dazu diese Töne sich in wogende Blumen verschlingen, aus einer Vergangenheit in die andre zurückfließen, immer leiser rinnen durch die vergangnen, hinter dem Menschen ruhenden Jahre – endlich nur murmeln unter dem Lebensmorgenrot – nur ungehört aufwallen unter der Wiege des Menschen – und erstarren in unsrer kalten Dämmerung und versiegen in der Mitternacht, wo jeder von uns nicht war.[7]

Almost always it is the vagueness, successive echoes, or gradual decay of tone that signalizes the spatial and temporal power of music.

If we turn to music itself for the conceptions underlying its tonal ideal, we find that the magical potency of tone is a recurrent theme of opera and programmatic works starting with the flute and bells of Mozart's *Zauberflöte* and often deriving from the demonic musicians of Hoffmann's tales. Music becomes less a physical event than the manifestation of the internal nature of an instrument or its material, or the voice of a spirit or of a supernatural force, and its tonal indefiniteness follows as a matter of course. An important associated conception is the mythic and legendary quality of music, or in general its distance from the everyday world. This motif is developed in numberless operas, romances, and ballads that deal with fairies, sprites, saintly heroines, and satanic or legendary heroes or make use of an oriental or medieval setting. In turn, medievalism is often connected with religious subject matter, which is another important source of the Romantic tonal ideal in dramas of saints and religious knights and in various re-creations of the style of Palestrina or Gregorian chant. Here the otherworldly suggestiveness of tone is coupled to the fused and diffused tonal ideal of a cappella singing, conceived typically in a reverberant church interior or in the still vaguer acoustic setting of heaven. Metaphysical material is as frequent as religious, and music is often connected with the supernatural (as in the Undine operas or in Wagner's *Holländer* and *Lohengrin*) or with the spirit of nature (as in the undulating patterns of water in Mendelssohn's *Melusine* and Wagner's *Rheingold*), and in particular with the mysterious voice of the forest (as in *Freischütz* and *Siegfried*). Or again, the metaphysical import of music may be envisaged in general, as in Victor Hugo's *Ce qu'on entend sur la montagne*, which conveys the large indefiniteness of cosmic music that Liszt's tone-poem brings to life with such power, or in the *Ring des Nibelungen,* where music gives voice to the being of all of inanimate and animate nature, very much in accordance with Schopenhauer's philosophical conception.

In the aesthetic and philosophical writings of the Romantic period we have the most explicit and convincing evidence that the tonal ideal of an epoch is bound up with its most fundamental ideas and attitudes. Jean Paul's *Vorschule der Aesthetik* conceives the vagueness and blending of music as its peculiarly Romantic qualities, for the essence of Romanticism is taken to be expanse and lack of confinement.[8] This is valid for visual art and poetry, not only for music, and indeed we find the same changes in sensuous ideal occurring within the sphere of each individual art. "Eine Statue schließt durch ihre enge und scharfe Umschreibung jedes Romantische aus; die Malerei nähert sich schon durch Menschen-Gruppierungen ihm mehr und erreicht es ohne Menschen in Landschaften, z. B. von Claude."[9] Poetry is subject to the same principles, some of its varieties qualifying as Romantic and others not.

Die altnordische, *mehr ans Erhabne grenzende fand im Schattenreiche ihrer klimatischen verfinsterten Schauernatur, in ihren Nächten und auf ihren Gebirgen zum Gespensterorkus eine grenzenlose Geisterwelt, worin die enge Sinnenwelt zerfloß und versank; dahin gehört Ossian mit seinen Abend- und Nachtstücken, in welchen die himmlischen Nebelsterne der Vergangenheit über dem dicken Nachtnebel der Gegenwart stehen und blinken; und nur in der Vergangenheit findet er Zukunft und Ewigkeit.*[10]

In this context, as though by necessity, the author has recourse to musical analogy: "Alles ist in seinem Gedichte Musik, aber entfernte und dadurch verdoppelte und ins Unendliche verschwommene, gleichsam ein Echo, das nicht durch rauh-treues Wiedergeben der Töne, sondern durch abschwächendes Mildern derselben entzückt."[11] And somewhat later on he writes again, still with particular reference to the tonal ideal of the time: "Die nordische Poesie und Romantik ist eine Äolsharfe, durch welche der Sturm der Wirklichkeit in Melodien streicht, ein Geheul in Getön auslösend, aber Wehmut zittert auf den Saiten, ja zuweilen ein hineingerissener Schmerz."[12] It is scarcely to be wondered at, then, that music appeared as the Romantic art par excellence, for a lack of objectivity, a fluent and transient character, is inherent to it. While we are scarcely aware of light as such, but only of its source or the object from which it is reflected, with tone it is the opposite, so that the spatial definiteness of the source always tends to be supplanted by the spatial indefiniteness of the wave motion of transmission. And is it not reverberation, for example, that explains the "eigenes anziehendes Zwielicht," the "fremdartigen . . . geistigen Schein," which Schumann finds surrounding the explicit patterns of music?[13] It was difficult to conceive of a specific Romantic movement in music, in his opinion, for this art was always Romantic.[14] The notion was widespread and occurs also in Jean Paul's *Vorschule:* "Es ist noch ähnlicher als ein Gleichnis, wenn man das Romantische das wogende Aussummen einer Saite oder Glocke nennt, in welchem die Tonwoge wie in immer ferneren Weiten verschwimmt und endlich sich verliert in uns selber und, obwohl aussen schon still, noch immer lautet."[15]

It is understandable, then, that reverberation appears as the chief characteristic of the Romantic tonal ideal in its literary descriptions. The quality is often misnamed "echo," but it is certainly the most important member of a family of properties that includes echo, diffuseness, extensiveness, fusion, and distance. The common effect of these is to obscure the tonal source, to prevent a clear perception of it by disguising its nature, concealing its position, and blending it with other sources simultaneously activated. The role of the local specificity of musical sources in the constitution of music had been emphasized by antiphony and the concerto principle during the seventeenth and eighteenth centuries, and an awareness of the identity, location, and activity of each singer and instrumentalist was an important feature of the high Baroque and Classical styles. But the tonal ideal of Romanticism employs every means to effect an opposite result. It selects instruments themselves difficult to localize; the tones of the glass harmonica, of the aeolian harp, and of the French horn (for various reasons we cannot here consider) are peculiarly unspecific with respect to their point of origin; they seem to come from everywhere and from no place in particular. It combines instruments or voices to produce literally extensive sources which cannot fail to create a somewhat diffuse impression because they do not in fact occupy a single position. It removes sources from the listener so that indices of direction and distance both become ineffective, the tone becomes weak, and the point of origin cannot be determined.[16] Finally it surrounds the tone with a halo of reverberation, which enlarges the apparent size of the source, prevents the detection of its position (because reflections from the surfaces of the room produce images that confuse perception), and provides a natural, omnipresent, and apparently inexplicable instance of the fading out of tone – its disappearance, it would seem, into some unknown land. Reverberation also increases tonal fusion, and in Wagner's Bayreuth theater, a long reverberation time of over two seconds adds its effect to that of an orchestra that is lowered and covered over, so that there is an initial fusion produced by internal reflections (as well as an interference with localization because direct sound is cut off). The resultant modification and blending of the tone, together with the invisibility of the instruments, effectively detaches the sound from the orchestra so that it can serve characteristic Romantic purposes. In general, the concert halls of the nineteenth century had reverberation times substantially longer than those of the first half of the twentieth century, and given its proper environment, the tone of Romantic music will take on a certain rich brilliance and an autonomous value, qualities altogether different from the objectivity of the late Baroque or the dry precision cultivated in the typical sound-absorbent setting of Neoclassicism.

In the whole circle of conceptions that accompany the Romantic tonal ideal, the aim is not solely the magical revelation of the being or essence of each instrument or singer or sonorous substance, but still more typically directed away from the medium of performance altogether; the horns of *Freischütz* or the *Ring* present not the soul of the instrument or of the metal of which it is made but of nature itself – of the forest or the Rhine; the choirs at the close of *Parsifal* evoke supernal religious conceptions or visions. Thus the tonal source logically disappears in perception, most characteristically in Wagner's mystic abyss, and instead it is the being of some represented object that is revealed to us. Romantic music is as little a representation of performing forces as it is a representation of extramusical objects, happenings, or specific ideas. It is therefore music of the most absolute kind in a double sense, but always with respect to conventional types of perception and understanding, which it rejects. The hunting horns in the second act of *Tristan und Isolde* can be taken as a model instance of this ideal, first in the fact that the instruments themselves are not susceptible of auditory localization, then in the association of the horns with the forest and in the soft and fused quality of their harmonies, further in the fact that the horns on stage represent those in the drama rather than themselves, and finally in the actual distance and vagueness of these represented hunting horns, which are invisible because of both distance and night and which are eventually confused completely with the rustling of leaves and the bubbling of a stream.

The very nature of auditory experience suggests that there are two opposed modes of hearing: possibilities or types to which any given historical attitude may be referred to help in defining it more precisely according as it partakes more of the one or the other. We may call these modes Classic and Romantic. In the first, hearing is perceptually oriented; the sources of sound are objects of interest; and since precision of location and the identity of the sound producer are of primary importance, hearing cooperates with vision and is subjected to it, as the sense of superior clarity and perceptual ability. In Romantic hearing, on the other hand, sound is not taken in its usual practical importance as an index of the location and identity of objects of the external world, but more in its own terms, in its peculiar sensational qualities, and in their meaning as a revelation of emotion and being – of the inner nature of life and the natural world. The individual singers and instruments are disregarded, and the tones they produce are not treated in the fashion of physical science, as signs of the presence and activity of sonorous objects, but are given another and more mysterious reference and at the same time typically detached from their productive agents by means of reverberation and blending. The Romantic mode of hearing is thus directed toward an invisible world and is in some sense religious, animistic, or metaphysical. It suggests constantly, in fact – and for this reason it delights in the subtle emergence and dying away of tone – a world that is imperceptible even to hearing, yet to which only hearing can give access.

Thus it is always the inner side, the Ding-an-sich, that Romantic music presents, not the aspect manifest to the senses. And music acts in its own ideal form and in its own right, appealing to hearing alone, or through hearing, to the soul and the organ of philosophic knowledge. In contrast, when hearing joins with vision in musical apprehension, the normal mode of sense perception is brought into play, which effects an objective awareness of external objects and events through the cooperative activity of the senses, so that hearing has its basis in adjustive behavior. But this mode of hearing puts us in touch with our external world and makes us attend to the musical performers; it does not elevate us beyond them to a world ideally above human experience altogether. The Romantic mode of hearing will understandably invoke the aid of night to establish itself; and darkness is indeed a factor with a deep affinity to all the various motivations of the Romantic ideal of tone, whether aesthetic, magical, religious, or metaphysical. The Novalis *Hymnen an die Nacht* and Wagner's *Tristan* frame a half-century of music in which night is a recurrent motif of artistic subject matter and darkness a natural concomitant; for a mode of hearing that involves vision belongs to the world of ordinary experience, with its practical and precise distinctions and its concrete emotions; and it is to these that the distance, fusion, and transcendence of the Romantic tonal ideal are most fundamentally opposed.

With the eyes excluded, imagined scenes are conjured up by a second, inward vision subject to the music. The passage we have cited from Wackenroder's *Herzensergießungen* continues its description of the effects of music as follows:

Dann hielt er sich mit seinem Körper still und unbeweglich und heftete die Augen unverrückt auf den Boden. Die Gegenwart versank vor ihm; sein Inneres war von allen irdischen Kleinigkeiten, welche der wahre Staub auf dem Glanze der Seele sind, gereinigt; die Musik durchdrang seine Nerven mit leisen Schauern und ließ, so wie sie wechselte, mannigfache Bilder vor ihm aufsteigen.[17]

The strength of Schopenhauer's conception of music, which appealed so strongly to Wagner and the young Nietzsche, is that it provided a metaphysical substructure that combined readily with epistemological considerations of the senses, thus making possible a universality and coherence that had no parallel and enabling it to account with the greatest success for all the properties of music as it was known and experienced at the time. The Romantic tonal ideal accordingly finds its most thorough justification in Wagner's essay on Beethoven, a work that adopts and extends the musical conceptions of Schopenhauer. Wagner distinguishes carefully and at length between two kinds of consciousness, one turned outward and the other inward: states that are thoroughly hostile to one another and cannot be efficacious simultaneously. On this distinction the opposition of visual art and music is founded, and then the essential incompatibility of seeing and hearing. We can find no place here for the details of the theory, but in the course of his discussion Wagner adduces a little story of his personal experience that conveys the basic notion quite well:

In schlafloser Nacht trat ich einst auf den Balkon meines Fensters am großen Kanal in Venedig: wie ein tiefer Traum lag die märchenhafte Lagunenstadt im Schatten vor mir ausgedehnt. Aus dem lautlosen Schweigen erhob sich da der mächtige rauhe Klageruf eines soeben auf seiner Barke erwachten Gondolier's, mit welchem dieser in wiederholten Absätzen in die Nacht hineinrief, bis aus weitester Ferne der gleiche Ruf dem nächtlichen Kanal entlang antwortete: ich erkannte die uralte schwermüthige, melodische Phrase, welcher seiner Zeit auch die bekannten Verse Tasso's untergelegt worden, die aber an sich gewiß so alt ist, als Venedigs Kanäle mit ihrer Bevölkerung. Nach feierlichen Pausen belebte sich endlich der weithin tönende Dialog und schien sich im Einklang zu verschmelzen, bis aus der Nähe wie aus der Ferne sanft das Tönen wieder im neugewonnenen Schlummer erlosch. Was konnte mir das von der Sonne bestrahlte, bunt durchwimmelte Venedig des Tages von sich sagen, das jener tönende Nachttraum mir nicht unendlich tiefer unmittelbar zum Bewußtsein gebracht gehabt hätte?[18]

Distance, echo, and fusion show how intimately tonal qualities are connected with the underlying philosophical conceptions. In what follows, the epistemological opposition is examined inside the concert hall, where a kind of paralysis of the sense of vision is attributed to the effect of music:

Wir erfahren diess in jedem Konzertsaal während der Anhörung eines uns wahrhaft ergreifenden Tonstückes, wo das Allerzerstreuendste und an sich Häßlichste vor unseren Augen vorgeht, was uns jedenfalls, wenn wir es intensiv sähen, von der Musik gänzlich abziehen und sogar lächerlich gestimmt machen würde, nämlich, außer dem sehr trivial berührenden Anblicke der Zuhörerschaft, die mechanischen Bewegungen der Musiker, der ganz sonderbar sich bewegende Hilfsapparat einer orchestralen Produktion. Daß dieser Anblick, welcher den nicht von der Musik Ergriffenen einzig beschäftigt, den von ihr Gefesselten endlich gar nicht mehr stört, zeigt uns deutlich, daß wir ihn nicht mehr mit Bewußtsein gewahr werden, dagegen nun mit offenen Augen in den Zustand gerathen, welcher mit dem des somnambulen Hellsehens eine wesentliche Ähnlichkeit hat. Und in Wahrheit ist es auch nur dieser Zustand, in welchem wir der Welt des Musikers unmittelbar angehörig werden.[19]

But Wagner has here unwittingly added a cultural dimension to his theory, for the modern reader will not fail to notice that although Wagner believes he is describing the inherent nature of listening to music, he is in fact describing a particular way of listening to music. Thus the contrast of two modes of knowledge, of two arts, of seeing and hearing, or of day and night can be interpreted as a contrast between two modes of hearing, the one assimilated to external perception and the other exploiting the peculiar values of the unaided sense. The tonal ideal of Romanticism is founded upon this autonomous activity of audition and its philosophical significance. By destroying the objective aspect of music it permits outer tones to become inner ones, thus reversing the process of utterance and revealing the intrinsic identity of man and nature.[20]

NOTES

From *Festschrift für Walter Wiora zum 30* (Kassel: Bärenreiter Karl Vötterle, 1967), pp.419–26.

1. *Werke*, Bd.1 (München 1960), pp.949–50.

2. Leipzig 1921, p.188.

3. *Kalligone* (1800). *Sämtliche Werke*, Teil 19 (Stuttgart und Tübingen 1830), Bd.2, p.14.

4. Op. cit., pp.188, 190.

5. *Werke und Briefe*, Bd.1 (Jena 1910), p.165.

6. Op. cit., p.948.

7. Op. cit., p.951.

8. *Werke*, Bd.5 (München 1960), p.88.

9. Ibid., p.87.

10. Ibid., p.89.

11. Loc. cit.

12. Ibid., p.92.

13. *Gesammelte Schriften* (Kreisig), Bd.1 (Leipzig 1914), p.250.

14. Ibid., p.26.

15. *Werke*, Bd.5 (München 1963), p.88.

16. In Jean Paul's *Flegeljahre* there is even an instance of a moving source (invisible as well as receding), to which I called attention in an article on Schumann (*Journal of the American Musicological Society* 17 [1964], p.345).

17. Op. cit., pp.188–89.

18. *Sämtliche Schriften und Dichtungen*, 5. Aufl., Bd.9 (Leipzig 1911), p.74.

19. Ibid., p.75. Wagner had commented on this conflict years before, in the essay *Ein glücklicher Abend*, where those who look at the performers are considered to be Philistines, and the devout listener seats himself where he cannot see the orchestra (ibid., Bd.1, pp.137–38). Closing the eyes is another variant of the same attitude, but with its own peculiar effects on the experience of listening; it has a special connection also with auditory imagery and the superiority of a private realization of music. For the

operatic audience vision would seem to have a positive function, but its role in the theater is nevertheless fully compatible with its suspension at concerts.

20. This equation occurs in the text of Isolde's final ecstasy in Wagner's *Tristan,* along with an excellent characterization of the Romantic ideal of tone. At the same time, the orchestration achieves the highest degree of tonal mixture and blending and even draws the voice into its unified texture.

9

Theory and Practice in Schumann's Aesthetics

OR THOSE who are interested in comparing theory and practice in the field of musical aesthetics, the composers of the nineteenth century possess a special attraction, since they often express themselves in words almost as readily as in tones. To some extent, however, the combination of theorist and practitioner in one person is illusory, for the writings of composers rarely come under the head of speculative aesthetics, and take the form of criticism, letters, or diaries, of literary works and tracts on technical theory, rather than the form of a philosophical treatise. Conceptions of music will be either implicit or incidental; they must be uncovered as the presuppositions of criticism or assembled into coherent form from occasional reflections. Although Schumann once projected a study of musical aesthetics, his writings in fact belong to the field of criticism, and thus to applied rather than speculative aesthetics; they constitute a second sphere of practice alongside his music and similarly call for explanation in terms of general principles. We may therefore examine the characteristics both of Schumann's music and of his criticism, in order to induce from them the notions that will serve as their theoretical foundation. But we shall be aided by various explicit statements found in his critical writings themselves, as well as in his letters, for if Schumann was little inclined toward systematic philosophy, he could hardly avoid reflecting occasionally on the underlying principles of his creative and critical activity. The time was one that spontaneously coupled music and philosophy; musical ideas assumed a new importance both in literature and in metaphysics; newspaper articles discussed the nature of music as a matter of course; musical philosophy even had its counterpart in philosophical music. We can logically expect that Schumann will represent such a major current of thought, for there is no one who reveals more clearly the dominant concerns of Romanticism. Nor was he an academic critic, for he wrote as the leader and propagandist of a new direction in music, a progressive movement of which he was also the outstanding representative as a composer. Under the circumstances, his work could not fail to embody a particular aesthetic attitude.

The path from practice to theory is one naturally suggested by our material, for Schumann's music and writings alike confront us with certain puzzles and paradoxes. These problems are all concerned with the nature of musical significance and, more specifically, with the way in which music is connected to external events, which was a vital issue for both Schumann and his century. The most various kinds of meaning are suggested not only by Schumann's music itself but by the titles, headings, and mottos of his instrumental compositions. References to specific objects are less frequent than vague intimations. Much of the significance was private and can never be completely known; indeed the enigma of which music was capable, and especially the mystery intrinsic to its nature, represented a major attraction for the Romanticist. Reminiscent of the Renaissance *soggetto cavato* is the use of the mottoes ABEGG, ASCH, GADE, and BACH in Schumann's keyboard works. Here names point to composers, to the town of Schumann's fiancée, and to a pianist disguised as a fictitious countess, although there is a specifically musical reference to style as well: the works based on BACH, for example, look to Bach's polyphony as a model. As we can see in the case of ASCH, such serial procedures are naturally suited to melodic transformation that seeks diversity in form and character.

In a few works we find a scale passage ascending through a seventh, a pattern called "papillon" by Schumann. Melodic quotation occurs in the use of the *Marseillaise* and the *Grossvatertanz* (or *Thème du XVIIème siècle*), and there is also a purely musical symbolism in the imitation of Chopin, Gade, and Mendelssohn; in various parodies of Bach, Beethoven, and Schubert; and in the adoption of stylistic features of traditional genres such as the gigue or the waltz. Often there is a reference to a literary genre closely associated with a musical style, such as the ballad or the romance. The diversity of programmatic inscriptions can be seen in the titles of the piano works, which range from the specificity of *Marche des Davidsbündler contre les Philistins* and *Kind in Einschlummern* to the atmospheric *Phantasiestück* or *Nachtstück* and comprise titles so rich in suggestiveness as *Kreisleriana*. A special class is formed by designations of imaginative narration: the titles *Fabel*, *Novellette*, *Romanze*, and *Ballade*, to which we may add the headings *Im Legenden-Ton* and *Balladenmässig*. This invocation of a storylike or fabulous content is complemented by the still more inviting vagueness of *Der Dichter spricht*, *Botschaft*, *Vision*, and *Traum eines Kindes* and by the strange effect of the absence of a title in three of the pieces of the *Album für die Jugend;* where the surrounding pieces all have names or head-ings, the nameless ones take on a curious character at once expressive and enigmatic. Graphic representation occurs in Schumann too: no verbal help is really necessary to point out the striking of the clock and the fading away of the sounds of the ball at the end of the *Papillons.*

Somewhat more detailed significance is given by verses that stand at the head of a few compositions. "Mai, lieber Mai, – Bald bist du wieder da!" is inscribed over one of the pieces of the *Album für die Jugend,* while another has the heading: "Weinlesezeit – Fröhliche Zeit!" Prefixed to the *Davidsbündlertänze* is the "Alter Spruch":

> *In all und jeder Zeit*
> *Verknüpft sich Lust und Leid:*
> *Bleibt fromm in Lust und seid*
> *Dem Leid mit Mut bereit.*

The *Phantasie* opus 17 carries the famous verses of Friedrich Schlegel as a "Motto":

> *Durch alle Töne tönet*
> *Im bunten Erdentraum*
> *Ein leiser Ton gezogen*
> *Für den der heimlich lauschet.*

And a specific picture is painted in the *Waldszenen* by the stanzas of Friedrich Hebbel that precede *Verrufene Stelle:*

> *Die Blumen, so hoch sie wachsen,*
> *Sind blass hier, wie der Tod:*
> *Nur eine in der Mitte*
> *Steht da im dunklen Roth.*

> *Die hat es nicht von der Sonne:*
> *Nie traf sie deren Gluth;*
> *Sie hat es von der Erde,*
> *Und die trank Menschenblut.*

Prominent in the work is the transformation of the melodic material of *Einsame Blumen,* the piece directly before *Verrufene Stelle,* but it is only the poetic program that reveals the full meaning of the musical relation-ship. Most interesting of all are the comments that appear during the course of a work: "Meine Ruh' ist hin," "Stimme aus der Ferne," or in the *Davidsbündlertänze*, "Hierauf schloss Florestan und es zuckte ihm schmerzlich um die Lippen" and "Ganz zum Überfluss meinte Eusebius Folgendes; dabei sprach aber viel Seligkeit aus seiner Augen." The remaining pieces of the *Davidsbündlertänze* are signed either by Florestan, by Eusebius, or by both, and similarly, the first edition of the Sonata in F♯ Minor was inscribed: "Clara zugeeignet von Florestan und Eusebius." All these indications are conceived for a performer rather than an audience, and still more extreme examples of this tendency appear in the "Innere Stimme" of the *Humoreske* and the *Sphinxes* of the *Carnaval*, which are not even to be played, so that music as well as meaning is directed to a completely private appreciation.

It is not so much the frequency and variety of these verbal indications that concern us, however, as the ambiguity that surrounds them. In this sense, the intended riddles of secret meaning conceal much deeper ones. Schumann himself seems to be uncertain about the content of his compositions; typically he will change his mind or make conflicting statements about programmatic significance. Thus the motto of the *Phantasie* opus 17 is in itself enigmatic, but the mystery is only increased when we learn more of Schumann's ideas. The work was dedicated to Liszt but was conceived as a memorial to Beethoven, with its movements entitled first *Ruinen, Trophaeen, Palmen;*[1] subsequently *Ruine, Siegesbogen und Sternbild, Dichtungen;*[2] and finally left unnamed. It contains, in fact, a number of thematic references to Beethoven. Yet in relation to the first movement Schumann wrote to Clara: "It is a deep lament for you."[3] And a year later he asks her about the same movement: "Doesn't it summon up many images in your mind?"[4] He half believes, as he says, that "it is really you who are the tone in the motto." The only hint of consistency in these views can be found in the melodic citations of Beethoven, for among these *An die ferne Geliebte* is conspicuous. In the deletion of the titles of the individual movements we have an example of Schumann's characteristic tendency to curtail or suppress original headings. Some of these appear only in his sketches or letters and are never made public; others occur in the first edition but not in later versions. The *Nachtstücke*, for example, were originally thought of as a *Leichenphantasie*,[5] and the movements were to bear the titles *Trauerzug, Kuriose Gesellschaft, Nächtliches Gelage, Rundgesang mit Solostimmen*.[6] In the symphonies in B♭ and E♭, programmatic headings of several movements were similarly discarded. And the intermezzo of the third *Novellette*, which was first published as a supplement to the *Neue Zeitschrift für Musik* in 1838, originally carried a motto from Macbeth:

> *When shall we three meet again,*
> *In thunder, lightning, or in rain?*[7]

The deletion of these verses, however, may have its explanation in Schumann's feeling that "the impression of a wild, fantastic play of shadows" was stronger when the intermezzo was heard in the context of the whole *Novellette;* thus verbal support would no longer be required. Again in the *Davidsbündlertänze,* the descriptions of the behavior of Florestan and Eusebius disappeared from the second edition, along with their signatures after the individual pieces. Even the title did not go untouched: *Davidsbündlertänze* became *Davidsbündler.* Did Schumann come to feel that guides to the meaning of his works were really not necessary? that the content was sufficiently obvious without them? or that the public had become educated and no longer needed the help it did originally? Did he feel that the headings restricted the imagination, or that they were a danger because they might be misconstrued? Or did he always regret having permitted any small glimpse into his personal affairs and feelings? Perhaps the headings did not give the significance of the music at all or even provide an index to its significance; they might have arisen as an additional poetic expression inspired by the music, which the composer could easily feel to be expendable. Or again, in removing them, Schumann might actually have changed rather than concealed the meaning of the music; did the pieces in fact remain the same without their titles? We are provided with a sudden and valuable insight into the first movement of the F♯ Minor Sonata when we learn that it was conceived as a *Fandango,* but this may in fact demonstrate that the elimination or change of a title will produce an intrinsic change in the composition.

The paradoxical practice of Schumann with respect to programmatic significance is seen most readily in the *Papillons,* which Schumann connected with Jean Paul's novel *Flegeljahre* (Years of indiscretion) in spite of the fact that much of the music had varied sources in the apparently more neutral sphere of earlier sets of dances. The novel deals with the twin brothers Walt and Vult, the one sentimental and poetic, the other worldly and disillusioned, and in particular, with Vult's unsuccessful attempts to lead Walt from a state of naiveté to one of sophistication. In the concluding episode, the brothers attend a masked ball: Walt as a coachman and Vult, in female dress, as a personification of Hope. Walt dances with Wina, whom they both love, talking philosophically of art and idealistically contemplating her beauty. Then Vult proposes that they change costumes, and in the role of Walt, dances with Wina and extracts a confession of love while Walt watches helplessly. But Vult returns home, jealous and angry, writes a farewell letter to his brother, and is preparing to leave him for good when he hears Walt arrive, pretends to be asleep, and is able to finish his packing as a sleepwalker. Walt has a long, cosmic dream in which finally he sees the glow of dawn across a vast and heaving ocean. When he asks his brother about the meaning of the dream, Vult tells him to remain in bed, and playing his flute, he leaves the house while Walt continues to listen to the tones fading into the distance without realizing that Vult will not return. In his own copy of *Flegeljahre*, Schumann marked a number of passages in the masked-ball narrative, assigning to them the numbers of the first ten of the *Papillons*, although in an order which differs somewhat from the sequence of the story.[8] The first passage describes Walt just after he has put on his costume:

i. As he came out of the little room, he asked God that he might happily find it again; he felt like a hero, thirsting for fame, who goes forth to his first battle.

The passage marked for the second piece continues the narrative:

ii. Because of a mistaken turn such as afflicted his life, he first entered the punch-room, which he took for the dance-hall. . . . Wina was not to be seen, nor any sign of Vult. . . . Finally, wishing to examine the overflowing anteroom, he came upon the real, resounding, burning hall full of waving figures. . . . A procreant aurora-borealis full of interlacing, zigzag figures!

The third passage contains a single, vivid image:

iii. He was attracted and astonished most of all by a giant boot that was sliding around dressed in itself.

The fourth is also brief and specific:

iv. Hope spun away quickly; a masked shepherdess came by and a simple nun with a half-mask and a fragrant bouquet of auriculas.

The nun turns out to be Wina, and the fifth passage concerns her encounter with Walt:

v. Now he stood for a second alone next to the tranquil maiden. . . . Fresh and charming, the half rose and lily of her countenance looked out from its half-mask as though from the sheath of a drooping bud. Like foreign spirits from two distant cosmic nights, they looked at each other behind the dark masks, like the stars in a solar eclipse, and each soul saw the other far distant.

Instead of following next in order, the passage marked for the sixth piece comes from a somewhat later stage of the story. Vult is speaking to Walt in justification of the change of costumes he has proposed, and he refers to the fact that Walt's costume is composite – part coachman and part miner:

vi. Your waltzes so far – do not take the description ill – have traversed the hall as good mimic imitations, partly horizontal, of the coachman, and partly vertical, of the miner.

The passage for the seventh piece precedes this slightly in the story and describes Vult's request that they exchange roles:

vii. He threw his mask away, and a strange hot desert-aridness or dry fever-heat broke through his gestures and words. "If you have ever felt love for your brother," – he began with dry voice and took the wreath off and undid the female costume – "if the fulfillment of one of his dearest wishes means anything to you . . . and if it is not indifferent to your joys whether he is to have the least or the greatest, in short if you will listen to one of his most earnest entreaties . . . "

The passage for the eighth piece again precedes this and describes Walt's ineffectual dance with Wina:

viii. As a youth touches the hand of a great and renowned author for the first time, he lightly – like a butterfly's wing, like auricula pollen – touched Wina's back and stood back as far as possible in order to look at her life-breathing face. If there is a harvest-dance that is the harvest, if there is a fire-wheel of loving rapture, Walt the coachman had both.

The ninth piece is connected with a later passage which gives Walt's reply to Vult's proposal that they exchange costumes:

ix. *"To that I can only give the answer, 'Joyfully.'" "Then be quick," replied Vult, without thanking him.*

The passage for the tenth piece is the last of all; it occurs somewhat after Vult's criticism of Walt's dancing, and describes the return of the brothers to the dance and the implementation of Vult's plan:

x. *As Walt entered, it seemed to him that everyone observed the exchange of masks. . . . Some women noticed that Hope now had blond hair behind the flowers instead of black as before. . . . Also Walt's step was shorter and more feminine, as was suitable to hopes. But he soon forgot himself and the hall and everything else as the coachman Vult without ado placed Wina . . . at the head of the English dance and now to her astonishment artfully sketched out a dance-pattern with her, and like some painters, seemed to paint with his foot, only with larger decorative strokes. . . . Towards the very end of the dance, in the hurried hand-reaching, in the crossing, in the rapid leading back and forth, Vult allowed Polish sounds to escape him more and more – only the breath of speech – only stray butter-flies blown to sea from a distant isle. This language sounded across to Wina like a strange lark's song in late summer.*

For the last two pieces of the *Papillons* there are no passages marked, and this would seem to corroborate the belief of Julius Knorr, who was one of Schumann's circle of Davidites, that these were written after the others and for the sake of completing the whole picture.[9] But Knorr makes no specific reference to *Flegeljahre*. He gives as the purpose of the *Papillons* the intention to paint the colorful fluttering, as though of but-terflies, at a carnival ball, and adds what he claims is Schumann's own interpretation of the individual pieces. Following the introduction, no.1 is the true opening melody; no.2 is the imposing impression of an illu-minated hall with the colorful sparkle of lights; no.3 is various trains of maskers crossing one another (in canon); no.4 is a teasing Harlequin who mixes among them; no.5 is a sketched polonaise; no.6 is a scene in the drinking room, with the music in the hall intruding; nos.7 and 8 are a continuation of this, which Knorr deems too lengthy to include in his account; no.9 is a tumult that arises as a result of a short pause in the music; and no.10 is, first, the dancers beginning to gather again and then their rapid assemblage as the music that had been heard in the dis-tance (in no.6) is resumed, only now close by and rougher in sound. What follows is described by Knorr as a kind of "Invitation to the

Dance": no.11, a free polonaise with trio, and no.12, the familiar *Grossvater* melody used in the manner of a *Kehraus* and later joined to the melody of the opening. The merriment dies down, and the crowd disperses; the tower clock strikes six, at which the noise of the carnival night is completely silenced. Arrived home, people seek quiet, but for a long time cannot put the echoes of the ball out of their heads. As far as the first ten pieces are concerned, the interpretations given by Knorr fail to agree almost completely with what we learn elsewhere of Schumann's conceptions. The last two pieces, however, might well have been composed in the interests of completeness, and in this event they would logically be related to the final chapter of *Flegeljahre*. Schumann does refer to the content of this chapter in the letters he wrote in explanation of the *Papillons*, and indeed the closing sentence of the novel originally stood as a motto at the head of the score: "Walt listened ecstatically to the discourse of the fleeing tones still sounding up from the street, for he did not notice that with them his brother was also fleeing." This conception seems to be contradicted, however, by the remarks Schumann added to the twelfth piece – "Das Geräusch der Faschingsnacht verstummt. Die Turmuhr schlägt sechs" – and indeed by the music itself, which clearly paints these events in accordance with Knorr's report. But such a picture is really not incompatible with the concluding episode of the novel, and the possibility remains that the end of the *Papillons* may describe both. The eleventh piece presents equal difficulties. Its prevailing character would tend to connect it with Vult's angry letter of farewell. But the fact that it is a polonaise with an inserted section which is extremely delicate and distant in quality suggests that it is related to the "Polish sounds" and the "stray butterflies" mentioned in the tenth passage Schumann marked, except that the dance involved there is clearly described by Jean Paul as an *Anglaise*. In any event, there is actually no secure reason for disputing the general sense of the evidence of Schumann's letters, which would make the last two pieces part of the *Flegeljahre* conception. A letter to the editor Ludwig Rellstab is relevant in this respect, and it also has an important bearing on the specific way in which the *Papillons* originated:

Less for the editor of Iris than for the poet and kindred spirit of Jean Paul I will take the liberty of adding a few words to the Papillons concerning their origin, since the thread that connects them is scarcely visible. You will recall the last scene in the Flegeljahre – masked ball – Walt – Vult –

masks – Wina – Vult's dancing – the exchange of masks – confessions – anger – disclosures – hurrying away – final scene and then the departing brother. – Often I continued to turn the last page over, for the end seemed to me only a new beginning – almost without knowing it I was at the piano, and thus arose one papillon after the other. May you find in these origins a pardon for the whole, which in its particulars very often calls for one![10]

In a letter written two days before, Schumann had offered a similar explanation to his family. He addresses a multitude of imagined butterflies as his messengers:

Then tell them all that they must read the last scene of Jean Paul's Flegel-jahre *as soon as possible and that the* Papillons *were really intended to transpose this masked ball into tone, and then ask them whether there is perhaps correctly mirrored in the* Papillons *something of Wina's angelic love, of Walt's poetic nature, and of Vult's lightning-sharp soul.*[11]

In these letters Schumann clearly states that the *Papillons* arose from the *Flegeljahre* and that the same factors that produced the composition were also represented in it and expressed by it. On the other hand, not only does he state just as unequivocally elsewhere that his titles are written after the music has been composed,[12] but we know in addition that some of the pieces included in the *Papillons* existed earlier in another form. The *Papillons* have a long and complex history involving numerous sketches and alterations.[13] Three of the pieces, numbers 1, 6, and 7, were in part derived from the unpublished *Sechs Walzer;* they were based respectively on waltzes 6, 4, and 5. The fifth piece is an arrangement of the trio of Polonaise 7 of the *Eight Polonaises* for four hands, which was written in 1828, and the eleventh piece draws on the third and fourth of these polonaises. In general, the atmosphere and concept of the waltz lie behind the *Papillons;* the pieces are variously transformed waltzes and, to a lesser extent, polonaises. Stylistically, in spite of their striking originality, they look mostly to Schubert, and also to Weber's *Invitation to the Dance,* and these specifically musical influences – like the scenes of the *Flegeljahre* – are a kind of content as well as a source of inspiration. Finally, to compound the confusion, the whole composition is called *Papillons,* a title that introduces still another concept of the musical significance. Indeed Castelli interpreted the work as "flirtatious, volatile, and coquettish," but Schumann rejected this notion as far from the mark.[14]

The butterfly was actually an important symbol for the Romantic era and a still more important one for Schumann himself; there can be no question that its meaning was much more profound than the immediate implications of its obvious qualities. Schumann was fascinated by it; his letters reveal that it was a recurrent image of his thought and outlook. In the letter to his family that we have cited, for example, Schumann appeals to the imagined butterflies as follows: "and tell my good brothers that I think of them affectionately and that their life must be as light as your flight and as deep as your meaning."[15] We are dealing with a ubiquitous and infinitely suggestive symbol, whose complex significance includes the notion of metamorphosis and thus possesses an affinity with the significance of the masquerade. The occasions on which Schumann is concerned with the butterfly are so numerous that they provide material for a separate study, but I cannot forbear citing a passage in one of the letters to his mother that poetically combines different kinds of meaning:

In many a sleepless night I have seen a distant image, like a goal – during the writing out of the Papillons *I felt unmistakably that a certain* independence *was striving to develop, which criticism, however, for the most part condemns – Now the papillons are fluttering about in the wide, beautiful world of spring; spring itself stands before the door and looks in at me – a child with sky-blue eyes. – And now I am beginning to understand my existence – the silence is broken – my letter is in your hands.*[16]

The butterfly is also the soul, a conception especially important to Schumann. In a letter to his friend Henriette Voigt, which contains this notion, the *Flegeljahre* appears both as a cause of the *Papillons* and as a text added later, and Schumann also reveals his uncertainty over how clearly the composition conveys its meaning to others:

As Florestan read off the letter, chance made a truly ingenious anagram – You wrote "Rochlitz, who for many long years has stood steadfastly at the side of every aspiring artist, etc." – but Florestan read "of every expiring" – That, in my opinion, rightly describes Rochlitz as a loving father who so often with tears of grief has pressed closed the eyes of many a great man and spoken at his grave. Florestan added that he also thinks of Lafayette in this connection, who often stood up boldly at the last gasp of a nation as a defender of the corpse – "What will you hit upon next, Florestan"? I said. Indeed that might provide a bridge to the Papillons: *for we like to think of the psyche fluttering up over the withered body. – You could learn much from me about this if Jean Paul had not taught it better. If you ever have a free minute, please read the last chapter of the* Flegeljahre, *where everything stands in black and white even to the giant boot in F-sharp minor (at the end of the* Flegeljahre *I feel as though the play (to be sure) were over but the curtain not fallen). – I will mention also that I have set the text to the music, not the reverse – otherwise it seems to me a "foolish beginning." Only the last one, which playful chance formed as an answer to the first,[17] was aroused by Jean Paul. Another question: Are not the* Papillons *clear to you in themselves? It is interesting to me to learn this.[18]*

A similar ambiguity exists in the *Bilder aus Osten,* an interesting parallel to the *Papillons* for which Schumann explained his literary inspiration publicly in a preface:

The composer of the following pieces, in the interest of their better understanding, feels that he may not conceal the fact that they owe their origin to a particular stimulus. The pieces were written namely during the reading of the Rückert Makamen *(Tales after the Arabian of Hariri); the book's marvellous hero, Abu Seid – who can be compared to our German Eulenspiegel, except that the former is cast in a mold by far more poetic and noble – and the figure of his honorable friend Hareth as well, could not be put out of the mind of the composer as he worked, which may explain the strange character of certain of the pieces. Beyond this, definite situations were not in the mind of the composer for the first five pieces, and only the last one may perhaps be regarded as an echo of the last Makame, in which we see the hero bring his life to a close in penance and remorse. May this attempt to give utterance in our art also to oriental modes of poetry and thought, approximately as has already been done in German literature, be not unfavorably received by those who are interested.*

Here again Schumann seems uncertain about whether his literary experience actually accounts for the character of the music; and again it is the final piece, although not without some doubt, that appears to arise more specifically from the story. That there is no easy solution to the problem of the meaning of the *Papillons* will now have become apparent. Perhaps Schumann's conception of music can be elucidated more readily by recourse to his critical writings and aesthetic reflections.

Poetic parallels of musical works are the outstanding feature of Schumann's early critical practice; to convey the nature of a composition to his readers, he will devise an imaginative program – a story or a scene. Beethoven's Seventh Symphony, for example, becomes a series of events in a wedding celebration. Here is the description of the Allegretto, put into the mouth of Florestan:

"But now it grows very quiet outside in the village" (Here Florestan reached the Allegretto and played fragments of it now and then), "only a butterfly chances by or a cherry blossom falls. . . . The organ begins; the sun stands high; slanting through the church, separate long shafts of light play with moats; the bells sound out – church-goers gradually take their places – pews are clapped open and closed – some peasants peer sharply into their hymnbooks, others look up to the choir gallery – the procession approaches – first choir boys with burning tapers and holy-water basins; then friends who frequently look around towards the couple accompanied by the priest; then the parents, the bridesmaids, and finally all the young people of the village. How everything now falls into place and the priest steps up to the altar and speaks now to the bride and now to the happiest of men, and how he recites to them the duties of the bond and its purposes, and how he then calls for the 'yes' that assumes so much for eternity and she pronounces it firmly and slowly – let me paint the picture no longer and do the Finale in your own way." . . . Florestan broke off and tore into the close of the Allegretto, and it sounded as though the sexton had slammed the door shut so that the whole church reverberated.[19]

This is characteristically a story within a story, and when Florestan interrupts his interpretation, Schumann at once takes it up. The use of a framework narrative is connected with an important practice of Schumann's which might be called "polyphonic criticism," for it readily permits differing views of the same work to be advanced in turn within a single unified setting. Apart from any other significance it may have, the expression of the various conceptions of diverse personalities and temperaments produces a unique kind of multidimensional objectivity.

In one of the reviews of Schubert, the interpretation includes even the optical projection of images, which are thrown on the wall by a deaf painter:

On the other hand, a whole carnival really dances through the "German Dances." "And it would be an excellent idea" Florestan shouted into the ear of Fritz Friedrich, "if you fetched your laterna magica *and followed the masked ball on the wall in shadows." – He ran out and returned jubilantly.*

The following group belongs among the loveliest. The room dimly lit – Zilia at the keyboard, the wounding rose in her hair – Eusebius in his black velvet cape, leaning over his chair – Florestan (dressed similarly) standing on the table and ciceroning – Serpentin with his feet around Walt's neck and often riding about – the painter a là *Hamlet, with staring eyes, parading his shadow-figures, of which a few spider-legged ones were already running from wall to ceiling. Zilia started, and Florestan may have spoken approximately as follows, although with everything much more elaborated:*

No.1. A major. Throngs of masks. Kettledrums. Trumpets. The lights dim. A perruquier: "Everything seems to be going very well." – No.2 Comic figure, scratching himself behind the ears and constantly calling "pst, pst." Disappears. – No.3. A Harlequin, his arms on his hips. Somersault out of the door. – No.4. Two stiff, distinguished masks, dancing, speaking little to one another. – 5. Slender cavalier, pursuing a mask: "Have I caught you at last, lovely zither-player?" – "Let me go." – She flees. – 6. An erect Hussar with plume and sabre sheath. – 7. Two harvesters, blissfully waltzing together. He softly: "Is it you?" They recognize each other. – 8. A farmer from the country, getting ready for the dance. – 9. The folding doors open wide. Splendid procession of cavaliers and noble ladies. – 10. A Spaniard to an Ursuline: "At least speak, since you may not love." She: "I would rather not speak, and be understood!"[20]

The theme of the masquerade at once calls our attention to the similarity between poetic criticism and Schumann's practice as a composer; both involve the addition of specific descriptions to musical works. At the same time, this review has a peculiar relevance to the problem of the *Papillons*, for it suggests that Schumann may have connected ideas of a masked ball with his earlier sets of dances right from their inception, especially since these dances were inspired by Schubert. In the composition of the *Papillons*, then, Schumann could have acted under the influence of *Flegeljahre* to select older compositions that were intrinsically suited to depict the events of the novel. The compositional process would remain essentially literary rather than musical, but it would not be so truly creative as in the case of pieces that had previously been unconnected with any programmatic idea. In any event, this sort of composition does not explain the nature of the creative process in music but only pushes the question further back. That Schumann's procedure in the *Papillons* may also apply to the *Carnaval* is indicated by what he says about this work in a letter to the pianist Ignaz Moscheles: "To decipher the masked ball will be a game for you; but I also probably need to assure you in all seriousness that the compilation as well as the headings came about *after* the composition of the pieces."[21] At least in a general sense if not in its detailed images, the masquerade appears to lie at the center of Schumann's imagination in his earlier works. It is even echoed toward the end of his life in the *Ball-Scenen* and the *Kinderball*, which as four-hand works would seem to return once more to the medium of his original inspiration. And it plays a part in forming the atmosphere of the *Faschingsschwank aus Wien*. But the concept seems to interrelate the early works in particular; Schumann thought of the *Intermezzi* as longer *Papillons*,[22] and the opening melody of the *Papillons* is quoted in the *Carnaval*, while the *Grossvatertanz* not only appears in the *Papillons* but is also cited in the *Davidsbündlertänze* and is used again in the *Carnaval* for the march of the Davidsbündler. The original title of the *Carnaval* was *Fasching. Schwänke auf vier Noten*,[23] a name that curiously contains and possibly prefigures the relationship between "Asch" and "Schumann." The *Carnaval* may have been a *Faschingsschwank* more properly than a document of Schumann's connection with Ernestine von Fricken; it was certainly in some sense both of these. In any event, the anagrammatic and musical relationship between the *Fasching* and Schumann's name must have provided the strongest possible reinforcement of his preoccupation with the subject of the masquerade, if not part of the reason for its prominence in his thought.

Poetic criticism is an important idiosyncracy of Romanticism; it runs its course from Heinse, through Wackenroder and Tieck and Hoffmann, to find its last and greatest representative in Schumann. It has obvious practical and pedagogic values, especially if the only alternative, as Schumann believed, is technical analysis; for the critic must somehow introduce his reader to musical compositions and provide insight into their nature. But what is the real significance of this variety of critical writing? If we accept Schumann's postulate that good criticism must

recreate the impression produced by the work of art itself,[24] we must regard the poetic description as in some way equivalent to the music. It
must either restate the content of a composition, or – if this content is
ineffable and cannot be conveyed in words – it must suggest the content
or direct the reader to it by producing an analogous or similar impression. Thus in revealing the nature of the work it will be a legitimate part
of criticism and even its foundation; for criticism is an effort to evalu-
ate, and evaluation must rest on a determination of the essential quality
of its object. At the same time, poetic criticism will be pedagogic in the
highest sense, since it will educate the public to the most significant
properties of music. Underlying Schumann's method is a defined scale
of values in which *Geist* and specific poetic meaning come first and are
followed by the lesser virtues of form, workmanship, and functional
suitability. But however well-turned a composition may be, and however perfectly it may realize the role of its genre, it must meet those demands of meaning that are probed by poetic criticism, or it will have
little value. To get at the content of a work is the most essential task of
the critic.

Yet poetic criticism is more than an instrument to this end: it is a
spontaneous activity for Schumann, an inevitable part of his musical
response and thus an indispensable part of his conception of music. He
objects to Berlioz's program for the *Symphonie Fantastique,* but what he
really wants is to create his own: "At first the program also spoiled all
my enjoyment, all my freedom of view. But as it receded more and
more into the background and my own fantasy began to create, I found
not only everything in the program, but much more."[25] Imagining external circumstances in response to music was indeed a habit of mind of
the whole era; poetic criticism had a counterpart in poetic listening, for
the auditor of the Romantic epoch created scenes and stories as an understood part of his musical experience. But even beyond the problem
posed by differing interpretations of a single work, we again meet with
the same ambiguity that exists in Schumann's compositional practice,
for the imagined circumstances tend to be imputed to the composer as
the causal determinants of his composition, just as though there were
no distinction at all between the effect of music and its stimulus.

As we have mentioned, Schumann's aesthetic theory was never realized in the form of a self-contained study; his early project of a philosophical work was never consummated, while his anthology of the

musical conceptions found in literature and poetry, which similarly remained incomplete, was more a historical than an analytical undertaking. Yet the observations scattered through his criticism, letters, and notebooks provide a convincing theoretical basis for his practice both as a composer and as a critic. Indeed the strength of this theory lies in its intimate connection with practice. What is evident at once is Schumann's concern with musical content and meaning and his belief that music is affected by every occasion of life. The literary influence that we have found so important is but an instance of a more general principle. Thus if literature is replaced by physical environment, for example, the Symphony in B♭ will become the counterpart of the *Papillons*. "To describe, to paint was not my intention," Schumann writes, "but that just the time in which the symphony arose affected its formation, and that it thus became precisely what it is, I certainly believe."[26] Some weeks later, however, in a letter to the conductor Wilhelm Taubert, he offers considerable information about descriptive details:

If you could breathe something of the longing for spring into your orchestra when it plays; it was chiefly this that affected me when I wrote the work in February 1841. Right at the first entry of the trumpet, I would like it to sound as though from on high, like a call to awaken – into what follows of the introduction I could then infuse how it begins to turn green everywhere, possibly even a butterfly flutters up, and in the Allegro, how everything gradually assembles that can be said to belong to spring. But these are fantasies that came to me after the completion of my work; only about the last movement do I want to tell you that I would like to think of spring's farewell in connection with it, that I therefore would wish it not to be taken too frivolously.[27]

We cannot determine whether the titles originally assigned to the movements of this symphony were thought of as describing causal circumstances or suggested images; in any event Schumann characteristically decided to suppress them; but the letter to Taubert clearly distinguishes cause from effect, describing the one as general and the other as specific and at least to some degree arbitrary. This is an important distinction; yet in general Schumann seems to subscribe to it no more in the case of physical environment than he does in connection with literature. His review of Schubert's C-Major Symphony, for example, while it conceives the cause and effect of the music separately, tends nevertheless to equate the content of the two and to find relevant in each case a re-markable fullness of detail:

However this may be, let us now refresh ourselves in the fullness of spirit that streams forth from this priceless work. This Vienna with its St. Ste-phen's steeple, its beautiful women, its public pageantry; girdled with countless bands by the Danube, the way it reaches into the blossoming plain that gradually climbs to higher and higher mountains; this Vienna with all its remembrances of the great German masters – must in truth be a fertile soil for the fantasy of the musician. Often when I contemplated it from the heights of the mountains, it occurred to me how Beethoven's eye had doubtless strayed restlessly across towards those distant Alps time and again, how Mozart may often have pursued dreamily the course of the Danube, which seems to dissolve everywhere into the brush and woods, and Father Haydn often have gazed at St. Stephen's steeple, shaking his head at so dizzy a height. If the pictures of the Danube, of St. Stephen's steeple, and of the distant Alps are compounded and covered over with a light aroma of holy Catholic incense, we will have a portrait of Vienna; and if now this whole charming landscape stands alive before us, strings also will be set into motion inside us that otherwise would never have be-gun to sound. On hearing the Symphony of Schubert, with the bright, blos-soming romantic life it contains, the city again arises before me more distinctly than ever, and again I find it perfectly clear how such works can be born precisely in these surroundings.[28]

Having given his own reactions, however, which essentially duplicate the environmental forces that he supposes to have acted on the Sym-phony, Schumann curiously goes on to emphasize that images and titles added to music have a relative and even an extrinsic nature:

I will not attempt to give the Symphony a foil; different times of life choose too differently in the texts and pictures they attribute to music, and the youth of eighteen often hears an international event in a composition where the adult sees only a provincial incident, while the musician has thought of neither the one nor the other and just has produced no more than his best music as he found it in his heart.

But the effect of the composer's environment cannot be questioned; Schumann states it as a general principle; it seems to determine the con-tent of the composition and to imply again that among the varied inter-pretations that may exist there will be one that is uniquely significant:

But that the external world, radiant today or darkening tomorrow, often takes hold of the inner life of the poet and musician we must indeed believe, and that in this Symphony there lies hidden more than mere beautiful song, more than mere sorrow and joy as music already has pronounced them hundreds of times, indeed that it leads us into a region we nowhere can remember having been before: to acknowledge this we have only to hear such a symphony. Here, aside from masterful technique in musical composition, we also find life in every fiber, coloring extending to the finest gradations, meaning everywhere, the sharpest expression of detail, and finally a romanticism diffused over the whole that we already know from other works of Franz Schubert.[29]

In a letter to Clara we find what is probably the most detailed explanation of how external influences act on Schumann and, through him, on his music:

But now I can also be very serious, often all day long – and do not let this annoy you – it is mostly happenings in my soul, thoughts about music and composition. Everything that takes place in the world affects me, politics, literature, people; I reflect on everything in my own way, and it then seeks to break through, to find an outlet in music. Thus also many of my compositions are difficult to understand because they are tied to distant interests, and often importantly, since everything of the time that is noteworthy takes hold of me and I must then restate it musically. And therefore so few compositions satisfy me, because apart from all deficiencies of craftsmanship, they also dawdle in musical sensations of the lowest variety, in common lyrical proclamations. The highest that is achieved here does not even reach to the beginning of my kind of music. The first can be a flower, the second is the very much more spiritual poem; the first an impulse of crude nature, the second a work of poetic consciousness.[30]

And he adds the important comment: "All this I really do not know while composing and it comes only afterwards." His theoretical position is clear, however: music is formed by climate, current events, physical surroundings, cultural setting, and literary experience; music itself may be added to the influences, although it is external to Schumann's works in a different sense and becomes part of their content in a different way.

But experience and environment affect the soul primarily and music only mediately. It is consistent then to focus attention on the soul itself, disregarding external forces, and to consider music as an autobiographical medium expressing the internal state and the mental and physical health of the composer. To some extent composition had the value of keeping a diary: Schumann could confide in music, clarify his feelings, and rescue them from mortality. Indeed he often made note, along with his musical sketches, of his thoughts and moods at the time a particular musical idea occurred to him; there can be no question but that he believed the one to have been fundamentally connected with the other; the music contained or expressed his inner state at the very time of conception, whatever else it might also signify. But if this state was worth recording, it was not only in support of the diary function of composition, for the verbal notation may also have served to reinstate the fullness of the musical conception at a later time; the notes alone might come to lack character or to be unfruitful in suggesting extended treatment when their emotional significance had been forgotten. The verbal comments would then play a role similar to that of titles and headings, for these serve to direct the listener's response into the proper channel; they are guides to the inner nature of the work. Yet in pointing to the actual causal forces of music, the brief comments appended to sketches were essentially private; Schumann felt strongly that workshop secrets were not for the public eye, and this may be the reason that he often deleted titles, having come to feel that they had crossed the line dividing pedagogy from autobiography. Larger counterparts of the private jottings, however, can occasionally be found in letters that undertake to explain finished compositions. In a letter to the conductor George Otten, for example, he describes the Symphony in C Major as follows:

I wrote the Symphony in December 1845, still half sick; it seems to me that one would have to hear this in it. Only in the last movement did I begin to feel myself again; actually I became better only after finishing the whole work. But otherwise, as I say, it recalls to me a dark time. That in spite of this even such sounds of pain can arouse interest shows me your sympathy. Everything you say about it shows me how exactly you know the music, and that even my melancholy bassoon in the Adagio, *which of course I wrote down at that spot with a particular predilection, did not escape you delighted me most of all.*[31]

The autobiographical meaning would seem to extend even to details. Some months later, a letter to his pupil Louis Ehlert discusses the musical effects of his recovery:

The late time of gloomy moods I happily have behind me; there fell in it the Second Symphony, the Studies for pedal-piano, and in part the Trio in D Minor. Since then I have been impelled into other spheres; the Christmas Album, the Spanish Liederspiel, and a Song Album that has just appeared will make this known to you – and a great deal more from this happy time still lies in my briefcase.[32]

Finally, a more general statement of the relationship between Schumann's life and his music can be found in an earlier letter to the composer Karl Kossmaly:

With some timidity I enclose a package of older works of mine. You will easily discover what is unripe and imperfect in them. They are mostly reflections of my wildly agitated former life; man and musician always strove in me to express themselves simultaneously; this is probably still the case even now, when I have learned, to be sure, more mastery over myself and over my art as well. How many joys and sorrows lie buried together in this little heap of notes your sympathetic heart will discern.[33]

Music is above all the language of the soul; "all week long," Schumann writes to Clara, "I sat at the keyboard and composed and wrote and laughed and cried all at the same time; this you will now find all beautifully depicted in my opus 20, the 'grand Humoreske.' "[34] Indeed we can feel in what he says to Simonin de Sire that in the development of this expressive language he saw his mission as a composer:

Often strange in appearance is the human heart, and pain and joy intermix in wild disorder. But you must still hope for the best; I feel there is much in me still, indeed often I am so rash as to believe that music as the language of the soul still stands in its beginnings. May a good genius then preside over such thoughts, and raise what still lies in the cradle to blossoming and powerful life![35]

And his remarks often leave no doubt that the feeling content of music is a real one; "I am now *living* some of the last Beethoven quartets in the best sense," he writes to the composer Hermann Hirschbach, "even to the love and the hate in them."[36]

In the development of music as an autobiographical medium of inner life, Schubert was the great pioneer; not only his use of harmonic nuance but his individual manner of progressing from one idea to the next is seen to represent an equally subtle expressiveness that escapes verbal formulation. Writing to Wieck in 1829, Schumann can hardly contain his excitement over this art, for which he finds a parallel in the writings of Jean Paul:

Schubert is still always my "unique Schubert," above all as he has every-thing in common with my "unique Jean Paul"; when I play Schubert, it is as though I were reading a composed novel of Jean Paul. . . . In general, there is no music besides Schubert's that is so psychologically *remarkable in the* course of its ideas *and their connection and in the* apparently *logical leaps, and how few have thus, as he has, been able to* imprint *a single individuality on* one mass of tone-paintings *so different among them-selves, and fewest of all have written so much* for themselves *and for their own heart. What a diary is to others, in which they* set down *their momentary feelings, etc., music paper really was to Schubert, to which he en-trusted his every mood, and his whole through-and-through musical soul wrote notes where others use words.*[37]

Schumann even seems to give the connection of music and life a pro-grammatic and normative formulation, for he has Florestan say, "I do not like those whose life is not in unison with their works."[38] This dic-tum, coming as it does from Plato's *Laches* (188c–e, 193d–e), has a moral rather than an emotional force, like the aphorism, "The laws of morality are also those of art,"[39] but it can for that very reason be taken to encompass every relationship of temperament and feeling.

But the fact of external influence in music does not in itself deter-mine the nature of titles, headings, responses, or poetic criticism. The invention of titles is not to be undertaken lightly, in Schumann's opin-ion; indeed, in choosing them the composer reveals his poetic sen-sitivity.[40] But this would imply that such signposts admitted of some latitude; they are certainly not arbitrary, but neither are they uniquely determined for any composition. Poetic criticism is subject to the same consideration, as we can see in the interesting practice of "polyphonic reviews," or in the course of Schumann's discussion of the C-Major Symphony of Schubert, where he acknowledges the variety of images a single work will provoke. Each individual response – provided it is that of a poetic nature – has its validity. But how is this possible? And which interpretation is to be equated with the causal circumstances of the mu-sical composition? Certainly the external constellation producing the quality of a given work is unique; how is it possible then that the description of its contents, whether by composer's designation or poetic criticism, may vary, even that it should vary, in Schumann's view, with the personality of the listener? Is Schumann's thesis here that the content of a work is relative: of one kind for the composer but of different kinds for different listeners? Or is the variety merely variation within the limits of a defined locus or field of qualities, so that the true meaning of the music possesses a certain generality with respect to external circumstance and feeling? But how again would such a generality of meaning result from a specificity of cause? Perhaps the same composition could arise from any one of a number of causes, just as it could stimulate any one of a number of responses.

We can in fact complete our picture of the formative influences on music by a theory of multiple causation, for not only do external forces necessarily act through the composer's subjectivity, but many of them can act simultaneously, some as relatively novel factors and others as more general or persistent forces, while the mental and physical state of the composer similarly possesses its own more lasting and inherent conditions that combine with all the externally induced tendencies. Thus literary experience, environment, health, temperament, and all the conditions of life are effective conjointly, although the pattern of the whole obviously may contain one or more dominant forces. This conception is actually borne out by Schumann's comments on particular works, and his remarks are thus often complementary rather than contradictory. We have seen an interesting example in the causal complex of the *Phantasie* opus 17, and many similar examples could be cited, particularly in the domain of vocal music, where at least one influence appears explicitly in the text. Thus the qualities of a composition may be attributed to natural surroundings or to a season of the year, and also to an emotional state or to the general circumstances of Schumann's life. Multiple causation is clearly a counterpart of polyphonic criticism and would appear to establish a total congruence between cause and effect, but certain differences still remain. An image produced by the music may correspond to one causal factor, or even be identical with it, but the whole causal constellation is clearly unique, while the total range of descriptions and effects is determined only in respect of appropriateness and would actually seem to be indefinite in extent. Nor does our formal equivalence come to grips with the problem of whether a correspondence factually exists between causal forces and subsequent descriptions, either in general or in detail. Must each poetic image find a justification in its resemblance to some original influence?

The answer Schumann provides to such questions lies, paradoxically, in a meaning of music that transcends life even as it expresses it, a meaning that is in part above verbal concepts and particular images. Specific assigned texts and pictures are possible but not necessary, and the creation of music may similarly proceed without any awareness of images or influences. Indeed we often find Schumann stressing the purely musical component of a composition and even the autonomous properties of music in general. In his review of Mendelssohn's *Schöne Melusine*, he recognizes that even in respect of description the peculiar capabilities of music cannot be conveyed by language:

And here those joyous images over which youthful fancy likes so much to linger may well come alive for everyone; those legends of the life far below the watery depths, full of darting fish with golden scales, full of pearls in open shells, full of buried treasures that the sea has taken from man, full of emerald castles built towering on top of one another, etc. – But this, we think, distinguishes the Overture from the earlier ones: that quite in the fashion of a fairy tale, it seems to talk to itself of such things and does not actually experience them. Therefore at first sight its surface even appears somewhat cold, or mute; but the life and motion in the depths can be uttered more clearly by music than by words, for which reason also the Overture (we admit) is better by far than this description.[41]

And in general, Schumann gives a large share of his attention to structure and compositional technique in their own right. "But we musicians stick first and foremost to the notes," he writes on one occasion, "and before we pronounce them, united as a whole, to be a masterpiece, we demand an accounting from every one."[42] There is no doubt in his mind as to the intrinsic and self-sufficient logic of music: "for in music in general a nonsensical statement is simply not possible; even a madman cannot suppress harmonic laws."[43]

Yet we cannot say that music is unaffected by outer experience, or that it is not representative of inner life and personality. In Schumann's view, music thus isolated would possess no more than routine correctness; it would be mechanical and empty, completely devoid of value; formal symmetry and well-conceived genre are in themselves insufficient. The heart of his conception is the notion of character, which he defined in a dictionary article as follows:

Character, musical, is possessed by a composition when a disposition ex-
presses itself predominantly, or so obtrudes itself that no other interpreta-
tion is possible, as in the Eroica Symphony of Beethoven or in the Military
of Haydn. In a higher sense it is even the moral background of the artwork;
for although music without words can represent nothing evil, yet the moral
man is connected in such a fashion with the aesthetic, the ethical nature
with the artistic, that whatever is created in unethical passion also can not
conceal its origin in the artwork. Characteristic music is distinguished from
pictorial (picturesque) in that it represents the states of the soul, while the
other represents the circumstances of life; mostly we find the two mixed.[44]

To Schumann, character is covariant with artistic worth; it is the property in which content or *Geist* manifests itself, for it will be evident and
unambiguous only if the music has been importantly determined by vital circumstances or ideas. Since it expresses the soul, its value is in part
ethical, so that pictorial music will be ennobled if it is also characteristic. Character is thus the ideal meeting ground of the external and autonomous constituents of music, and if Schumann belittles concrete
descriptions, he means not to advocate an empty musical autonomy but
a specific kind of expressiveness: "The headings I added later. For is not
music always sufficient and articulate in itself?"[45] The listener requires
neither titles nor causes; even in the case of the *Pastoral Symphony* he is
injured because "Beethoven did not trust him to divine its character
without his assistance."[46] Character will in fact always elude in some
measure a hermeneutics of particular images; these can be at best illustrative, analogous, or suggestive.[47]

But if the specifically musical import of a work cannot be captured as
such by any given concrete description, it does not for that reason come
into being uninfluenced by the composer's external experiences. Yet in
general we cannot determine how these experiences enter into the musical significance, for artistic creation is only partly conscious; beneath
the surface is a process intrinsically unknowable, and somehow connected, in addition, with divine inspiration. In his conception of musical composition, Schumann reflects the Neoplatonic outlook of his
time. The operation of genius, fantasy, and imagination cannot be
known. But these are the primary forces of creation, as opposed to reason and craft, so that the essential import of music becomes fundamentally inexplicable and is most emphatically not to be conveyed by any
simple mechanism or analogy. Imagination does not convert the mate-

rial of life into music in a demonstrable fashion, so that each circumstance produces a corresponding tonal expression. At times the composer is aware of the factors that determine his musical ideas; his mood at the time of composition, the season of the year, a particular scene or event, manifestly form or guide the music. Yet often he can point to no source; the musical fantasy appears to generate its patterns spontaneously and autonomously. Particular images that seek to give an account of causal circumstance are still unessential, since the compositional process transmutes external forces into a musical character that is partly autonomous; they may serve again as illustrations, analogues, or guides, but in respect of a knowledge of the true formative influences on the music they now take on as well a tentative character, for creation is largely unconscious and for the most part escapes analysis and understanding. It fuses external and musical components in a manner that generally cannot be defined, and this is the central reason for the paradox of Schumann's practice. It is a problem that never ceases to occupy him. In one of his early reviews he writes, "With a sigh I continue – in no other criticism is demonstration so difficult as in the case of music."[48] And after surveying the epistemological bases of science, poetry, and the other arts, he continues, " – but music is an orphan, whose father and mother no one can name." The metaphor is well chosen, for orphans do have parents, but a mystery of identity accompanies the certainty of their existence. The review of Sterndale Bennett's programmatic *Sketches* is more explicit about the variable and generally unknown participation of the parental factors:

In which way, for the rest, the Sketches arose, whether from inner to outer or the reverse, does not affect the matter and no one can decide. The composers usually do not know themselves; one says one thing and the other another; often an external picture takes the lead, often again this is called forth by a melodic phrase. If only music and independent melody remain, let us not rack our brains but enjoy.[49]

In a discussion of Spohr's program symphonies the importance of specifically musical values is stressed still more, as a corollary of Schumann's distaste for composing to a program laid down in advance.[50] He had called such a procedure a "foolish beginning" in his letter to Henriette Voigt about the *Papillons,* and influenced now by the theory of the unconscious forces of creation, his attitude becomes one of scorn. For Schumann wishes to preserve the mystery of musical composition, perhaps partly because of a belief in its divine nature; but his desire is reinforced by the legitimate feeling that music must contain its own justification. The danger of working from a program is doubtless the production of purely picturesque music, of description rather than character. The creative process must be left to go its own way; conscious control would rob it of its peculiar strength and unconscious wisdom. Looking deeper than the alternating contributions of music and image, Schumann here envisions them in a miraculous synthesis. What he seeks may be music "before all else," but it is clearly not music alone, or as autonomous:

We admit to having a prejudice against this kind of creation, and perhaps share it with a hundred learned heads who to be sure often have strange ideas of composition and always call upon Mozart, who is said to have imagined nothing in connection with his music. As we have said, however, many probably have the prejudice, even the non-learned, and therefore if a composer holds a program up to us before his music, I say: "Before all else let me hear that you have made beautiful music; *afterwards I can also find your program pleasant." . . . the battle is already beginning to flare up again over that-which-may-not-be-thought-of in composing and the opposite. The philosophers really imagine the matter as worse than it is; certainly they are wrong when they believe that a composer who works according to an idea sets himself to it like a preacher on Saturday afternoon and schematizes his theme according to the usual three parts and works it out in general in a suitable way; certainly they are wrong. The creation of the musician is totally different in nature, and if an image, an idea hovers before him, he still will feel himself happy in his work only when it advances to meet him in* beautiful melodies, *borne by the same invisible hands as the "golden vessels" of which Goethe somewhere speaks.*[51]

The most comprehensive discussion of the whole texture of ideas connected with the unconscious nature of creation is found in the important review of Berlioz's *Symphonie Fantastique.* Schumann finds fault here not with the practice of composing to a program, but with making the program public, and indeed with the exposure of any of the circumstances of creation. "Men possess a peculiar modesty in front of the workshop of genius: they want to know nothing at all of the causes, instruments, and mysteries of creation, just as nature also manifests a certain delicacy in that she covers over her roots with earth."[52] Beyond this, as we have seen, a program restricts the poetic fancy of the listener, and it implies that the character of a work is not evident without assistance. In what follows, Schumann explains musical character as an outcome of the compositional process, thus establishing a connection between the two principal conceptions of his aesthetic theory:

As to what concerns the knotty question in general of how far instrumental music may go in the representation of thoughts and events, many are here too anxious in their attitude. We are certainly wrong if we believe that composers set out pen and paper to realize the miserable intention of expressing, describing, or painting this or that. Yet let us not place too low a value on fortuitous external influences and impressions. Unconsciously alongside the musical fantasy an idea is often continuously active, alongside the ear the eye, and this, the organ always active, then holds fast amidst the sounds and tones to certain contours that can condense and develop themselves into distinct forms with the advancing music. Now the more the thoughts or images produced with the tones carry within them elements related to music, the more poetic or plastic in expression the composition will be, – and the more fantastic or sharper the conception of the musician is, the more his work will exalt or arrest us. . . . Indeed even smaller, more particular images can lend so charming and definite a character to music that one is astonished at how it is able to express such traits. Thus a composer once told me that while he was writing, the image of a butterfly swimming along on a leaf in a brook intruded itself upon him; this had given the little piece the delicacy and naiveté that somehow only the image may possess in reality.

Schumann completes the picture by adding an anecdote that concerns the problem of interpretation:

In this fine genre painting Franz Schubert in particular was a master, and I cannot forbear adducing from my experience how once during a Schubert March the friend with whom I was playing answered my question about whether he did not see very specific figures before him: "Indeed! I found myself in Seville, but over a hundred years ago, amidst Dons and Doñas walking up and down, wearing dresses with trains, pointed shoes, pointed swords," and so on. Strangely enough we were one in our visions even to the city.[53]

But precision in musical representation would actually destroy the true basis of Schumann's delight, which is the mysterious ambiguity of character and its challenging vagueness as an index to the creative process. This is the great enigma that underlies and suggests all the other riddles he is so fond of adding to his compositions. Just as he is astonished when the Spanish visions of his duet partner correspond to his own, on occasion he will wonder whether his imagination does in fact hit upon the scene that a composer has sought to embody in his music. Thus in a letter to Mendelssohn he writes about one of this composer's pieces that "it seemed to me to come as though out of an old chronicle, when the 'players' blow their trumpets for the tournament and the knights will not appear and the musicians now grow impatient, *etc., etc.* Tell me, am I wide of the mark, or was something of the sort in your mind?"[54] Even his own works are mysteries to Schumann, and the images he finds in them come to him as discoveries that reveal previously unknown details of the process of creation. "In the Davidstänze," he writes to Clara, "the clock strikes twelve at the very end, as I have discovered."[55] Similarly the marked passages in his copy of *Flegeljahre* could well be discoveries of originally unrecognized influences in the composition of the *Papillons,* especially since the music does not follow the order of the story.

Schumann speculates even about the autobiographical basis of his works; in reference to his emotional state during the composition of the Andante and Variations for Two Pianos, he writes to the conductor Johannes Verhulst, "their tone is very elegiac, I believe I was somewhat melancholy when I composed them."[56] The element of doubt is characteristic, but where Schumann's own compositions are concerned it is often peripheral. Thus in spite of the detail of the images he finds in one of the *Fantasiestücke,* opus 12, he still seems to seek the confirmation of Clara, but he is not so much questioning the appropriateness of his program as he is seeking evidence of the mutual sympathy of their natures:

Later, when I was finished, I found to my delight the story of Hero and Leander in it. You know it well. Leander swims every night through the sea to his beloved, who waits in the lighthouse and with burning torch shows him the way. It is an old, beautiful, romantic tale. When I play "die Nacht" I cannot forget the picture – first how he plunges into the sea – she calls – he answers – he through the waves and happily arrived on land – then the cantilena, when they are in each others arms, – then how he again must leave and cannot tear himself away – until the night again en-

velops everything in darkness. But tell me whether this picture fits the music for you also.[57]

Schumann is also rather tentative about the butterfly that flutters up in the introduction of the B♭ Symphony, but here the image seems to be no more than a suggested aid to interpretation.[58]

Whether images provide information about the creative process or are poetic fancies partly determined by the listener, while it may be a matter of interest and curiosity, is in fact of no consequence with respect to the musical substance itself. As concrete entities of a visual or conceptual nature, cause and effect are actually of equal relevance; to the intrinsic character of music, with its strange generality, the one is as unimportant as the other. Thus, life experience may be an essential constituent of music; but paradoxically, a knowledge of the particular experience bearing on any composition is not in general an essential factor in the comprehension of the music. It is here that Schumann's aesthetics has led to the most divergent interpretations. If we can understand a musical work in its own terms, then the meaning of music is in a sense independent of its causal influences; these are present in the musical content not in any literal way, but only as transformed into tonal shape. They constitute a specific meaning of the composition, but in their specific form an unessential one. Thus the music transcends them but bears their imprint in its character, and the appreciation of this character, in its peculiar duality, belonging simultaneously to life and to the "absolute" sphere of tone, constitutes understanding of the work. Specific cause and program become pedagogical and dispensable, although descriptions have an independent value, when the original influences bearing on a work are unknown, as poetic penetrations of artistic character. Such devised programs in effect say: these conditions could have formed the composition in question. Generally unaware of the forces shaping his work, the composer will select titles and headings that reveal his own sensitivity to the values of his music. This was an important undertaking in a time that could not refrain from interpretations, for the composer had to protect his compositions from clumsiness, excess, and inappropriateness.[59] But fundamentally, Schumann felt, it was often well to omit verbal indications altogether. If the musical character has a generalized emotional nature, yet a definite one, we will lose little in the absence of any title or heading. In a work like *Vogel als Prophet,* on the other hand, or *Verrufene Stelle,* the content is so specific that we cannot fully appreciate the character without a knowledge of the program; the verbal description is an essential part of the poetic whole.

If we turn back for a moment to the problem of the *Papillons,* we will find relevant to its solution a surprising number of the principles that have been reviewed. A wide range of causal factors is to some extent recognized by Schumann. His letter to Henriette Voigt described the last piece only as arising from *Flegeljahre,* but he also seems to have acknowledged the compositional process more explicitly as a new collocation of older pieces under the specific influence of the novel, for he writes to Gottfried Weber, the editor of *Cäcilia:*

> to the Papillons *[I must add] that they arose* in part *from the last chapter of the* Flegeljahre *of Jean Paul, and that I then assembled them in such a way that one might remark in them something of the masked ball and perhaps of Wina's eye behind the mask.*[60]

He even cites the effects of his surroundings and of the whole cast of his life in a letter to Theodor Töpken:

> *That you know the Papillons, of which much arose in Heidelberg and in its beautiful surroundings, makes me very happy, as it must give you at least an indication of my life.*[61]

Thus, conceptions of the masquerade, of the butterfly in both its ephemeral flight and its metamorphosis, of the soul, of Schumann's own achievement of independence and individuality, of Heidelberg and its pleasures, of sets of dances and their hidden relationships as an expression of the masked ball, even of the style of Schubert both in its external features and its psychological suggestiveness, and finally of Jean Paul's *Flegeljahre* – all these formed a natural unity of associations that entered variously into the process of creation, and all the more variously because this process was so extended in time. Schumann could never fully analyze such a compound, especially after it had become absorbed by the unconscious and combined again with more mysterious and specifically musical components; he could only surmise and wonder and again create poetically, but now in words and images, on the basis of the finished and tangible musical product. And he could ask his family for confirmation as to whether his pictures were indeed suitable ones (and therefore likely causes), or tell Henriette Voigt how important it was to him to know whether the musical character was indeed self-sufficient. We cannot doubt, however, that part of Schumann's curiosity over the appropriateness and relevance of specific circumstances was really wonderment over the way music seemed automatically to contain the nature and structure of particular happenings – a metaphysical issue he never examined directly.

The belief that life and art are one has become a platitude of Schumann research. An endless stream of scholars and biographers has repeated the truism that we cannot understand the music except through the man, that Schumann's life has the most direct bearing on the nature of his art. We have taken up this concept with regard to detailed connections, but we may apply it also even to the choice of genre and medium. Then the solo piano piece, with its shifts and contrasts of mood, will become a reflection of the individuality of the youth who is given to introspective examination of his reactions and feelings. With the intimate twoness of love, the musical range is expanded almost by necessity – a necessity upon which Schumann comments without consciousness of this particular cause – to the wonderfully sensitive dialogue of piano and voice, its explicit content love in all its nuance and beauty. As a matter partly of economic success, the paterfamilias looks more to society, to fame and large achievement, and these new interests and ambitions are reflected in symphonic, dramatic, and choral works. The number of performers alone thus appears to be not a purely technical aspect of the music, but an almost literal representation of the relationships of life; and although the regular succession of media in Schumann's career has more than one cause, it would seem wrong not to consider the interpenetration of art and life as an important basis of explanation. Thus even in the largest possible perspective his musical career will mirror his view of life: "And so it is throughout in human life: the goal we once strove for is no more a goal: and we seek and strive and long, always higher, until the eye breaks and the breast, and the shattered soul lies slumbering in the grave."[62] From the broad scope of this poetic and tragic picture, in a descending scale, there follows the succession of other, more particular relationships between outer experience and musical practice: the content of the piano works, expressing Schumann's strong literary interest and revolving about the atmosphere and dark significance of the masked ball; the varied feelings of the love songs, including such specific features as a young girl's sentimental idealization of an older man in *Frauenliebe und Leben* – for Schumann was eight years older than Clara, and Chamisso was over forty when he married a girl of eighteen. These concerns are succeeded by new kinds of motif: by the cosmic pictures of man embodied in Faust and Manfred, by graphic impressions of Rhenish scenes, by religious feeling. In each case, the effect is not simply due to external circumstance as the occasion for the adoption of a particular genre; the relationship is not the looser tie between the eighteenth-century function or commission and its musical product but a deeper and more thorough transformation of the composer's experience into the substance of the music; to this even the demands of commissions and special occasions must be subservient if a given work is to have artistic value. In addition, Schumann's life was filled with the music of other composers and with the sonorities and capabilities of the different musical media, and this series of experiences similarly became part of the content of his compositions. Needless to say, the detailed expression of experience in musical content fades somewhat in Schumann's later music, although without affecting the general validity of our thesis; increasing neoclassical tendencies meant a greater objectivity and a greater opaqueness of musical materials, and hand in hand with this new compositional practice went new theoretical conceptions that stressed workmanship rather than genius. By his own earlier views, of course, the later Schumann would stand condemned, or at least be harshly judged, just as he often has been by historians; reliance on an arduous learning of technique spelled talent rather than genius, and if the older composer cannot find praise enough for the value of learning to do things well, the younger one cannot sufficiently express his disdain for discipline in musical theory or his admiration for the sovereign and untutored ease of genius.[63]

Nevertheless the foundations of neoclassicism are present in the very center of Romanticism; even as a youth Schumann described understanding as the guide of fantasy,[64] and his subsequent practice as a critic by no means neglects the question of formal coherence, just as the meaning of his music never destroys its aesthetic and structural integrity. Both realism and dramatic vividness are essentially absent from his works, perhaps more through conviction in the one case and more through inability in the other. Although there are outstanding exceptions, the musical content is typically generalized feeling and mood, more suggestive than concrete; specific depiction and detailed narration are secondary to inner experience, with its indefinable qualities, its vagueness, its tantalizing evasion of verbal fixation. Indeed it is Schumann's own personality, divided into Florestan and Eusebius, that informs much of the substance of his music; enthusiasm and reverie remain as essential emotional contents even after the personifications have disappeared. Thus the detailed poetic excursions of Schumann's criticism could hardly be literal renditions of specific meaning. And his ambivalent attitude toward program music is due precisely to its literal tendencies; he insists that the detailed program is not the criterion by which musical success is to be measured; music must satisfy us in its own terms. But although music inevitably follows its own inherent laws, to take it in its own terms is not really to follow it in its purely musical aspect, but in its presentation of the kind of content to which it is suited. Schumann simply wishes to cast aside realism when he speaks of purely musical values, but what he actually sets in the place of external imitation is a different kind of content: inner experience captured in musical character. It is only logical then that what predominates in Schumann's work is the vaguely suggestive character-piece: the richly associative quality of dance motifs, the implicit invitation contained in the ballad or romance to follow a story. But what story? Just this legendary atmosphere, to be filled in ad libitum but in accord with the prevailing tone, was what the Romantic composer sought. The imaginative construction of ever new types of character added to the stock of inherited qualities. Sometimes a phrase was taken from life, from a sailor's song or a tarantella; at other times the whole atmosphere was created altogether artificially, as in the suggestion of oriental character. But it was always the undefined nature of the result that was important, and it was this very lack of definition that Schumann understood by Romanticism. It is difficult to conceive of a specific Romantic movement in music, he believes, for music is always Romantic;[65] behind its explicit melodies there is a mysterious and suggestive light, like the glow of dawn.[66] His own music could hardly find a more adequate characterization; and if we add to such a vague and distant quality the thoroughly personal nature of the experience called for by this aesthetic, and the introspective personality of Schumann in particular, the inappropriateness of dramatic representation becomes as conspicuous as that of realism. It is only because Manfred is akin to Schumann that his depiction can become convincing.

We may now turn briefly to the province of vocal music, in the hope that it may be profitably examined as part of the general question of musical significance, and that the Lied will prove amenable to the same explanatory principles that apply to the piano piece.[67] The piano itself certainly does not mean to Schumann what it does to Chopin; it is a universal instrument of expression, but it is not a specific world closed off from the rest of music. Indeed, in Schumann's case it appears to have absorbed and concentrated an early musical experience of surprisingly wide range, and it continues to suggest the varied colors of orchestral instruments and to evoke the expressivity of the human voice, although not the feeling of its conceptual definition. The Schumann Lied, on the other hand, dissolves its particular images in more general tonal qualities and feelings, in a haunting aroma of sentiment; we view the words through a veil that softens and transfigures their explicit message, and the effect is encouraged by the poetry itself, for it possesses the very same tendencies. But the lyrical piano is then no longer so far from the almost incorporeal vocal tone. And the astonishingly beautiful *Berg und Burgen* in the Heine *Liederkreis,* for example, can become very much like an emotional intensification of the F-sharp major *Romanze* of opus 28, while in the light of the song, every change and new departure in the melodic flow of the piano piece seems to take on an increased meaning and a more specific expressiveness. Piano and voice prove their underlying identity in Schumann's Lieder by their intimate give and take, their equal participation in the expressive substance. This essential interchangeability can be seen not only in the melodic alternation of the two but also in the remarkable force of the piano postlude. In the haunting and introspective postludes of *Am leuchtenden Sommermorgen* and *Die alten, bösen Lieder* it is as though for the first time we discern the true nature of the character-piece. But why does the piano become endowed with such eloquence in this context? Melodic expression is revealed as a peculiar composite of specific occasions and the deeper significance of tone – a compound in which the experience is universalized and the tonal element enhanced in poignancy. Evidently the concrete meaning of the poem illuminates this character and makes the final statement of the piano a climactic moment that distills and concentrates the essence of the Lied. The postlude becomes a perfect incarnation of Romantic aesthetics, and it contains the key, if only we might grasp it and set it into words, of the nature of music as it was realized in that era: a mutual

enhancement of concrete experience and tonal mystery, the one trans-
figured and the other made deeply relevant to human life.

If we inquire finally into the sources of Schumann's outlook, we can
logically take the influence of extramusical experience as our guide. It
will be literature, then, that will appear as the basic formative force affecting alike his music, his criticism, and his aesthetic theory. Surrounded from childhood by a literary atmosphere, Schumann turned
first to this art rather than to music, and the whole subsequent cast of
his thought was determined by his early experience. The fact that one of
his youthful projects, to which he returned at the end of his life, was the
compilation of the musical views of the great poets of various epochs,
shows clearly that he must have received his main concepts of the nature and powers of music from literary works. What he found in music
would thus almost inevitably have been a personal version of what his
favorite authors found in it; and what he admired in Schubert and
Beethoven and Bach he saw in the light of Jean Paul and Hoffmann and
Wackenroder. Above all else, the works of German Romantic literature
eulogize the strangely affective power of musical tone; they find excruci-
ating delight in the sound of the musical glasses and the aeolian harp.
But music is affective in a very special manner that simultaneously in-
tensifies and resolves individual feelings and can justly be called cathar-
tic. For the emotional variety found in music has little to do with the
Affektenlehre and paradoxically possesses a certain sameness: it is always
deep and inarticulate, both sad and consoling, and characterized by
mystery and infinite longing. Yet its single quality encompasses all the
feelings of life, at once absorbing, transforming, and expressing them,
and granting them a measure of transcendence over reality but not the
accessory or fictional property of images.

   The universality of music answers to every need of the human heart,
although especially to the Romantic desire to express the feeling of
nameless and insatiable longing. In this unfulfilled longing all the arts
were to coalesce, but the spirit that suffused the whole was that of music, and the hidden or explicit wish of many an author of the time was
to become a composer, so that he might better succeed in an expressive
endeavor for which words were inherently too concrete and earthbound. This desire was consummated in Schumann's career; turning
from literature to music, he carried with him the nocturnal atmo-

sphere, the masked-ball motif, and the morbidity and effusiveness and dreamlike imagination of poetry. Not illogically, the strange powers of music were connected with cosmic forces; as the emotional quality of music dissolved the real feelings of life, it was easily regarded as above them; still more obviously was music superior to individual occasions; it was a manifestation of the supernatural and put us in touch with a supernal realm. The divine nature of genius and inspiration followed as a matter of course.[68] And in the epochal dichotomy of immediacy and distance, of classic and romantic, static art was aligned with the first and music with the second. Philosophic writings reinforced these conceptions; the cosmic motif appears with Dalberg and Herder and is developed in Schelling and Schopenhauer; the close connection of music with feeling is most prominent in Hegel and reached Schumann in the writings of Amadeus Wendt. The cosmic connection is not a dominant one in Schumann's thought, although it is present. His central notions arise from the peculiar quality of tonal experience and its equivocal relationship to life. Like the heroes of Romantic literature, Schumann turned to music both to flee from life and to pour out his feelings, to escape into a higher world and simultaneously to give expression to his experience. His sensitive and introspective personality was an instrument of peculiar capabilities that transmuted the baser material of life into tonal form. In the dreamlike suggestion of distance that clothes the texts of his Lieder, we see this transmutation as though in process of occurrence; the result is an ideal embodiment of the dual attachment of Romantic music. Schumann's image of genius could equally well have been his image of music: a tree with its roots covered by earth and its crown turned toward heaven.[69]

We have not fully grasped the nature of this music, however, if we conceive it only as bearing the imprint of extrinsic events. Metaphysical theory, the philosophy of literary creation, and the practice of poetic criticism all direct our attention to an opposite process, in which music does not take up experience but produces it.[70] As a primary creative substance, music gives rise to all the phenomena of the world, and nature is everywhere animated by *Stimmung*. The almost imperceptible sounds of the Jews' harp and the ocarina suggest this background of cosmic import, and in the action of the wind on the Aeolian harp ethereal music seems to be made sensible. It is not in the least strange, then, for Schiller to describe the first stage of literary creation as the presence of a musical mood. All poetry – as a creation of particular ideas and fictions – grows from and looks back to a metaphysical source in music, which is poetry in a more fundamentally creative sense.[71] In the composition of Lieder, it will thus be quite logical to write the poem after the music, a procedure that indeed was not uncommon in the Romantic period. And the importance of the postlude in Schumann's Lieder will be matched by that of the prelude, by instances, such as we find in *Mein Herz ist schwer,* in which the voice appears to arise as a concretion of the mood or spirit of an instrument. The same consideration applies to poetic criticism or to verbal mottoes and headings, all of which may point not only ahead, as causes to be transformed into musical character, but back to the tonal force that produced them, and now with the greatest hermeneutic value. And even beyond this, since poetry arises from tone, music will become its logical interpreter,[72] just as poetry interprets music that arises from literature. In every case, music gives the inside of events, the ontological substrate of images. In the final scene of *Flegeljahre,* Walt's dream contains the mysterious halflight of dawn, the vagueness and distance by which life adumbrates music; and just as literature strove to become music, the meaning of his dream is in fact given by music – by tones that proceed from an indefinitely receding source and thus do not belong to the objective world of perception.

NOTES

From *Journal of the American Musicological Society* 17, no.3 (1964): 310–45. © The American Musicological Society. This article is a somewhat expanded version of a talk given at Yale University on 22 April 1963.

1. Friedrich Gustav Jansen, ed., *Robert Schumanns Briefe, Neue Folge,* 2nd ed. (Leipzig 1904), p.420.

2. Clara Schumann, ed., *Jugendbriefe von Robert Schumann* (Leipzig 1885), p.281.

3. Ibid., p.278. This is amplified a few years later (ibid., p.302): "Die Phantasie kannst Du nur verstehen, wenn Du Dich in den unglücklichen Sommer 1836 zurückversetzest, wo ich Dir entsagte; jetzt habe ich keine Ursache so unglücklich und melancholisch zu komponiren."

4. Ibid., p.303.

5. Ibid., p.301 (letter of 7 April 1839 to Clara).

6. Ibid., p.309 (letter of 17 January 1840 to Clara).

7. See Friedrich Gustav Jansen, *Die Davidsbündler: Aus Robert Schumann's Sturm- und Drangperiode* (Leipzig 1883), p.230.

8. These are given, rather carelessly, by Wolfgang Boetticher, in *Robert Schumann: Einführung in Persönlichkeit und Werk* (Berlin 1941), pp.611–13. The chapter in question is no. 63, the next to the last; see *Jean Pauls Sämtliche Werke, Historisch-kritische Ausgabe, 1. Abteilung, 10. Band: Flegeljahre* (Weimar 1934), pp.462–72.

9. For Knorr's discussion of the *Papillons,* which appeared in his *Führer auf dem Felde der Klavierunterrichtsliteratur* (Leipzig 1861), see Martin Kreisig, ed., *Gesammelte Schriften über Musik und Musiker von Robert Schumann,* 5th ed. (Leipzig 1914), vol.2, p.456.

10. *Jugendbriefe,* pp.167–68 (letter of 19 April 1832). Schumann wrote two closely similar letters a short time afterward, directed to the editors Gottfried Fink and Ignaz Castelli; the first can be found in Boetticher, op. cit., p.613 (27 April 1832) and the second in *Neue Folge,* pp.35–36 (28 April 1832).

11. *Jugendbriefe,* pp.166–67 (17 April 1832).

12. In a letter of 15 March 1839 to his admirer Simonin de Sire, Schumann writes, "Die Ueberschriften zu allen meinen Compositionen kommen mir immer erst, nachdem ich schon mit der Composition fertig bin" (*Neue Folge,* p.148); other examples will be considered below.

13. See the valuable study by Wolfgang Gertler, "Einleitung," *Robert Schumann in seinen frühen Klavierwerken* (Wolfenbüttel-Berlin 1931).

14. *Neue Folge,* p.43 (letter of 5 April 1833 to his friend Theodor Töpken).

15. *Jugendbriefe,* p.166 (17 April 1832).

16. Ibid., p.174 (8 May 1832).

17. This may mean – although the idea is speculative – that the last piece was conceived originally in terms of the *Grossvater* melody, and that Schumann then discovered (to his astonishment, as we may imagine) that this traditional tune combined polyphonically with the initial "papillon" melody of the work. "Chance" might then represent the action of the subconscious forces of composition, which in selecting the *Grossvatertanz* for the final piece would be reflecting the peculiar quality of the end of the novel to which Schumann has just described his reaction. Schumann's conception of the nature of the compositional process will be discussed below.

18. *Neue Folge,* pp.53–54 (22 August 1834).

19. *Gesammelte Schriften,* vol.1, p.122. As Florestan indicates (ibid., vol.1, p.121), his account is based on an interpretation found in the *Cäcilia* of 1825 (ibid., vol.2, p.386).

20. Ibid., vol.1, pp.202–3.

21. *Neue Folge,* p.92 (23 August 1837).

22. Ibid., p.40 (letter of 5 April 1833 to Theodor Töpken).

23. Ibid., p.537.

24. *Gesammelte Schriften,* vol.1, p.44. Schumann expands his remark in a

footnote: "In diesem Sinne könnte Jean Paul zum Verständnis einer Beethovenschen Sinfonie oder Phantasie durch ein poetisches Gegenstück möglich mehr beitragen (selbst ohne nur von der Phantasie oder Sinfonie zu reden) als die Dutzend-Kunstrichtler, die Leitern an den Koloss legen und ihn gut nach Ellen messen."

25. Ibid., vol.1, p.84. The same idea is expressed by Eusebius (ibid., vol.1, p.28): "Deinen Ausspruch, Florestan, dass du die Pastoral- und heroische Sinfonie darum weniger liebst, weil sie Beethoven selbst so bezeichnete and daher der Phantasie Schranken gesetzt, scheint mir auf einem richtigen Gefühl zu beruhen."

26. *Neue Folge*, p.223 (letter of 23 November 1842 to Spohr).

27. Ibid., pp.224–25 (10 January 1843).

28. *Gesammelte Schriften*, vol.1, p.462.

29. Ibid., vol.1, pp.462–63.

30. *Jugendbriefe*, pp.282–83 (13 April 1838).

31. *Neue Folge*, p.300 (2 April 1849). Schumann similarly says about the *Overture, Scherzo, and Finale:* "Das Ganze hat einen leichten, freundlichen Charakter; ich schrieb es in recht fröhlicher Stimmung" (ibid., p.434; letter of 5 November 1842 to the publisher Friedrich Hofmeister).

32. Ibid., p.319 (26 November 1849).

33. Ibid., p.227 (5 May 1843).

34. *Jugendbriefe*, p.299 (11 March 1839). General formulations can be found among the aphorisms of Eusebius: "Die Antichromatiker sollten bedenken, dass es eine Zeit gab, wo die Septime ebenso auffiel wie jetzt etwa eine verminderte Oktave, und dass durch Ausbildung des Harmonischen die Leidenschaft feinere Schattierungen erhielt, wodurch die Musik in die Reihe der höchsten Kunstorgane gestellt wurde, die für alle Seelenzustände Schrift und Zeichen haben" (*Gesammelte Schriften*, vol.1, p.22); and again: "Die Musik ist die am spätesten ausgebildete Kunst; ihre Anfänge waren die einfachen Zustände der Freude und des Schmerzes (Dur und Moll), ja der weniger Gebildete denkt sich kaum, dass es speziellere Leidenschaften geben kann, daher ihm das Verständnis aller individuelleren Meister (Beethovens, Fr. Schuberts) so schwer wird. Durch tieferes Eindringen in die Geheimnisse der Harmonie hat man die feineren Schattierungen der Empfindung auszudrücken erlangt" (ibid., vol.1, p.27). Florestan is quite in agreement, and his statement has something of a mortal tone: "Das wäre eine kleine Kunst, die nur klänge und keine Sprache noch Zeichen für Seelenzustände hätte!" (ibid., vol.1, p.22).

35. *Neue Folge*, p.110 (letter of 8 February 1838).

36. Ibid., p.158 (30 June 1839).

37. *Jugendbriefe*, pp.82–83 (6 November 1829).

38. *Gesammelte Schriften*, vol.1, p.18.

39. Ibid., vol.2, p.170.

40. "Nur geschehe solche Andeutung durch Worte sinnig und fein; die Bildung eines Musikers wird gerade daran zu erkennen sein." *Gesammelte Schriften*, vol.1, p.361.

41. Ibid., vol.1, p.143.

42. Ibid., vol.2, p.297.

43. Ibid., vol.1, p.22.

44. Ibid., vol.2, p.207.

45. *Neue Folge*, pp.101–2 (letter of 22 September 1837 to Moscheles).

46. *Gesammelte Schriften*, vol.1, p.83.

47. They can also be described as fictitious, if not arbitrary. The framework narrative used in Schumann's critical writings enhances this fictional quality, and in permitting several views to be advanced, it emphasizes it still further. The use of multiple interpretations is a method certainly capable of conveying a more adequate sense of the musical character. In his essay on Beethoven's Ninth Symphony, on the other hand, Schumann runs riot with arbitrary and absurd reactions, doubtless in reflection of a current pastime (ibid., vol.1, pp.39–42).

48. Ibid., vol.1, p.44.

49. Ibid., vol.1, p.368.

50. Ibid., vol.2, pp.129–30.

51. Loc. cit.

52. Ibid., vol.1, p.83.

53. Ibid., vol.1, pp.84–85.

54. *Neue Folge*, p.255 (18 November 1845).

55. *Jugendbriefe*, p.275 (11 February 1838).

56. *Neue Folge*, p.229 (19 June 1843).

57. *Jugendbriefe*, pp.286–87 (21 April 1838). The next day Schumann again writes about *Die Nacht* in a letter to Karl Krägen (*Neue Folge*, p.120): "Später habe ich die Geschichte von Hero und Leander darin gefunden. Sehen Sie doch nach. Es passt alles zum Erstaunen."

58. See the letter to Taubert cited above.

59. "Man hat diese Überschriften über Musikstücke, die sich in neuerer Zeit wieder vielfach zeigen, hier und da getadelt und gesagt, eine gute Musik bedürfe solcher Fingerzeige nicht. Gewiss nicht: aber sie büsst dadurch ebensowenig etwas von ihrem Wert ein, und der Komponist beugt dadurch offenbarem Vergreifen des Charakters am sichersten vor." *Gesammelte Schriften*, vol.1, p.361. The analogous danger of misguided poetic criticism is best illustrated by the satirical discussion of Beethoven's Ninth Symphony (see footnote 47).

60. *Neue Folge*, p.46 (11 January 1834).

61. Ibid., p.40 (5 April 1833).

62. *Jugendbriefe*, p.20 (letter of 28 April 1828 to his mother). Schumann himself transfers this outlook to the progression of musical genres; a letter written nearly twenty-three years later to the military officer August Strackerjan provides an example (*Neue Folge*, p.335; 13 January 1851): "Der geistlichen Musik die Kraft zuzuwenden, bleibt ja wohl das höchste Ziel des Künstlers. Aber in der Jugend wurzeln wir alle ja noch so fest in der Erde mit ihren Freuden und Leiden; mit dem höheren Alter streben wohl auch die Zweige höher. Und so hoffe ich, wird auch diese Zeit meinem Streben nicht zu fern mehr sein."

63. The contrast, expressed also in terms of the preoccupations of Schumann's life, can be examined by comparing the

"Denk- und Dichtbüchlein" (*Gesammelte Schriften*, vol.1, p.17ff.) with the later "Musikalische Haus- und Lebensregeln" (ibid., vol.2, p.163ff.).

64. *Neue Folge*, pp.7–8 (letter of 5 August 1828 to the song composer Gottlob Wiedebein).

65. *Gesammelte Schriften*, vol.1, p.26.

66. Ibid., vol.1, pp.249–50. Schumann applies the characterization to the music of Stephan Heller.

67. Certainly the literary inspiration that is found in instrumental works becomes even more conspicuous and concrete in vocal music. Schumann writes to Moritz Horn about *Der Rose Pilgerfahrt:* "Gewiss eignet sich die Dichtung zur Musik, und es sind mir auch schon eine Menge Melodien dazu durch den Sinn gegangen" (*Neue Folge*, p.339). The beauty of Schumann's Lieder, more than in the case of other composers, is dependent upon the values of the poetic texts and upon his sensitivity to them. Even the experimental forms of his later vocal music owe their origin to the inspiration of poetry. He writes about *Schön Hedwig:* "Es ist eine Art der Composition, wie wohl noch nicht existirt, und so sind wir immer vor Allem den Dichtern zu Dank verbunden, die, neue Wege der Kunst zu versuchen, uns so oft anregen" (ibid., p.372; letter of 8 May 1853 to Carl van Bruyck).

68. Creation was not only unconscious but also in touch with destiny, and in plumbing the creative process Schumann discovers supernatural forces along with natural ones. He tells Clara how, during the composition of the *Nachtstücke,* the images he saw, the title he conceived, and the emotions that affected him were all joined by a mysterious intimation (*Jugendbriefe*, pp.300–301; letter of 7 April 1839): "Von einer Ahnung schrieb ich Dir; ich hatte sie in den Tagen von 24. bis zum 27. März bei meiner neuen Komposition; es kommt darin eine Stelle vor auf die ich immer zurückkam; die ist als seufzte Jemand recht aus schwerem Herzen: 'ach Gott.' – Ich sah bei der Komposition immer Leichenzüge, Särge, unglückliche, verzweifelte Menschen, und als ich fertig war und lange nach einem Titel suchte, kam ich immer auf den: 'Leichenphantasie' – ist das nicht merkwürdig – Beim Komponiren war ich auch oft so angegriffen dass mir die Thränen herankamen und wusste doch nicht warum und hatte keinen Grund dazu – da kam Theresen's Brief und nun stand es klar vor mir." The letter brought news of his brother Eduard's imminent death. Schumann attributes a similar unconscious prophetic power to Mendelssohn, as expressed in the musical character of his C-Minor Piano Trio: "Wundervolle Stellen sind darin. Jetzt, nachdem er so früh scheiden musste, kann ihr Sinn Niemandem mehr verhüllt sein" (*Neue Folge*, p.451; letter of 3 December 1847 to the publisher Hermann Härtel).

69. *Gesammelte Schriften*, vol.1, p.121.

70. The mutual inspirational force of poetry and music can be thought of as a general law of Schumann's aesthetics (indeed it goes back to his early belief in the interrelation of all the arts); he was by no means unaware of it, and it finds

ingenious expression when he comes to review Spohr's *Die Weihe der Töne* (ibid., vol.1, pp.65–66), which is based on a poem that in turn celebrates music: "Man müsste zum drittenmal nachdichten, wenn man für die, welche diese Sinfonie nicht gehört, ein Bild entwerfen wollte; denn der Dichter verdankt die Worte seiner Begeisterung für die Tonkunst, die Spohr wiederum mit Musik übersetzt hat." Properly speaking, the series that ends with poetic criticism starts with the music of the cosmos, as the review subsequently makes clear. It is feeling that unites the successive stages, and fundamentally Schumann's aesthetics is an elaboration and exemplification of Beethoven's "Mehr Ausdruck der Empfindung als Malerei"; but Schumann realized that Beethoven himself had no need of the alternate phases of objective realization, whether in image, word, or nature: "Als Beethoven seinen Gedanken zur Pastoralsinfonie fasste und ausführte, so war es nicht der einzelne kleine Tag des Frühlings, der ihn zu einem Freudenruf begeisterte, sondern das dunkle zusammenlaufende Gemisch von hohen Liedern über uns (wie Heine, glaube

ich, irgendwo sagt), die ganze unendlichstimmige Schöpfung regte sich in ihn" (loc. cit.).

71. Is this the reason for the peculiar suitability of the terms "poet" and "poem" in Romantic music? Or does the explanation lie in the relative specificity of musical character? About the word "Dichtungen" Schumann writes to Clara (*Jugendbriefe*, p.281; 13 April 1838): "Nach dem letzten Wort suchte ich schon lange, ohne es finden zu können. Es ist sehr edel und bezeichnend für musikalische Kompositionen, denke ich."

72. As a youth of eighteen, Schumann writes to Gottlob Wiedebein (*Neue Folge,* p.6; 15 July 1828): "Ihre Lieder schufen mir manche glückliche Minute, und ich lernte durch diese Jean Pauls verhüllte Worte verstehen und enträthseln. Jean Pauls dunkle Geistertöne wurden mir durch jenes magische Verhüllen Ihrer Tonschöpfungen erst licht und klar, wie ungefähr zwei Negationen affirmiren, und der ganze Himmel der Töne, dieser Freudethränen der Seele, sank wie verklärt über alle meine Gefühle."

10

The Aesthetic Theories of Richard Wagner

WITH SURPRISING regularity, Wagner's treatises and essays in the field of aesthetics fall externally into five groups separated from one another by intervals of ten years, the dates in question running from 1840 to 1880. Undoubtedly the most original and influential of these works are those he wrote just at midcentury, from 1849 to 1851, during the first years of his exile in Switzerland. The major writings of this group are *Art and Revolution, The Artwork of the Future, Opera and Drama,* and *A Communication to My Friends.* They reveal Wagner at the most important turning point of his career, in his late thirties, about to begin the composition of the *Ring,* and in the process of formulating and clarifying the aesthetics that was to underlie the great operas of his maturity.

The leading conceptions of these Zurich treatises are the social role of art, the completeness of the artwork, and the primary position of feeling as an aesthetic value. Art is a mirror of society, reflecting – in Wagner's time – the extreme degradation of man. Ideally, art is a rite, a type of public religious service that commemorates the deeds of a hero by means of dramatic presentation. This ritual, as Wagner projected it for the future, is superior to Hellenic tragedy in its encompassing character: it is not limited to an aristocratic class or to a single nation but is rather for all mankind, fulfilling what are really the optimistic ideals of the Enlightenment, so powerfully expressed in Beethoven. The artwork of the future is even a product of the people; it is literally a cooperative creation, and thus besides presenting social values in its content, it provides the example of a model society of artists, governed by mutual love. In all this, Wagner is obviously the revolutionist turned prophet.

From this large social context, conceived even more broadly as an expression of nature, the artwork derives one of the bases of its completeness. The object of art is to present man in his entire and unspoiled nature, for it is nature, and in particular human nature, that – in the spirit of Rousseau – is able to rescue man from depraved taste and to point the way to true art. Behind this conception is the powerful vision of evolution, partly in the Hegelian sense of the progress of reason and partly in the mechanistic sense of Charles Darwin, whose influential ideas were yet to come. There is thus a natural continuity and a progress from nature to life to man and finally to art, the natural product of man. The artwork is to display man in his full reality, surrounded by a natural environment, in his social intercourse with his fellows, speaking a language that expresses both his feeling and his ideas in their native union, and accompanied (somewhat inconsistently) by an orchestra which fulfills the emotional intent of his speech, consummates his gesture, and reveals his stream of consciousness – his life in time – with its memory and its foreboding. Man is present in entirety: physically, intellectually, and emotionally. To this complete art all the separate art varieties must contribute: the plastic arts of architecture, painting, and sculpture, and especially the arts of man: dance and poetry and music. Also all the senses are enlisted, primarily the higher ones of vision and hearing, but by implication, those of touch and smell as well. One sense alone, like a single art, gives only a partial picture of man; by this standard (among others) the isolated art is condemned; the togetherness of the senses is essential for a complete experience.

Closely related to the completeness of the artwork, the expression of feeling remains as Wagner's chief properly aesthetic goal. The view of art as an expression of feeling, which in some form or other is so characteristic of musical aesthetics, is in Wagner's case part of a rather simplified anthropology which looks upon man as a creature of heart and mind. Human experience and activity are composites of two elements, feeling and understanding. Feeling is expressed in tone and gesture, intellectual activity in speech and written language. This body-mind relation is a constant background of Wagner's theorizing. In terms of the inevitable historical perspective: what was originally a harmonious natural unity has become split apart, and the independent overdevelopment of the intellect runs hand in hand with all the diseases of civilization. In putting together again the whole humpty-dumpty of nature, art is a redeeming force; but the new unity it achieves is essentially a suppression of the complexities of conceptual thought. In his healthy natural state, man is never devoid of feeling. Emotions accompany all his ideas, and the spontaneous consummation of thought into deed is not only in itself an expression of feeling, but prevents the excessive reflection that characterizes inaction, along with the divorce of thought from feeling.

But Wagner's concern with feeling went beyond its place in a restored natural balance of man's faculties and was exaggerated into that heightening of the emotional character of art which was really his central aesthetic endeavor. It is tied to his notion of the purely human, of the essential humanity that is found in every nation and place and time and that he sees manifested in the ideals of ancient Greece and of the Renaissance. Although Wagner has a secure understanding that the personality is formed only in a social setting and that its nature is constituted by an impress of social forces, he somewhat illogically conceives a constant and eternally true human nature that can be separated from the accidents of a particular environment. Thus his epochal decision against historical subject matter and in favor of myth. What is left of man when a particular setting of civilization is removed is precisely that core of emotional life that is universal, or so Wagner believed.

As the man of nature is unencumbered by the details of a historical surrounding, so was he also free of the complexities of civilized speech, for his thought was free of the entanglements of intricacy that plague modern intellectual life and the spoken drama as well. The mythical hero spoke a tonal speech – still partly alive in the German *Stabreim* – which constantly conveyed the emotional aspect of his ideas. This heightened speech was accompanied by a heightened action. Real life was intensified in the musical drama by a selection of powerful emotional moments, which also absorbed and concentrated the innumerable reinforcing occasions of life. The orchestra further strengthened the emotions of the action by renouncing a musically autonomous structure and reducing its contribution largely to individualized expressive phrases, endlessly juxtaposed and repeated, especially in sequence, so as to increase their impact by elemental devices of rhetoric. And still additional emotional power was achieved by presenting feelings in time, so that we see them develop and gather force, and become persuaded of their inevitability. At the same time, the orchestra unrolls the full depth of inner life by contributing both the recollections and the intimations that give emotional experience its richness and unique character. Thus in every way, the Wagnerian artwork was calculated to intensify feeling; its monumental emotionalism was the result of the implicit principle that, in the realm of feeling, quantity was quality. But the mainspring of the whole machinery was an anti-Biedermeier mentality which drove art to a level intended to be well above bourgeois sentimentality, although in fact the heroic realm devised there contained only inflated editions of Wagner's own sentimental images.

It is notorious that Wagner the social prophet was as unsuccessful as Wagner the revolutionist. Bayreuth became a fashionable tourist spot for rich Philistines. But this in itself is no argument against the ethical mission of art and no demonstration that the artist is best unconcerned with social implications. Yet like the utopian political schemes of the time, Wagner's social philosophy of art is hopelessly impractical. His aesthetics, on the other hand, deserves extended consideration, for the concern with completeness and with emotions is peculiarly equivocal with respect to the relationship of art and reality – a relationship for which the nineteenth century seems to have struggled unsuccessfully to find a formula. If art appeared as an escape from the everyday world to a superior realm in the outlook of early Romantic aesthetics, the realism of the second half of the century too easily identified it or at least confused it with everyday life itself, and even developed procedures and aesthetical laws to increase the resemblance. As early as in Berlioz's monodrama *Lélio,* the protagonist is the composer himself, telling us the passions and ideals of his own life, an equation of art and reality that here significantly turns the programmatic *Symphonie fantastique* into an explicitly dramatic work. But this curious and symptomatic composition reveals a problem to which the drama – as a highly representative art – is always subject. It is the same problem of illusion that is responsible for the eternal play-within-a-play, for the conception of all the world as a stage, and for the closing *la commedia è finita.* Wagner grasped the factors of choice and abstraction that entered into the procedure of the creative artist; he even criticized the homely bourgeois spoken drama and its concern with social problems. But his own selective and formative activity was dedicated to the production of a world that was also subjected to external standards and consequently influenced by psychological principles. Yet drama is no more condemned to this course than any other art, although significantly, Wagner looked upon it as a type of poetry rather than as an art in its own right and as the highest type of poetry precisely because of its closeness to life.

The notion that *The Ring of the Nibelungs* is governed by a type of realism may seem amusing if not utterly ridiculous, but it is an illusionistic art nevertheless, even if it seeks reality in a fancied primeval man. Like the early Romantics, Wagner still fled the Philistines, but he no longer tried to escape into a transcendental world. Instead, he sought the intensity of an art that would transform society, and that, in spite of its mythological setting, was essentially a sphere of commonsense materialism and common sensuousness. There he confused reality and semblance just as he did in his own life, weeping over the plight of his characters and intruding his personal feelings into the drama, particularly through the medium of the orchestra. Thus the emotional involvements of life were looked for in art. Its appeal to a wide audience was a corollary. The purely human demanded for its understanding no technical schooling, no special adeptness in the subtleties of an artificial medium. In perfect exemplification of Nietzsche's poor opinion of drama, the artwork of the future was obvious and rather crude in its effects; it commanded its audience by emotional force instead of working out its own destiny as a special medium whose apprehension would require refined taste and effort.

But an aesthetic that bases art on heightened real-life emotion seems mistaken in its fundamental conceptions; real-life emotions are doubtless best left to real life, and we demand instead from art its special emotions, peculiarly bound to the medium that conveys them. Thus the wholesale condemnation of separate arts cannot be sanctioned; any art creates a sufficient ideal world, and Wagner fails to see this essential characteristic only because his gaze is so steadily fixed on completeness and physical presence. It is not even strength of emotion that art seeks, but rather idiosyncratic quality, and this only as a concomitant, often only as a by-product, of a special constructive endeavor that finds its own delight in the inherent properties of the medium it exploits and in the particular problems each work poses. We are inclined to look upon drama itself as such an ideal sphere, whose nature is constituted by the qualities of action taken for themselves. Wagner knew that drama hinges upon action, but he persisted in regarding it nevertheless as a composite art which could sum the effects of the separate arts. He overcame, or solved, the problems of space and time by presenting the reality of which they were abstractions; but this is nothing less than a failure to court the particular virtual space and time that are the very primitive substance of the individual arts. No doubt for the drama these realms of manifestation are not directly the matter to be formulated; the dramatic action is an entity with properties both spatial and temporal. But even this Wagner overlooks: his spatial-temporal framework is less a distinctive environment of his art than a direct imitation of the space and time of everyday experience. Thus Wagner transmits the drama to us not as a special medium with its own values, but rather as a mixed genre with the values of real-life emotion. Beyond this, his aesthetics entails the fallacy that the emotional impact of multiple sensory experience can be derived by adding up the effects of each sense mode taken separately, an operation that certainly is not justified, as we can see at once in the mutual inhibition that can arise between two senses. But it is a fallacy anyway to regard a summed experience as aesthetically superior to an experience defined in terms of a particular expressive medium, whether this appeals to only one sense or not.

What role does music play in this aesthetics of drama? In terms of his favorite analogy of physical love, Wagner sees music as a woman, a receptive ocean of unformulated possibilities which takes into itself the procreative force of poetry and thus gives birth to the complete artwork. Music is passive; its nature is defined only by the male personality with which it falls in love; alone it is powerless to create. This sounds so much like unconscious self-justification that it may very well have its origin in the nature of Wagner's musical genius, which was neither self-motivating nor productive of absolute musical values but gave birth only to offspring stamped with the likeness of a defined fertilizing factor as well as with the lineaments of music. Like its sister arts, dance and poetry, with which once it was lovingly joined in mutual artistic endeavors, music has its independent history, of which Wagner, dominated by the evolutionary view and the device of historical demonstration, gives his usual thumbnail sketch, offered in all earnestness, but remarkable in its naïveté. Never without its concrete connections to folk dance and folksong, music nevertheless put these folk motifs to work apart from their original context, and by elaborating them, it developed an astounding independent growth. In the fullness of its development, however – as an instrumental art – it was never really autonomous; it remained essentially an extended dance, united to its origins not only in its rhythm but in its very structure. The Classical symphony is still an expansion of the dance, and its melody an outgrowth of folksong. In the course of this egoistic advance, music reached the limits of its separate life. Taking upon itself expressive and poetic purposes, it longed, in Beethoven, for a reunion with language, with real contexts. What it could achieve alone in this respect, it achieved in Beethoven: a progression of moods, a psychological tendency missing in his predecessors, an internal drama which proceeded from struggle to joy but which beyond this was powerless to make known its specific emotional message. Beethoven did even more than this, for he demonstrated the solution to the problem of music, the necessity for its recourse to the word and also the new freedom and development that this alliance made possible. The demonstration is found not so much in the setting of *Freude, schöner Götterfunken,* which merely exposes the power of folk melody, but clearly in *Seid umschlungen, Millionen,* where music is fertilized by the word and succeeds to a characteristic definite expression, breaking through the formal structure that has imprisoned it from the days of its original union with dance and song.

Thus Wagner's aesthetics of musical drama includes an aesthetics of music, an aesthetics that is concerned with the insufficiencies of the art. Music is an expression of feelings, but it is both indefinite and limited and therefore must lean on a more complete experience. What it represents in this larger setting is the constituent of feeling – the inner life; but its new emotional powers necessarily involve a new exactness, an increase in the ability to express the various particular contents of speech and gesture and external experience. Independent music has in any event reached the end of its existence, a presumed state of affairs that must have seemed quite borne out in fact in 1850.

The elaborate and powerful philosophy of musical drama contained in this central group of treatises is also found elsewhere in Wagner's writings, although the psychological and political aspects are not so conspicuous in the other dramatic essays. But operatic theory is not Wagner's only contribution to aesthetics. He is often concerned with a vastly different matter: with the properties of music itself, and in particular, with the Beethoven symphonies. As a matter of fact, Wagner's changing conceptions of the Beethoven symphony give a complete picture of his development as an aesthetician. In this relatively neglected but impressive aesthetics of instrumental music, we discover to our surprise that music alone is a thoroughly satisfying and absorbing experience, requiring no supplementation by the other arts. Naturally this point of view, influenced at first by E. T. A. Hoffmann and later by Schopenhauer, represents an element more or less indigestible to Wagner's dramatic theory, and countless pages of prose are dedicated to assimilating it.

The Paris essays of 1840 and 1841 describe music as a unique experience which cannot be conveyed in words. Interpretive stories only direct us to an essence which remains inherently untranslatable. Absolute music does not deal with human emotions but with a suprahuman realm of elemental feelings.

These insights are later more detailed and deeper. The 1857 essay on Liszt contains early evidence of the contact with Schopenhauer. Music presents the essence of all ideas. It is the best medium for those intuitions impossible to express in language. It even becomes divine, a type of inaudible *musica coelestis,* of which heard music is only a restricted version. In 1860, in the middle of an operatic treatise, we read that music is an absolutely autonomous language, fundamentally different in character from conceptual thought but in no way inferior in force or in subtlety.

In the Beethoven essay of 1870, which must rank as Wagner's highest achievement in musical philosophy, music stands far removed from the other arts: it presents the inner core of all phenomena, an insight that Wagner the composer had grasped in the *Ring* before Wagner the philosopher expounded it in theory. In contrast to the waking world of light, the world of sound is a dream world, unknown to the waking consciousness except in the form of an allegory – a manifest dream. The other arts arise from the contemplation of phenomena, but music has its origin in the cry, the direct emotional expression. The other arts are analogous to the church, but music is like religion itself. So powerful is the experience of music that it paralyzes vision; when we listen to it we do not respond to visual stimuli. Musical harmony, the truly characteristic element of the art, is beyond time and space, and it is only in rhythm that music makes contact with the visual world. Thus Palestrina is religion free from dogma – timeless, spaceless music; while in secular music the plastic element is dominant, and music is entangled in appearance. The true category of music is not beauty but the sublime. To be sure, its first effect is that of contemplation freed from the strivings of the will; but this is no more than the impact of pure form, and thus the concern of empty music. The inner meaning of this form is revealed by Beethoven, whose music transcends beauty and has a character of sublime serenity and joy.

In the last group of aesthetical essays, dating from 1879 and 1880, absolute music is removed from earthly concerns; it has a character of supreme radiance that even transcends sense perception. It is not concerned with the common seriousness of life nor is it merely amusement or wit – it never makes us laugh. Beethoven's Seventh Symphony presents truthful shapes, but it presents them neither to sight nor to hearing. It is a rushing and tumultuous torrent of delight, a realm of lofty ecstacy. Wagner's interest in sensuous experience gives way before the more spiritual outlook of advanced age. The nullity of the phenomenal world, the reversal of the will to live: these are the ideal content of all true religions, and they can be conveyed only by music – but significantly, only by absolute music, which separates itself from the Church and eliminates the dogma of religious texts. The Beethoven symphony is the successor of Christianity, and music becomes the new religion of pity and sympathy, an ideal exactly the opposite of the total physical expression of Siegfried.

Thus Wagner is led to a complete contradiction in purpose. His aesthetics as a whole contains two different allegiances, two different areas of thought which stand in opposition, and it is easy to see why his labors as an aesthetician are devoted chiefly to a resolution of the conflict – a complex effort of forty years that can be followed throughout his prose works and throughout his operas. This is a story we cannot take space to tell, but its nature can readily be deduced from the general state of affairs in nineteenth-century musical aesthetics.

The key factor here seems to be an essentially new problem: namely, how to come to terms with the greatest novelty on the artistic horizon – the development of the art of pure instrumental music. Musical instruments themselves were obviously no novelty, and their use throughout musical history can be taken for granted, especially in conjunction with dance and vocal music. But within the world of conscious and impressive art, the efflorescence of a specialized music for instruments alone was an epoch-making occurrence. For the first centuries of its growth, during the Baroque and Rococo eras, this art found no adequate philosophic or aesthetic treatment; it was handled with the concepts of vocal music, or not handled at all. The Enlightenment looked upon it as a kind of speech, but inferior to vocal music in its lack of clarity, a notion fostered by the whole temperament of French aesthetics. At best it was a design devoid of significance. But whether as a relatively imprecise language of the affections or as a pleasurable design, it was in any event condemned to the lowest position among the arts. Professional aestheticians and philosophers – and the line can be traced from Kant back to Plato – were unable to regard it highly, much less account for its force. Seemingly divorced from conceptual thought, it could hardly deserve serious consideration. Now this was a view that might never have called for correction in a world of Baroque suites and fantasias and variations, or even in the face of the fugue and the concerto grosso; while the Rococo symphony was almost an endorsement of such an attitude, if not actually to some extent its consequence. But the instrumental music of Beethoven imperiously demanded another conception. With the first measures of this music the condescending smile vanished from the face of rationalistic philosophy. The literary aestheticians of Romanticism stepped into the field, and only in Romantic literature and philosophy did this significant new artistic manifestation receive full recognition. It was not merely accepted but almost immediately elevated to the highest position both in art and in philosophy itself. Only by the middle of the century, however, had this metaphysical furor settled down to a more precise and specifically aesthetic treatment. This is the great contribution of Hanslick, who grasps the peculiar value of absolute music and sets its aesthetics on the final downhill section of its route toward scientific analysis. But the path traveled had led through the cosmic awareness of early Romantic literature to the persuasive but still poetical codification in the philosophy of Schopenhauer, which dominated the imagination of the creative artist throughout the century.

Thus that complex and paradoxical era of romanticism and realism worshipped absolute music while it went ahead writing songs, character pieces, concert overtures, program symphonies, tone poems, and operas. This strange contradiction between professed faith and actual production constitutes the background of Wagner's prolonged effort to reconcile his own ideal of absolute music with the oppositely directed tendencies so powerfully expressed in the artwork of the future. The pattern for such a reconciliation would seem to have been provided by Schopenhauer himself, for if music is the essential core of phenomena, if it presents the will of the world, then combined with another art, it must supply noumenal character to the representation of a Platonic idea and thus raise art to a more comprehensive intuition of reality. In such a view, music is not an enhancement or a coloring of a poetic text, for example, nor does it simply add human feelings to external facts, but is really the essential part of the matter, while the text becomes incidental and illustrative. This was actually a conception developed by nineteenth-century aesthetics, although it is no more than a passing thought in Wagner's writings.

But is it inevitable that there be a conflict of interest between absolute music and musical drama? In the nineteenth century, the significance of pure instrumental music was found variously to reside in the cosmic power of tone itself, in the peculiar emotional quality of music, valued either for its vagueness or its sublimity (but in any event supramundane), and finally in the special structural beauty that was peculiar to the art. Now the crux of the matter, as Wagner well understood, was whether the combination of music with visual art and language would cancel or curtail its unique virtues. That it did so was difficult to deny, and while today we are more inclined to think of opera and instrumental music as separate arts, each with its own values, for Wagner, bent on monolithic endeavors and grandiose final solutions, there was no room for two arts different in kind, while his evolutionary prejudices corrupted his judgment with the attractive picture of one leading to the other as a higher form. His temperament further demanded that he make his decision in favor of drama. Thus he had to prove that in this drama music would not sacrifice the values of its autonomy, but that on the contrary, it would find its highest fulfillment. Music was obviously advancing along the line of increasing expressiveness, but however much it tried, it could not increase its capabilities in this direction without the help of poetry. Modulations that made no sense at all within the framework of the symphony were expressive and thoroughly satisfactory in drama. As an isolated art, music was eternally condemned to conventional structures and regular rhythms descended from dance, this fact itself being proof that music was necessarily attached to real-life contexts.

It appears from this that the compatibility of musical and dramatic ideals in aesthetics entails a limited notion of the nature of instrumental music, and Wagner's operatic aesthetics would certainly support the contention that he had no insight at all into absolute music. He gives little indication of any faith in the philosophical powers of tone. He finds the expressive qualities of music poor because they are undefined, and incapable of improvement because they are incapable of definiteness, of distinct human quality. Of its formal properties he is equally critical: routine symmetry of phrases, recurrence rather than progressive change, and limited variety – variants of one underlying mood – rather than true thematic contrast. In what really amounts to a repetition of the traditional polemics of philosophy, absolute music is arraigned as inarticulate from the standpoint of thought, and frustrated and unfulfilled as an instrument of emotion.

But belittling and ignoring the values of instrumental music were activities peculiar to Wagner's dramatic theory. Another side of his nature was aware of the Beethoven symphony not as a tortured struggle for definite expression, but as the seat of tonal and expressive and structural values on a plane high above human feelings and earthbound symmetries. This was an art that radiated a sublime joy, whose compelling and wonderfully intricate structure completely eluded the processes of reason, whose very material provided entry into the nature of being. But again, these were glories that a particular and realistic dramatic action could only trammel and destroy.

The problem was not confined to Wagner's aesthetics. His operas themselves – weighted so heavily on the musical side – seem to labor under the same burden. They attempt to include symphonic logic. They even find room, against the strictures of theory, for formal musical sections. Time and again the dramatic action slowly dissolves into self-contained music. And perhaps most characteristically of all, great prominence is given to tone itself, especially in the elemental form of sustained triads and triadic motifs. In this mystic preoccupation with the elemental and the supernatural, so impressive in the preludes to *Lohengrin* and to *Rheingold* and in the religious service of *Parsifal*, Wagner came closest to a reconciliation – almost a fusion – of music and drama. Here the experience is somehow both purely musical and significative at the same time, but the catalytic agent is the tonal ideal of Romanticism. This same ideal makes *The Ring of the Nibelungs* less a variant of Feuerbach's conceptions than a musical version of *The World as Will and Idea*. And the identification of music and religion which we have with equal clearness both in *Parsifal* and in the essay on *Religion and Art* of 1880 is only a final transformation of early Romantic aesthetics, with its tonal metaphysics and its cosmic feeling. Thus the peculiarities that make Wagnerian opera what it is may have their source in an aesthetic dilemma. The absolute musical ideals of their composer belong to the Romantic youth of the century, his operatic theory to the later realistic trends in which psychology and evolution play so important a role. But the earlier outlook never died, and without knowing it, Wagner found a place for it in his music as well as in his aesthetic theories.

From "The Esthetic Theories of Richard Wagner," *The Musical Quarterly* 44, no.2 (1958): 209–20, by permission of Oxford University Press. The article was presented as a paper at the 1957 national meeting of the American Musicological Society in Los Angeles.

11

The Formation of Wagner's Style

P ERSONAL individuality of style in Western music seems to have run its course from Josquin to Stravinsky and to have achieved its most striking expression during the nineteenth century, when music was released more and more from the constraint of public styles grounded in social function. Ideas of progress, evolution, and original genius, which had come to occupy a dominant position in thought and culture in general, were accordingly able to exert their full influence on artistic creativity.

The church and the aristocracy, which had provided traditional stylistic definition, were no longer vital forces, and the middle classes, while furnishing a new market for routine and facilely attractive music, were also ideologically committed to personal liberty and individuality – beliefs that combined readily, as it turned out, with the most various political programs.

In Wagner's case, the dynamic potential of this state of affairs was realized with remarkable success, since Wagner combined creative genius with extraordinary executive ability and ruthless political opportunism. The works he composed as a student and fledgling in music testify more to his effectiveness and his will to succeed than to his originality. Unlike Schumann, whose individuality of style was manifest quite early in his career, Wagner continued to reveal his dependence upon imitation and models for a considerable time. But while Schumann's innovative brilliance was gradually succeeded by styles closer to convention, Wagner's individuality began to bring forth an apparently endless series of radical innovations with a creative power that has rarely been equaled. Indeed the stylistic individuality of each succeeding work is so pronounced that it obscures the personal features of style common to all of them, just as in a larger framework the personal styles of the individual composers of the nineteenth century obscure the epochal features common to them all.

Except for the *Seven Compositions for Goethe's "Faust"* (1831) and the operatic fragment *Die Hochzeit* (1832), Wagner's early works, dating from 1830 to 1832, are almost all piano sonatas, overtures, and symphonies. They quickly graduate from the status of student exercises and achieve both performance and publication. Since Wagner set out to combine the arts of Shakespeare and Beethoven, it is not surprising to find that the most important model for his early music is Beethoven, who is imitated in the thematic invention, the motivic workmanship, the more general structural layout, and the emotional content. There are other influences, to be sure; we can hear the buoyancy of Rossini or Schubert in the Sonata in B♭ Major, opus 1 (in the second theme of the first movement), and Wagner said that the Symphony in C Major (1832) sought to fuse the styles of Beethoven and Mozart. But the voice of Beethoven is generally uncontested by any other, particularly in the large Fantasia in F♯ Minor, opus 3, and in the concert overtures. The theme of the *König Enzio* Overture bears an unmistakable resemblance to that of the *Leonore* overtures, a resemblance that may have a particular explanation in the drama for which it was composed, for the action involves the underground imprisonment of the hero, who is joined in his fate by his beloved. We can also observe the influence, both in *Die Hochzeit* and in the overtures, of Beethoven's powerful concluding sections of jubilation and triumph. And in the last section of the fantasia, earlier themes are summarily dismissed, one after another, by indignant recitative passages – a scheme that was certainly suggested by the last movement of Beethoven's Ninth Symphony.

In the C-Major Symphony, Wagner employs a rising major third (C–E) without accompaniment at the opening of the slow movement, just as Beethoven had done in the "Hammerklavier" Sonata. The tonality of the movement (A minor) is thus initially indecisive, the relative major is suggested (particularly in the symphony, for this is the key of the preceding movement), and there is an effect of anticipation or questioning. Beethoven prefixed the motif to the slow movement as an afterthought. In its brevity, its indefinite quality, and its rising inflection, it does not simply provide an introduction to the theme and the movement but becomes an entranceway into an expressive world and also sets this world off, removes it to a distance. To Wagner this motif had a mystical quality. It recurs in the movement as a kind of motto, its questioning unsatisfied. The Beethovenian background of the motif is reinforced by the passage that follows it, which is reminiscent of the Allegretto – again the slow movement – of Beethoven's Seventh Symphony, a movement that must have fascinated composers of the Romantic period, opening as it does with a suspended minor chord that unveils a distant realm. Here we come upon an evocative "mute" accompaniment to which only subsequently a haunting melody is added. The slow movement of Wagner's symphony clearly compounds elements that had a certain modern appeal at the time. It does not yet transform these elements appreciably, but it does select them from a particular point of view; it regards them in a new way. The materials are essentially unchanged; they are transformed only in the act of perception and use.

Wagner's symphonic works of 1830–32, which lack individuality and are hardly more than competent, are distinguished structurally by a consistent use of motivic manipulation. This is the central feature, as we might expect, of a Beethovenian and generally Classic style. But the motivic technique is in no way individualized, nor has it been made part of the newer stylistic trends of 1830.

In addition to motivic technique but also incorporating it, another Beethovenian characteristic of great importance in the formation of Wagner's style is the crescendo, especially in the large sequential form that distinguishes Beethoven's development sections. The prominence of the crescendo in the early symphonic works increases in the later overtures of the thirties, developing into an intrinsic and decisive constituent of Wagner's later style. We find particularly in the overtures what may be called an obsession with the crescendo – a circumstance of particular interest when we recall that the crescendo was an original and essential factor of the Classical symphonic style as well as a characteristic device of the opera buffa overture, in which it enjoyed a vogue in Rossini's hands that even exceeded its enthusiastic reception as part of the Mannheim style. The Beethoven crescendo presents dramatic and portentous power; that of Rossini a fever pitch of excitement. Wagner adopts both (there is an example in the *Liebesverbot* Overture of the Rossini style), but that of Beethoven becomes crucial to Wagner's style and to its large mural effect. The overtures, most notably the *Columbus* Overture, reveal this feature in the process of adoption and transformation; it becomes the substance of the music and takes over much of the duration of the work. The crescendos in the later national overtures, on the other hand (*Polonia* and *Rule, Brittania*), are frankly there for audience impact only. But it is Beethoven, in any event, who is the major musical source of Wagner's large style and overwhelming power. The two men are connected by a common rebelliousness of spirit, which in Wagner continually threatens to become fanaticism.

In the operas of the 1830s – *Die Feen, Das Liebesverbot,* and *Rienzi* – Wagner continues to be dependent on outside styles and techniques, many of them now fashionable ones, in subservience to particular changing goals of success. The operas contain a highly diversified succession of selected stylistic features and devices, all directed to the end of dramatic effect; Wagner's mastery of operatic technique can rarely be called into question. But what characterizes these works above all else is the impressionability of their composer. The songs Wagner wrote in these years tell the same story. In all the works of the 1830s, to be sure, there are isolated passages that can be found relatively unchanged in Wagner's mature works, but they do not alter the derivative character that prevails; unsupported by their context, they do not become effective constituents of style. Wagner remains strangely slow to develop his individuality, in part perhaps because of the range of his musical sensitivity but also because of the complexity of the stylistic world surrounding him as well as the intrinsic complexity of opera in particular (in Germany, it was still a descendant of the "mixed style"). On the other hand, his many journeyman years as a dramatic conductor obviously provided the best possible foundation for his type of synthetic mentality and for his career as a whole.

In *Die Feen* (1833–34), Wagner looks to German Romantic opera as a guide to subject matter, form, and style. The sustained triads of the opening, which provide an entrance into the supernatural realm, remind us at once of the opening of the *Midsummer Night's Dream* Overture. The melodies at times have a chordal construction, with an enthusiasm that derives unmistakably from Weber; or again they become affective and chromatic, in the fashion of Spohr. There is a ballade also, which in spite of its unusual satiric character, displays all the conventional features of the genre, including a foreboding trill and a shift to the major mode. Even in the colorful sequence of events, the inclusion of comic scenes, and the role of magic in the action, Wagner created a characteristic Romantic opera, one that was typically inattentive to the unity of the action and to the logic of the succession of events.

With the unexpected progression of the opening triads (which constitute one of the recurrent motifs of the opera), and with other such fundamental motifs of Wagner, we reach a type of stylistic feature in which it is often not possible to distinguish imitation or borrowing from the characteristics of the style of the period. To be sure, the features of public style must come from somewhere; there can be little question that they originate in the invention of individual composers. But this invention may in fact be a series of inventions, each in itself inconspicuous and unimportant but all contributing to a significant stylistic innovation that will thus be a joint and impersonal accomplishment. Furthermore, anonymity will have a counterpart in the dissemination of such a characteristic. A composer may not know how he comes by it, whether he has adopted it from the public domain or from a particular use in the work of a particular composer; and – still more important – it will not really matter which path he followed. The triadic succession in question was a natural part of a generally increasing interest in nonfunctional chordal connections, and consequently ubiquitous – even spontaneously arising in different places or through different and simultaneous chains of influence. Among such public features of style, some centuries old but now securing a new currency, are the undulating patterns that refer to water or waves, or those connected with the rustling of leaves, or those inevitable cadential patterns (either designating the cadence or revealing its immanence), hardly programmatic at all, which seem always to be more definitely formulated than others. It is at the cadence that the expressive accented appoggiaturas of Romanticism are usually encountered, although they are also, like the expressive turn, more widely distributed.

It is characteristic of Wagner in all his works that he is extraordinarily sensitive to the existence and to the incipient formulation, however vague and ill defined, of such public motifs; that he displays them and insists on them relentlessly; and that he succeeds in giving them a definitive form – really, *the* definitive form. This is the more general aspect of the formation of his personal style, as contrasted with the specific borrowings, whether literal or transformed. What we are gradually coming to see, however – although it is clearly a logical requirement of any intelligible style and thus does not need any empirical demonstration – is that the variegated and individual styles of nineteenth-century composers, while they indeed obscure public features of style, cannot replace these entirely.

Wagner's power in the formulation of public motifs can be seen readily in the case of a chromatic cadential pattern that occurs in the music of many composers during the first half of the nineteenth century, typically in a form such as we find in the last movement of Wagner's Piano Sonata in A Major:

Example 1. Wagner, Piano Sonata in A Major, mm.70–71.

There is a prominent example in Marschner's *Vampyr* (in the terzett "Wie, mein Vater," act 1, no.8), which may well have been a particular influence on Wagner:

Example 2. Marschner, *Vampyr:* Terzett, mm.35–37.

In any event, the same extension of the initial tone of the cadence reappears in the Overture to *Rienzi,* where the cadence is used in conjunction with a number of related patterns (known particularly through their use in Beethoven), from which it seems to extricate itself finally as a climactic conclusion. And one finds another example in the terzett at the end of act 2 of *Der fliegende Holländer.*

Example 3. *Rienzi,* overture, mm.185–87. *Holländer,* act 2; Terzett, mm.35–36.

There is something of a festive and courtly character in this chromatic cadence, a quality that Wagner discerns and develops and which he finally displays brilliantly on trombones in the introduction to act 3 of *Lohengrin:*

Example 4. *Lohengrin,* prelude to act 3, mm.45–49.

This form of the cadence had appeared a number of times many years
earlier, in the last act of *Die Feen,* but without a clearly defined significance. Its use in *Lohengrin* represents a fulfillment. Wagner has taken a
pattern relatively undefined in a "programmatic" sense, grasped its potential for expression, so shaped it and so deployed it in an appropriate
context that it sums up the entire history of its own use. As a consequence, every earlier instance of the pattern tends to be heard in terms
of Wagner's final conception, taking on something of its specific character and appearing as an incompletely realized and not fully formulated
predecessor. Beyond this, Wagner has made use of the occasion to display his skill in motivic relationship: the prefatory minor third leaps
upward to the high point, thus contrasting with its closing descent.

   Das Liebesverbot (1835–36) derives much of its astonishing variety of
style from opéra comique and opera buffa but adds to such elements, as
Mozart had done, serious features both of style and of action. The combination, of course, is a characteristic feature of Shakespeare's *Measure
for Measure,* which is the source of the plot. Indeed the serious side of
the opera is by far the predominant one. *Fidelio* is its stylistic model.
The heroism and idealism of Isabella are like those of Beethoven's hero-
ine, while the perfidy of Ferdinand in the central intrigue is the counterpart of Pizarro's villainy. The general effect of the opera, however, is
one of a colorful juxtaposition of styles, the sources of which range
from *Fidelio* to the buffa ensemble and include the Rossinian crescendo
mentioned above as well as that sustained triadic progression by thirds
which plays such a prominent role in the nineteenth century (and in
Tannhäuser, Lohengrin, and *Parsifal*) as a symbol of religiosity. The
overture is strikingly similar to the overture of Hérold's *Zampa,* which
also vividly projects the diametrical opposites of frivolity and severity
that constitute the core of the action – and the central musical
contrast – of *Das Liebesverbot.* The scene in which Isabella pleads for
her brother's life is cast in a mold of Beethovenian nobility of feeling;
the burning passion of the melody that conveys Ferdinand's lust pro-

duces a tour de force in the use of melodic turns and appoggiaturas, the symbols then current for intensity of feeling.

Rienzi (1838–40) is influenced mostly by Spontini and Meyerbeer. It makes consummate use of the outstanding features of French grand opera. There are incisive dotted rhythms, massive choruses, and a large display of forces. The libretto again features the selfless fidelity of sister to brother, here to the total exclusion of amorous relationships. Of the first three operas, *Rienzi* stands nearest to Wagner's personal nature, dealing as it does with political forces and with an impressive male figure moved by idealism. But it is a Wagner conquering Paris and in a sense Rome also; German national sentiment is sacrificed to foreign success and foreign style. In the 1840s there was to be a return to German models, which increasingly control and subordinate the French elements that remain.

In *Dors, mon enfant,* one of the songs Wagner wrote in Paris in 1839–40, conspicuous use is made of an upper grace-note ornament of a semitone or a whole tone:

Example 5. Wagner, *Dors, mon enfant.*

Dors ____ en-tre mes bras, en fant plein de char-mes! Tu ____ ne con-nais pas les sou-cis, les lar-mes;

Since Wagner wrote his French songs at least partly to make himself known in Paris by having a French singer present his music, he was doubtless making use of a vocal embellishment that was fashionable as well as effective. The embellishment enters *Der fliegende Holländer* (1841) by way of the spinning song, which was one of the first sections of the opera to be composed, but in various forms it penetrates this most German of operas. At the same time, the melody of the spinning song bears a certain resemblance to that of *Dors, mon enfant* in a more general way. Whatever other factors may underlie the connection of rocking a cradle and spinning, cyclical repetition is clearly a basic factor in their resemblance. Also relevant to the influence of French style on the opera is the existence of a later autograph version of Senta's ballade in French (to say nothing of a German version, *Schlaf, mein Kind,* of the cradle song).[1] But if the grace-note device is originally French, it is used in a most characteristically German fashion, as a ubiquitous unifying

motif that appears throughout the opera in the most astonishingly varied forms and contexts.

The semitone and the whole-tone version each has its own significance, both in general and in the opera; their connection with minor
and major respectively is obviously fundamental. The alteration of major and minor in itself has played a prominent part in music; the most
well-known example in Wagner's time was probably that of Schubert.
But another Germanic model for the alternation can be found in
Beethoven's Ninth Symphony, a much more influential stylistic source
for Wagner than was Schubert.

Example 6. Beethoven, Symphony no.9: first movement, mm.120–23.

Here the lowered and natural forms of the sixth degree, which become
the two versions of Wagner's embellishment, are strongly emphasized
factors in the alternation, although it is hardly likely that this passage
had any direct influence either on *Dors, mon enfant* or on the embel-
lishments of *Der fliegende Holländer*. There is, nevertheless, in the spinning song especially, a conscious use of the relationship between the
ornamentation and the appoggiatura; Wagner so connects the two intrinsically that they come to comprise jointly a fundamental feature of
Romantic melody, persisting in particular through all the changes in his
own melodic style.

There are other ways in which the Ninth Symphony seems to have
influenced *Holländer*. Indeed the relationship between the two can be
taken as a touchstone of Wagner's stylistic maturity, for it involves a typically Romantic transformation of material rather than the more or less
literal reproduction that characterizes his earlier works. The mysterious
sustained fifths of the opening of the symphony become fortissimo in
the opening of *Holländer;* the quiet descending fifths of the violins become the fortissimo ascending fifths of the horns; and Beethoven's
crashing and forbidding theme itself is transformed into the opening
motif of Senta's ballade. Quiet mystery and cosmic cataclysm become
demonic presence and its fearful legend.[2]

Behind this Romantic use of given material there exists a whole frame of mind concerning the musical past; rather than being objectivized and retained, history is creatively transformed by the new perspective of the composer and put to use as an integral part of a novel stylistic complex. Very much of a piece with this use of the Ninth Symphony is Schumann's "poetic" view and transformation of Bach's polyphony and Bach's motifs. And Beethoven's feeling that it would no longer do simply to write a fugue, but rather that one must make a poetic use of the fugue, indicates the same attitude.

In the case of Wagner's *Holländer,* there is in the background not only Beethoven's Ninth Symphony but also the vivid and fantastic imagination of a child acutely sensitive by nature to tonal impressions. The Ninth Symphony and even the tuning of an orchestra had already become fraught with the supernatural well before the creation of *Holländer.* The central place of the Ninth Symphony in the formation of Wagner's style is also heralded by his youthful piano arrangement of the score (1830). Ten years later, a performance of the symphony conducted by Habeneck in Paris made a powerful impression on him; it seemed to focus all the varied ideas and feelings that impinged upon him during his visit. At the furthest remove from his native environment, Wagner experienced a momentous change in orientation. The restless journeyman's period had finally culminated in the act of carrying a French grand opera to Paris in search of success at all costs. But the bitter disappointment of the pilgrimage, the poverty and distress, the crisis of imprisonment for debt – all these factors conspired to pave the way for an oppositely directed course back to Germanic material, Germanic style, and to Germany itself. Wagner's despair found expression in a number of vivid and autobiographical stories, and it also released his independence and originality of style, grounded now in the radical transformation of given material. The composition of the *Faust* Overture and *Holländer* signals a new creative intensity, rooted in Wagner's innermost nature; he began to consider subsequently a number of dramatic projects based on German history and legend – namely, *Die Sarazenin, Tannhäuser, Lohengrin,* and *Die Bergwerke zu Falun.*

The figure of Faust was an eminently appropriate part of this complex of associations. The *Faust* Overture, the only remaining movement of a projected *Faust* Symphony, shares the satanic mood and the key and the intensity of *Holländer;* it is no longer the routine prolongation of the Classical symphonic tradition but the expression of a thoroughly modern transformation of the symphony as it is found at about the same time in Mendelssohn and Schumann. Indeed, Wagner produced in his *Faust* a work that is fully entitled to a status equivalent to that of Schumann's powerful *Manfred* and *Genoveva* overtures, and he did so some years earlier.

There remain, nevertheless, many traces of French style in *Tannhäuser*, in particular the jaunty processionals, the large mass scene of the second-act finale, and the saccharine "Song to the Evening Star." The stylistic diversity is further increased by the adoption of a popular Männerchor flavor in the hymns, which is evident at the very opening of the overture. Yet a comparison with *Rienzi* shows how far Wagner had removed himself from the world of grand opera. The influx of German feeling and German elements of style that was initiated in Paris is carried out in the 1840s by a progressive elimination of foreign influence. Wagner abandons the path of Gluck, Mayr, and Meyerbeer, which had its point of departure in the mixed style of the eighteenth century, for this route would no longer suffice. The creation of a truly national opera demanded a different and more distinctively German basis. Foreign models, however, are succeeded by German ones. And it is doubtless this general change in the mode of formulation of Wagner's style that produces the new stylistic homogeneity of *Lohengrin*. But just as *Holländer* was based to some extent on Marschner's *Vampyr, Lohengrin*, that masterwork of breathtaking perfection and stylistic consistency, is derived to a certain extent from Weber's *Euryanthe;* the dramatic structure is quite similar, and so is the buoyant, courtly air that is typically captured in dotted rhythm. Some influence seems to have been exerted by Auber's *Muette de Portici* as well, with respect to the formal layout of Elsa's bridal procession.[4] Indeed multiple influence must be kept in mind as an ever-present possibility, perhaps more the rule than the exception, and this is true of specifically musical properties as well as of external motivation and suggestion.[5] A great composer's mind is an incredibly rich, essentially inexhaustible storehouse of musical experience; ideas of every kind are always summoned up, consciously and unconsciously, in response to whatever musical project is undertaken. Simultaneous influences are even more a matter of course if we consider the vast variety of components that enter into a work under construction: dramatic action, complement of voices, orchestration, recitative style, orchestral and vocal melody, rhythmic patterns and types of harmonic progression, formal plans of numbers and scenes and acts, expressive and emotional character, and so on. What is more natural than that some familiar opera should act as a model with respect to dramatic plan, while a melody or an orchestral effect of entirely different origin is taken up at the same time – or at some time during the process of composition?

The three Romantic operas of the forties are the culmination of the genre; and they prepare the way for the still more impressive stylistic development of the second half of Wagner's career. In this final formative process, all the earlier elements of novelty, originally without particular significance, were able to find their predestined place in a congenial context. What was called for by the intrinsic tendencies of music in general and of Wagner's style and aesthetic thought in particular was a transition from symmetrical melody and balanced melodic phrases to a freely constructed continuity in which symmetry was simply one possibility among others. This freer style operated with vivid and varied motifs rather than with melody, and these were assembled at first successively and then, with increasing frequency, simultaneously. The logic of continuity could be achieved in limitless juxtaposition, parallelisms, and antitheses. Coherence often required considerable repetition and sequence, but this apparent lapse into elementalism, like the balance of melodic phrases, was now part of an inexhaustible complexity that could support every shift of feeling and every turn of events in the external action. Motifs could even be extracted from a larger melodic whole, as they are from the theme with which *Parsifal* opens. This is, in a sense, a return to a Classical symphonic technique of fractionation, which is understandably evident in *Die Feen* but unimportant in succeeding operas. Characteristically, though, the opposite takes place, and Wagner weaves wholes of varying extent from motifs as units, through a variety of types of repetition and juxtaposition. An entirely new mentality is necessary in the composer, a new type of imagination that is more realistic and less a manifestation of formal musical schemata. In Wagner's melodic phase, however, and especially in the three operas of the forties, his typical method of construction was not entirely foreign to the style that developed after 1850, for he worked by ringing melodic changes on an unvarying rhythmic pattern, so that the melody itself – although clearly articulated into phrases – was yet granted a certain freedom of indefinite extension.

The consistency of Wagner's later style was such, however, that it could bind together the most diverse elements. In its complex and changing relationships between orchestra and voice, it encompasses and unites an astonishing variety of material. The formation of this diversified vocabulary of motifs and melodic phrases, which varies in its nature according to the needs of the conception of each successive opera, is easily abetted by the adoption, often unchanged, of earlier original phrases and motifs that are amenable to Wagner's later purpose. There is an unerring sense of what is conformable to the musical world of each later work and at the same time, of course, an equally unerring sense of what must be rejected as too subservient to older melodic formalities, too neutral to become part of the new programmatic character of the motivic invention. It is a change, in a word, from Romanticism to realism, whether the vividness or specificity in question is external, psychological, or as Wagner finally conceived it in accord with Schopenhauer, metaphysical. The consistency of a mature style is apparently due in part to borrowing from oneself, which is the closest approximation to an inventiveness that cannot be traced to its source at all. There follow two examples of earlier motifs which in their original occurrence have a merely incidental status but which, essentially without transformation, Wagner turned to excellent programmatic account in *Der Ring des Nibelungen.* The first is from the Fantasia in F♯ Minor (1832) and the second from an extended version of an aria from Marschner's *Vampyr* that Wagner had written for his brother in 1833.

Example 7. Wagner, Fantasia, m.213.   Example 8. Marschner, *Vampyr:* aria, mm.21–23.

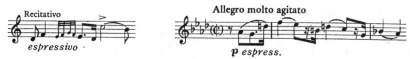

In the remarkable transformations of musical character that result from the operation of Wagner's imagination on the music that is his starting point, a new aspect of the use of borrowed material comes to light – an aspect that has as little to do with plagiarism as it does with the adoption of public musical configurations or with the duplication of style for purposes of compositional training. For a level of novelty is achieved in the products of Wagner's maturity that reduces the musical source of the creative process to unimportance, even to irrelevance. The original material,

which is no longer really the origin of the end product but rather a musical constituent fused to a programmatic one and drawn up into a new
imaginative or "poetic" complex, becomes part of a private workshop
method. Just as this is true of the Ninth Symphony with respect to *Holländer,* it remains true of *Hans Heiling* with respect to *Der Ring des
Nibelungen* or of *Jessonda* with respect to *Tristan und Isolde.* As in the use
of the Tarnhelm, we see only the transformed object, which is the effective
one, and the magic resides in the transforming power. By comparing the
point of departure with the result, however, we can gain some insight into
the *modus operandi* of this power. There follows an illustrative passage
from *Tristan,* which appears to derive, perhaps through a process of transformation of which Wagner was not conscious, from Spohr's *Jessonda:*

Example 9. *Jessonda* (1823), act 1, finale. *Tristan* (1857–59), act 1, scene 5.

To this let us add two passages of the *Ring* that similarly seem to have
been prompted by Marschner's *Hans Heiling:*

Example 10. *Hans Heiling* (1833), act 2, no.9. *Die Walküre* (1854–56), act 2, scene 4.

Example 11. *Hans Heiling,* act 2, no.12. *Das Rheingold* (1853–54), scene 4.

Das Rheingold (1853–54), scene 4

In connection with a possible psychology of musical influence, it is of interest that the passages of *Jessonda* and *Tristan* are both concerned with death, the one in *Tristan* in a double sense, while the scene of *Hans Heiling* in which the Queen of the Earth Spirits warns Anna that Heiling must be returned to his realm corresponds to the scene in which Brünhilde tells Siegmund that he must follow her to Valhalla, and the motif of Marschner that is compared with Wagner's musical description of the Nibelungen is initially sung by a chorus of gnomes rising out of the earth (the text is "Aus der Klüfte Schlund, durch der Erde Grund drängt hinauf, empor an das Licht hervor").[6]

But we are concerned primarily with the *difference* between Wagner and his predecessors. Wagner deepens the supernatural by making it elemental and metaphysical, and he makes it a logical part of an encompassing system of relationships. This is seen at once in a comparison of *Holländer* with *Vampyr,* or of course the *Ring* with *Hans Heiling.* There is an equally obvious difference between the chromaticism of *Jessonda* and that of *Tristan.* While Spohr's chromaticism is ubiquitous in *Jessonda,* permeating inner lines, characterizing many approaches to cadences, and giving rise to passages almost literally the same as those of *Tristan,* it is not developed systematically into a language in its own right; it does not create a world alternative to that of tonality; nor is it charged with symbolic significance. Even in this sense, however, Wagner's achievements have predecessors. There is a passage in Schumann's *Genoveva* that glows with the guilt of passion when Golo, unable to control his desire, kisses the sleeping Genoveva; both the music and its meaning could easily come from *Tristan.* Indeed the roots of symbols often reach back into the past. But just as Spohr's chromaticism lacks the systematic elaboration and logical coherence of Wagner's, so do the individual instances of chromatic symbolism in the first half of the nineteenth century lack that concrete integration into an articulated sphere of meaning that Wagner created with each work. Only Liszt appears to have been working along the same lines.

More specifically, turning now to the three examples we have cited, when we compare the earlier passage with the later one in each case, what comes most forcefully to our attention is the intensification Wagner has effected, the compelling consequentiality of his formulation. The passage from *Tristan,* to be sure, incorporates a powerful rise and fall of feeling in place of the more static comparisons of *Jessonda;* but this too, of course, is part of Wagner's forcible logic of expression. And in the passage from *Die Walküre,* it is striking how Marschner's weak terminal descent is replaced by an insistent and logical upward sequence. Wagner accomplishes this change by introducing the additional motif of questioning at this point, as the text suggests. He closely integrates the motif into the melodic line of the initial phrase, extracting it, as it were, from the neutrality of its form in Marschner's melody. This procedure serves to increase further the convincing and definitive character of his melodic structure. At the same time, it is also an adaptation of symphonic technique: the question motif is really a part of the opening theme, and it overlaps itself in its sequential repetition. Toward the end of this scene, the motivic manipulation appears in the modern guise of transformation, which is connected characteristically with programmatic significance, in this instance with Brünhilde's decision to allow Siegmund to live.

It becomes evident here how Wagner both adopts and extends Classical symphonic methods of construction, with the enhancement of the drama as his goal. He opens up new horizons of melodic formulation by means of economical and incisive interrelationships that are impelled by sheer strength and directness of feeling. And the larger form that controls the motivic workmanship is given by the course of the dramatic action.

These same factors enter also into the passage from *Rheingold.* Again there is a logical progression from one motif to another, from accumulation to the subjugation it is based on, and there is an elemental simplicity and portentous significance which remain inaccessible to the music of *Hans Heiling.* But the essential features of Wagner's style that produce this result are seen more clearly in the process of formation of the style than they are in the style considered only in its finished form. This may indeed be true more generally in nineteenth-century music, as opposed to the sphere of public material that is characteristic of Baroque and Classic music, so that the method of the present investigation might profitably be applied more widely – to a comparison, for example, of Marschner or Weber with Beethoven or of other nineteenth-century composers to their predecessors, taking care in each instance, of course, that the earlier composer was well known to the later one. For a transformational mentality, as opposed to a reliance on public themes and motifs and progressions, is nothing less than a corollary of the notion of originality and creative genius. There must indeed exist a community of style, but if originality is a dominant value, then disguise and metamorphosis will prevail. It is this rationale, then, rather than the mysterious action of some evolutionary Zeitgeist, that explains why the formation of Wagner's style is largely a *trans*formation.[7]

NOTES

From *Music and Civilization: Essays in Honor of Paul Henry Lang,* ed. Edmond Strainchamps and Maria Rika Maniates in collaboration with Christopher Hatch (New York: W. W. Norton 1984), 102–16.

1. The French manuscript of the ballade (New York Public Library) was called to my attention some time ago by Richard Koprowski. The German version of the cradle song can be found in *Richard Wagners Werke,* ed. Michael Balling (Leipzig 1912–ca.1929), vol.15, *Lieder and Gesänge.*

2. It is also possible that the "redemption" section of the ballade melody derives from the slow movement of the Ninth Symphony, in which case Wagner would have converted the contrast be-

tween two movements of a symphony into a contrast between the two themes of a single "programmatic" movement (the ballade strophe or the *Holländer* Overture). A dramatic juxtaposition of this kind, of course, was not possible within one movement of a Classical symphony, for in Classical style, even thematic contrast was controlled by a governing principle of coherence.

3. *Mein Leben* (Munich 1976), 36.

4. See Hans Redlich, "Wagnerian Elements in Pre-Wagnerian Opera," *Essays Presented to Egon Wellesz,* ed. Jack Weurup (Oxford 1966), 145–56. See also John Warrack, "The Musical Background," *The Wagner Companion,* ed. Peter Burbidge and Richard Sutton (New York 1979), 85–112.

5. I have examined some examples of such multiple factors, largely extramusical ones, in "Theory and Practice in Schumann's Aesthetics," *Journal of the American Musicological Society* 17 (1964): 310–45 (reprinted as chapter 9 in this collection).

6. In the relationship between Schubert's *Erlkönig* and the Prelude of *Die Walküre,* the musical similarity would again seem to be grounded in a common subject matter.

7. But transformation also characterized Wagner's treatment of the musical material within any one of his own works. Borrowing and internal technique involved the same basic process – a conclusion that seems merely to confirm common sense. A moment's thought suggests, however, that the relationship may be quite different in other stylistic periods. The use or adaptation of public material in the eighteenth century, for example, both in Baroque style and in Classic, bears no such simple relationship of identity to the compositional technique of the time. This type of relationship, therefore, which apparently has never been considered previously, doubtless represents another new investigative tool for the student of style.

12

Wagner's Conception of the Dream

I T IS WELL KNOWN that Wagner was familiar with a great many different types of narrative and dramatic literature; his interest extended from legend and epic, through ancient Greek drama and the tragedies of Shakespeare, to the Italian, French, and German opera of his time. Of all the dramatic genres that influenced him, German Romantic opera was certainly the most important, and we can in fact consider his achievement to consist in the perfecting of this operatic genre and in its transformation into the musical drama.

German Romantic opera – at the furthest possible remove from the realistic and social concerns of French opera – frequently dealt with dreams and with dreamlike situations. The presence of elements of this kind in the action was an automatic consequence of the sources of Romantic libretti in medieval narrative, the comedies of Shakespeare, and the tales of Gozzi; another basis existed in the Singspiel from which Romantic opera evolved, for this popular genre often made prominent use of supernatural figures and highly imaginative action. Every important aspect of the dream was involved in these traditions: its strange content, its illogical succession of images, its illusory character, and its revelatory power.

The strangeness of the figures and scenes of the dream often seems to underlie the fantastic and demonic stories of E. T. A. Hoffmann, which became an inspirational force in Romanticism.[1] That the unexpected sequences of images in the dream, uncontrolled either by logic or by external reality, also became a feature of Romantic opera can be seen at once in the chief criticism to which the genre was subjected, notably by E. T. A. Hoffmann and Carl Maria von Weber: that there was no overall unity to the action and that the sequence of events was unmotivated. Indeed Wagner's dramatic conceptions were to a great extent formed as a response to this criticism. And only a glance at the *Magic Flute* – a powerful influence, along with *Don Giovanni*, on the development of Romantic opera – will reveal a highly variegated series of images, apparently devoid of any logic of succession or coherent meaning: dreamlike as a whole but also with individual scenes and figures of striking unreality. The wonderful and the marvelous are an intrinsic part of the dramatic conception. And the juxtaposition of different orders of humanity and especially of different realms of being – of the human and the supernatural – continually produces scenes that have an ambiguous and dreamlike quality. Equally striking in both *Don Giovanni* and the *Magic Flute,* this juxtaposition unquestionably becomes the central motif of the action of Romantic opera, the point of entry both of the miraculous and of the dramatic tension, so that in one way or another, ideas of the dream will almost always be at hand.

The illusory quality of dream images – along with their revelatory power – was a more complex area of significance. Are we dealing in a given case with a vision or with reality? with an image or an actual supernatural visitation? with a deceptive picture or true clairvoyance? Is the drama itself a literal representation of the experience of life or an artificial construct of the imagination? Drama is of course always a representation, even when it is a rite or a cultic action, but it makes a difference whether we stress its verisimilitude and continuity with life or its illusory quality. Visions are similarly equivocal, and if we are often invited to consider the whole action as a dream, we are similarly left in doubt as to whether particular figures are figments of a dream or apparitions that are "actual." The appearance of a god or spirit or ghost is a time-honored feature of drama and opera, descended doubtless from the deus ex machina; *Don Giovanni* provides an example that was particularly influential in the formation of nineteenth-century conceptions of opera. But in Romantic opera it may not be known or ever disclosed whether the vision has been an actuality. In the case of a vision, however, actual means supernatural, so that little difference remains between reality and dream.

The property of illusion can obviously be restated as the suggestion of reality, and this in turn entails the exclusion of any explanation or explanatory hypothesis that will account for dreams within the established framework of scientific knowledge. It also entails the eventual possibility of distinguishing the situations and events of the dream from those that factually occur. The suggestion of reality, however, implies not only that a dream may seem real but also that reality may be a dream. Thus any dramatic incident or scene, or even an entire drama, particularly when strange events or supernatural figures are in question, may be illusory rather than factual, and to this must be added the complication that what we see on stage is always a representation in itself. In recollection, of course, recent dreams are generally distinguished without difficulty from actuality. But even when a dream is known to be such, the question of meaning still persists; the images have always presented an enigma. What has caused them if not the external world? Their strange relationships to reality make it inevitable that a significance will be seen in them which lies outside our ordinary channels of knowledge. Indeed this remains true in modern psychology, except that the revelatory properties are interpreted with respect to inner life and the subconscious instead of to the external natural and supernatural world.

Wagner's first complete opera, *Die Feen* (1833–34), is based on a fairy tale of Gozzi. Searching through the forest for the fairy realm in which he hopes to find his wife, Ada, the hero Arindal comes to doubt her existence. "Was it all then a dream?" he asks.[2] Subsequently he is overcome by sleep and then awakened by the sound of her voice, whereupon two conceptions of the dream make their appearance, one of them literal and the other again questioning whether reality is not a deception: "Where am I? / Ah, to what blissful realm / Has my lovely dream carried me? / And there, ha, if I do not dream, / Is it not my wife?"[3] A similar situation arises again toward the end of the opera, as Arindal is awakened from a sleep of exhaustion that heals his madness: "Who calls to me? / Ah, where, where / Has my gentle dream *(Wahn)* carried me? / I heard my wife calling! / Oh, God, how the gloomy night is brightened into day by her voice!"[4] The synesthetic experience described here anticipates the theories Wagner was later to develop connecting sound with the dream.

In *Der fliegende Holländer* (1841), another feature of the dream closely associated with the supernatural makes its appearance: the prophecy and clairvoyance. Also the dream is more than an unimportant incident of the action, or a turn of events that rather mechanically advances the story: it has crystallized into a special type of scene – the dream narration. Senta's mortal lover, Erik, who is soon to lose her to the Dutchman, tells her of a dream he has had to warn her of what will happen; he has foreseen the arrival of his legendary competitor, Senta's meeting with him, and their departure together. Wagner heightens the action by coupling with the narration a simultaneous clairvoyant trance in which Senta has a daytime vision that exactly follows Erik's dream.

Wagner's stage directions read: "Senta sinks down exhausted in the armchair; with the beginning of Erik's narration she falls into a kind of magnetic sleep, so that she seems also to be dreaming the dream told by him."[5] When Senta's tension reaches a certain pitch, she interrupts and joins in the narrative. She is carried away by excitement, and Erik takes her agitated behavior as confirmation of the truth of his dream. This coupling of day and night dreams is the first instance we come upon of a central feature of Wagner's conception of the dream: his theory of two contrasted types.

Die Sarazenin, a libretto that Wagner sketched in 1841 and completed in 1843 but never set to music, contains a dream scene that is the mainspring of the action. The irresolute hero Manfred is aroused to fight for his throne by a dream of a ghostly military procession led by his father, Kaiser Friedrich II. Wagner's stage directions call for the Kaiser to stop momentarily and gesture to Manfred, who is to respond in his sleep with a convulsive movement. The dream ends with the appearance of the Saracen woman Fatima, who is Manfred's half-sister. She calls, summoning him to action. The characteristic ambiguity is present in that Manfred at first takes her to be a supernatural figure, and indeed, even in contradicting him she betrays something of a supernatural status, for she says, "He whom you have just seen in your dream has sent me!"[6]

In the justly famous dream scene of the first act of *Lohengrin* (1847), Elsa relates a prophetic dream of the supernatural hero who will arrive to fight on her behalf. This is the outstanding narrative of its kind in Wagner's Romantic operas, and possibly also the most impressive fulfillment we have of the Romantic thesis of the kinship of music and the miraculous. It remained Wagner's conviction throughout his life that the elevated sphere he sought to enter in drama, with its heightened action and its transcendence of the everyday, demanded music for its realization, and in the musical description of Lohengrin, as Elsa tells her dream, and still more in the musical depiction of his arrival, two of the most powerful dramatic effects of the opera are achieved, which in the composer's characteristic fashion, transform fantasy into actuality and make the unreal real.

Götterdämmerung, finished in 1874 but in its original form sketched out in 1848, or well before the other operas of the *Ring*, is as traditional with respect to dreams as it is in other ways. The sinister visitation in which Alberich reminds Hagen of his evil mission is intensified in its

impact by an artful maintenance of ambiguity throughout. Hagen is in-
structed to sing "softly and without moving, so that he seems throughout to continue sleeping, although his eyes remain open and fixed."[7]
And to Alberich's question, "Are you sleeping, Hagen, my son? – Do you
sleep and not hear me, whom rest and sleep betray?" he answers, "I hear
you, evil dwarf: what do you have to say to my sleep?"[8] effectively saying
both no and yes to the question.

The end of the scene does not decide the issue. Night is just beginning to give way, Alberich gradually disappears from view, and his voice
fades away with the admonition "Be true, Hagen, my son! Trusted hero,
be true! Be true! – true!"[9] Hagen, "who has remained unmoving in his
position, stares motionless and with fixed eyes toward the Rhine."[10] We
are never sure whether the visit was dream or fact, and we are sure that
Hagen is not sure. This is a culmination of the Romantic tradition of
ambiguity; or more properly, it draws from this tradition its logical
consequence, which makes dream and reality (or really dream and supernatural presence) one and the same. Beyond this, the fact that
Hagen's eyes are open and unseeing connects the scene with Wagner's
later theories of the dream, which have broad philosophical implications and have a still more important place in the dramatic conception.
The strangeness of this visitation is seen more clearly when it is contrasted with the annunciation scene of *Walküre,* in which Brünnhilde
appears to tell Siegmund of his coming death. Here ambiguity is displaced in the opposite direction: toward definition of one of the alternatives rather than their identification and fusion. To be sure, the supernatural figure carries with it – as it always does – something of the
atmosphere of a vision, and Sieglinde is asleep at Siegmund's side during the Valkyrie's visit, but there is hardly a doubt in his mind that he is
witnessing an actual occurrence and just as little in ours that we are witnessing the representation of one.

Sleep as such is occasionally an event of no special significance in
Wagner's dramas; in the later works the figures of Jesus, Hunding, and
Sieglinde come to mind. But the later operas show an unusual interest
also in magical rather than natural sleep – dreamless but enchanted.
Brünnhilde is put to sleep before Siegfried is born and is awakened by
him as her lover. Fafner sleeps on indefinitely, guarding the gold, until
Siegfried awakens him and kills him. More significantly, such deep, pro-
longed, and apparently dreamless sleep is connected with conceptions

of night, with death, and with eternal peace but also with the occurrence of nightmares. It is also connected with traditional attributes of the dream – prophecy and clairvoyance – but of enhanced and deepened power; Erda sleeps eternally but is in touch with the total course of world events; she possesses wisdom rather than the particular predictive ability conferred in an individual dream. "I know the past," she sings in *Das Rheingold* when she rises out of the earth to warn Wotan; "I see also becoming, and the future."[11] In Siegfried she reveals more explicitly that dreaming in some sense is part of her sleep: "My sleep is dreaming, my dreaming thought, my thought the sway of wisdom."[12] But her desire is for a sleep that will be dreamless: "Let me again descend: Let sleep end my knowledge!"[13]

Another strange figure with an insatiable appetite for sleep is Kundry. Always exhausted in her role as penitent, she is overcome by an irresistible need for sleep: "Only rest do I seek. Sleep! Oh, that no one wake me!"[14] She too, like Erda, commands wisdom. As Gurnemanz says to Parsifal: "She spoke the truth; for Kundry never lies, and she has seen much."[15] She is also torn out of sleep by what seem to be incipient nightmares that have the force of epileptic seizures: "No! No sleep! Terror grips me!"[16] The stage directions read "Looking up fearfully," and then, "After a hollow cry she trembles violently; then she lets her arms fall weakly." And when she is awakened by Klingsor to her role as seductress, very much as Erda is summoned out of the earth by Wotan, she screams out piercingly[17] and then seems incapable of coherent speech: "Ah! – Ah! – Deep night – Madness! – Oh! – Rage! – Oh! Misery! – Sleep! – Sleep! – deep Sleep! – Death!"[18] It is not only Klingsor who awakens her but her curse, imposed when she laughed at Jesus on the cross. This compels eternal repetition of her role as the primeval sorceress, just as it condemns her to the ceaseless compulsion to service in expiation. Her torture can be stilled only in eternal sleep, and in this she is closely related to a number of Wagner's male characters. The Dutchman calls out in his despair: "Eternal destruction, sweep me off!"[19] Wotan echoes him: "One thing only do I yet will: the End—the End! – "[20] And Tristan longs for death, fully expects to destroy himself when he drinks the potion, and finally does so when he tears the bandage from his wound. Amfortas similarly, unable to bear the suffering of a wound that will never heal, orders his knights to drive their swords into him: "Up, ye heroes! Kill the sinner with his torture!"[21]

As we might expect in a summary final work, the view of sleep in *Parsifal* is remarkably complex and comprehensive, incorporating as it does ideas of night and death, of expiation and freedom from guilt, of wisdom, of rest and peace paradoxically joined to misery and madness, even perhaps something of renewal and transformation, since it is always through collapse and sleep that the reversible metamorphosis of Kundry occurs. Only the dream that gives particular visions or prophecies, the dream that is remembered as such and is still readily interpreted, is absent.

In *Tristan,* the action is concerned with night as opposed to day, but the conception of night is remarkably comprehensive, and it is understandably permeated with various notions of sleep and dreaming. One of the two Wesendonck songs that are designated as studies for Tristan has the title "Träume" and provides music precisely for the nocturnal love scene of the second act. Although the song text is by Mathilde Wesendonck rather than Wagner, it can hardly for that reason be discounted. It asks for an explanation of wonderful dreams that enrapture the sense of the poetess, blossoming more beautifully each hour and each day: dreams that stream into the soul to paint an eternal image of dedication and total forgetfulness of the world; dreams that, like the spring sun, kiss the blossoms out of the snow so that they grow and bloom, dreamingly give forth their aroma, glow softly on the breast of the beloved, and then sink into the grave. The poem is clearly intended to convey Mathilde's sentiments to Wagner, her feelings of a deep and all-absorbing love and veneration, but it looks pessimistically nevertheless at the tragedy of mortality: the image is eternal, but the dreams themselves, visited upon a mortal creature, are much like a flower. What *Tristan* deals with is in fact not too different from this, although infinitely expanded and intensified, for the opera concerns a love that is consuming and eternal, but that nevertheless – or perhaps fittingly – can be consummated only in death. Some equation of this love to a dream may very well have played a part in the original conception, and in the sections of the large love scene that derive their music from "Träume," there is an unmistakable dreamlike quality. But the main conceptions associated with night are broader than that of an idyllic love dream. Indeed it is the day to which Wagner assigns the traditional dream vision, along with the ambiguity of deceptive reality. When King Mark and his followers interrupt the lovers, Tristan dismisses them as a daytime hallucination: "Day-spirits! Morning dreams! False and empty! Avaunt! Give way!"[22]

In the first act also, after drinking the love-potion, he cries out, bewildered, "What did I dream of Tristan's honor?"[23] And when shortly before this he proposes "Dream of omens!" as a toast,[24] he drinks to what is still a daytime dream, although the omens are of death. Although the concept of dreaming does occur in connection with night as normally understood, it is not applied explicitly to the sphere of night in the new sense, to death and love. Yet there are indications that special notions of sleeping and dreaming are present implicitly, similar to those we have come upon in the figures of Erda and Kundry. The origin of part of the love music in the Lied "Träume" is such an indication. And there is another when King Mark asks Tristan to account for his actions: "The unfathomable, fearfully deep, mysterious ground – who will reveal it to the world?" Tristan answers: "My King, that – I cannot tell you; and what you ask, that you can never learn."[25] This whole exchange, and the very language in which it is couched, cannot fail to suggest Wagner's theories of deep sleep, which are made explicit in his later operas and essays, and which deal in these same terms with the problem of interpreting the deep dream and even with the impossibility of conveying such an experience to the daytime world of reason.

In contrast to day, then, night is conceived not as the time of dreams in the usual sense, but as a realm of direct contact with being: a realm that surrounds and underlies life, and is known in deep, dreamless sleep, in the experience of love, and especially in death, when human love is superceded by the bliss of union with the universe. Night is the dark country from which Tristan comes and to which he returns, but also the death – his mother's death – from which he is born, and the cosmic darkness from which he awoke. These larger meanings do not wait upon the conclusion of the opera to become manifest; they can be found throughout, both explicitly and implied, particularly in the love scenes. In the second act, Tristan lives in the world of night, which he previously awoke to, as he says, only in dreaming. A supposed death-potion has now opened the door to this world, although his experience in it is really one of love; yet he longs for death, which he has come to equate with love, as an alternative to day. We are obviously not dealing here with a dream in either the customary sense or the sense that daytime life is an evil dream of deceit and treachery. Many of the ramifications of Wagner's conception appear in Tristan's invitation to Isolde to return with him to his homeland:

> On the land that Tristan means,
> the sun's light never shines:
>   it is the dark night-time land
>   from which once my mother sent me forth
>   when the one she conceived in death
>   she brought to light in death.
> What was, when she bore me,
> her retreat of love,
> the wonder-realm of night,
> from which I then awoke –
> that Tristan offers you,
> thence he leads the way.[26]

The characteristic interplay of meanings can be seen in the double sense that the action finally bestows upon "thence he leads the way." This one passage unites many varied meanings of dark land, love-retreat, night, and death. And the ideal toward which the whole action moves is more one of dream than of nothingness. Wagner's programmatic clarification of the meaning of the Prelude makes this clear, for after describing, quite in the vein of Schopenhauer, how the music depicts the repeated striving of the heart for a satisfaction in which it always sinks back exhausted into a renewed longing, he turns to the final intimation of supreme bliss:

> it is the bliss of dying, of no-longer-being, of the final redemption into that wondrous realm from which we stray the furthest when we strive to press our way in with the most impetuous force. Shall we call it death? or is it the nocturnal world of wonder from which, as the legend tells us, an ivy plant and a grape vine once grew upwards in ardent embrace on Tristan and Isolde's grave?[27]

The opera itself culminates in a kind of drowning or submergence, in which the individuality of consciousness is extinguished. But this death of individuality that is typified by night is thought of as an ideal of love, in which the individual senses are absorbed into a single unified sentience. A synesthetic universe is uncovered that is aromatic, kinesthetic, and sonorous, although significantly, not visual. Immersed in aromatic waves of sound, in the cosmic breath of the universe, the will is stilled, not momentarily, as in terrestrial love, but permanently.

In *Die Meistersinger,* the dream appears in a new guise: as the bearer of inspiration to the creative artist. This function is akin to prophecy in having some supernatural or divine foundation; but among other things, the inspirational dream of *Die Meistersinger* is connected, except in one striking instance, with daytime rather than night, thus providing an interesting contrast to *Tristan,* in which the day is odious and the morning dream hateful. Since *Die Meistersinger* is concerned essentially with aesthetics, the dream occupies a central position in the action and dominates much of the third act. On the morning of the song contest, Walther tells Sachs that he has slept only a little, but soundly, and that he has had a wonderful dream. This Sachs takes to be a good omen and asks Walther to relate it. But Walther replies: "I hardly dare even to recall it; I fear to see it vanish."[28] Sachs uses this normal feeling about dreams, here so well stated, as the basis upon which to define the nature of creative activity. The term *dichten,* "to poetize," is central, for since Schumann, in the 1830s, it had become the characteristic concept for artistic creation in general and was applied to music as well as to verbal art:

> *My friend, just that is the poet's work,*
> *that he interpret and note his dreams.*
> *Believe me, man's truest illusion*
> *is opened to him in dreams:*
> *all creative art and poetizing*
> *is nothing but the interpretation of a clairvoyant dream.*[29]

Creation consists, then, in interpreting and fixing the images of dreams. The process is accomplished, as Sachs explains at length to Walther, by the use of rules. In the ensuing action, when Sachs asks Walther to dictate his dream to him, we are witness to a lesson in artistic creation, which turns dream into poetry:

> W: *How I might begin it I should scarcely know.*
> S: *Tell me your morning dream!*
> W: *Through the good teaching of your rules it is as though it was*
>   *erased away.*
> S: *Now just take the hand of poetry:*
>   *Many have found through her what is lost.*

> W: *Were it then not dream, but poetry?*
> S: *Both are friends, they stand gladly beside you.*[30]

When Sachs has Walther sing his song for Eva and says to her, "Listen, child! This is a master song,"[31] Wagner's self-flattery confirms our impression that the opera describes his own experience of the creative process. The description is best illustrated by *Die Meistersinger* in particular, however, because of its elaborate incorporation of older styles and techniques and its fusion of them with progressive and inspirational features. Both the procedure and the theme can be found elsewhere, notably in *Tannhäuser,* but not nearly in so prominent a form.

The role of the dream in artistic creation is borne out by Wagner's way of introducing a song. Walther invokes the dreamlike state, which Sachs suggests is reinstated at each performance by a strange modulation reminiscent of the unusual sequence of chords associated with Brünnhilde's magic sleep. If the strange succession symbolizes the dream, doubtless by means of unusual association as the common term, the chordal texture in itself – which also introduces Tannhäuser's song – seems to represent also the unconscious or natural harmonic reservoir from which melody is born.

In the quintet of *Die Meistersinger,* which crystallizes everyone's happiness, Eva sets the tone by greeting the awakening morning and its dream of bliss. Then the dream concept is taken up by each person in turn, always in application to the whole present situation rather than to Walther's song. It is applicable because of the happiness of the moment: reality cannot be so perfect, and thus ambiguity is suggested. "Is it just a morning dream?" asks Eva. "Is it still the morning dream?" says Walther. And David and Magdelene wonder if they are awake or dreaming and guess that "it is probably just a morning dream." Each confesses not to be able to interpret or explain what is happening. Only Sachs is characteristically reflecting on the preceding evening, also not really a dream, but likewise forgoes interpretation: "It was a beautiful evening dream: the meaning I scarcely dare to give."[32]

In the final version of the prize song, the twin Stollen are ingeniously worked out in parallel depictions of contrasted dreams, the first of "Eva in Paradise," the second of "the Muse of Parnassus." "Glowing in the roseate light of dawn" becomes "The night enclosed me in evening twilight"; the "wonder-tree richly hung with fruits" becomes a "laurel tree brightly pierced with stars"; and most important, "to gaze in the blissful dream of love" becomes "I gazed in the waking dream of poetry."[33] This is an explicit dream typology, even though it stands on its head what we find elsewhere in Wagner. Love is assigned to the morning, as it is consistently in *Die Meistersinger,* rather than to night as it is in *Tristan.* And artistic creation is assigned to night, rather than to morning as it is earlier in the act when Walther tells of his dream. The typology has an interesting implication in that the plan of day followed by night agrees with that of the first two acts of the opera, which have daytime and nighttime settings respectively. This scheme is found in other operas of Wagner, but here the acts, like the Stollen, are also parallel opposites in their content and detailed structure. This confirms the impression that the opera as a whole is conceived as a bar form;[34] and it may also be a key to our understanding of the last act that the Abgesang of the prize song is in some sense a synthesis of the two Stollen, so that a Hegelian plan is here superimposed on a bar form, which follows a basically different principle:

> *Day of grace overflowing,*
> *to which I awoke from the poet's dream!*
> *That which I dreamed – Paradise –*
> *in celestial newly transfigured grandeur*
>   *lay bright before me,*
>
>   . . . .
>
> *in the gleaming day of the suns*
> *won through the victory of song,*
> *Parnassus and Paradise!*[35]

This may mean – although it is difficult to be sure – that the first Stollen has provided the experiential basis for artistic creation in a dream of love, the second the poetic vision necessary for the poet to undertake his task, while the Abgesang depicts the actual fulfillment of the creative project, now reality rather than dream, but as artistic reality, still perhaps only an image. This is borne out, with still further complication of the matter, by the comment of the people as Walther finishes his song: "Rocked as in the most beautiful dream, I hear it well, yet hardly grasp it!"[36] Walther's audience, of course, in some way represents Wagner's audience, and their reaction to the song represents our reaction to the opera, so that this single suggestion of a dream has a double effect on the complex interplay of reality, dream, and art.

From Wagner's personal experiences both as a listener and as a composer, we know that he was predisposed to find an intrinsic connection between music and visions; he not only possessed a synesthetic nature but in addition to this was strongly inclined toward the demonic and mysterious—a tendency particularly bound up with his tonal and musical sensitivity. In his autobiography he tells of the magical pleasure he felt as a child in hearing an orchestra that was very near him:

Even the tuning up of the instruments set me into a mystical excitement: I remember specifically that the bowing of the fifths on the violin seemed to me like a greeting from the world of spirits – which I must mention in passing had a completely literal sense in my case. Even when I was a little child, the sound of these fifths coincided exactly with the ghostlike, which had always excited me. I remember still in later times never walking past the little palace of Prince Anton at the end of the Ostallee in Dresden without terror; for in this neighborhood I had once and then repeatedly heard the tuning of a violin close at hand, that seemed to me to come from the stone figures with which this palace is fitted out.[37]

Many years later it still made a strange impression on Wagner when he actually met the violinist who lived in this area and who had unwittingly been his childhood "mysterious ghostly being."[38] The account in the autobiography continues:

As I now also saw the well-known picture in which a skeleton plays the violin to a dying old man, the ghostlike quality of precisely these sounds impressed itself with particular force on my childhood fantasy.[39]

Wagner tells also of daydreaming as a youth, when he attended concerts nearly every afternoon, and listening with "blissful terror"[40] to the chaotic sounds of the orchestra tuning up. The tone of the oboe, which seemed to awaken the other instruments like a ghostly invocation, never failed to set all his nerves into a feverish tension, and the swelling unison of the overture of *Der Freischütz* announced to him that he had entered "the magic realm of terror."[41] He was also especially affected by the introduction of Beethoven's *Fidelio* overture, and when his sisters subsequently told him of Beethoven's death, which added to the still very vivid and incomprehensibly tragic impression that Weber's death had made upon him, he was filled with strange fears that were not unrelated to the very early "ghostly terror"[42] over the violin fifths.

The production of ghostly daydreams by music explains how Wagner came to turn the Romantic connection of music with the supernatural into a central principle of his dramatic theories. The stories of Hoffmann were a powerful stimulus to his imagination, and his very first operatic effort, which remained a fragment (*Die Hochzeit*),[43] combines music with a secret and unaccountable passion of demonic force. This is true not only in the very fact of the operatic medium and in the somber style of the music but also in the action itself, which features a mysterious bond between an organist and the tragic hero.

But the evocation of the supernatural by music is only one side of the coin; we know also that dreams or at least daytime reveries provided inspiration to Wagner as a composer. There is a striking instance in the autobiography when he tells of the beginning of the composition of the *Ring*.[44] His efforts had been fruitless for months, and he had finally undertaken a trip to Italy, but he was plagued by restlessness and could not find the peace for creative work. Dysentery added to his misery, and it was intensified by seasickness, brought on by a stormy steamer trip to Spezia. Completely exhausted, he sought out a hotel room there, only to find that it was situated on a narrow, noisy street. The night was passed in fever and sleeplessness, but the next day Wagner forced himself on a walk through the pine woods of the surrounding hills. Everything seemed bare and desolate, and he could not understand what he was doing there. Returning to his room in the afternoon, he stretched himself out, deathly tired, on a hard daybed to await sleep. It did not arrive, but instead he fell into a kind of trance,[45] in which he suddenly had the sensation of sinking into a powerfully flowing stream of water. The rushing noise of this soon became the musical sound of an E♭ major chord, which flowed along ceaselessly in the wavelike motion of figured arpeggios. These presented themselves as melodic figurations of increasing motion, but the pure E♭ major triad never altered, and its persistence seemed to give an infinite meaning to the fluid element into which he sank. With the feeling that the waves now were rushing along high above him, he awoke from his half-sleep with a violent start, recognized at once that the prelude of *Das Rheingold* had come to him, and realized also that the vital stream of his life was to flow to him only from within, not from without. Wagner's inspiration here – the elemental wavelike motif of the Rhine – was nothing less than the musical foundation of the whole *Ring* tetralogy. His dream was strikingly synesthetic and bears a distinct resemblance to the description given at the close of *Tristan,* of submergence in waves of sound.

Wagner's prose writings present what seems like an elaborate super-structure resting on these autobiographical accounts; they provide theoretical conceptions of the dream that are an explicit counterpart of the ideas embodied in his operas. The early stories and essays of 1840 and 1841, "Ein deutscher Musiker in Paris," are often thinly disguised autobiography, accounts of his experiences and imaginings which are ascribed to a "friend." It is not surprising to find a familiar description of the effect of the oboe in the story "Ein Ende in Paris," although here the sound of the instrument is apparently imagined rather than real. The friend of the writer tells of a succession of the most various dreams. "In between them it often seemed to me that I heard the lamenting, ghost-like tone of an oboe; this tone penetrated all my nerves, and pierced my heart."[46] The second of the "Pariser Berichte" of 1841 twice mentions specific dreams to music. One of these occasions – which is reminiscent of Hoffmann in that it takes place during a performance of *Don Giovanni* – consists of an image of two black knights engaged in fierce combat, here summoned up, oddly enough, by the wrong opera;[47] the other is significant in that the dreams occur to violin playing, that of Henri Vieuxtemps.[48]

Very much as in his youthful attendance at orchestral concerts, Wagner is also concerned in his early essays with the capacity of music to produce a vague revery. *Der Freischütz* has this effect, he finds in a report about the opera written in 1841,[49] for it has a special atmospheric quality that is peculiarly German. And in the essay "Über deutsches Musikwesen" (On the Nature of German Music) of 1840, which belongs to the set "Ein deutscher Musiker in Paris," Wagner maintains that revery is a characteristic of the German sensitivity to music: of the listener's response and of the music itself. In addition to the nationalism that Wagner here espouses, he also takes up the Romantic belief that instrumental music is the ideal art.

What wonder that the serious, deep, and visionary German turns to precisely this genus of music with a stronger partiality than to any other? Here where he can give himself up entirely to his dreamlike phantasies – here he feels himself free and in his home.[50]

In the main bulk of Wagner's essays and treatises, which were written around mid-century, conceptions of the dream seem altogether absent.

These works represent Wagner the realist, who views art as a concentration of life and places aesthetics in a social and political context. It is not until the last two decades of his life that ideas more akin to those of the earlier, Romantic writings make their appearance.

The essay "Über Staat und Religion" (1864) turns to the dream to elucidate the nature of divine revelation. In so doing, however, it also casts light on Wagner's conception of the dream itself. Revelation can be conveyed to the people only in a kind of allegory, Wagner argues; for it is something that is inexpressible, that has never been perceived, and that is grasped only in immediate intuition. There is thus a need for a translation into the language of everyday life, with its basically erroneous outlook of naive realism, so that what is revealed may become an object of the only kind of knowledge possible in this sphere. But the necessary allegory, Wagner continues, is related to the mystery of revelation very much as the dream told by day is related to the actual dream of night; for the narrative of a dream is too caught up in and distorted by the impressions of everyday life either for the narrator to feel satisfied that what was most essential has not escaped entirely or for the listener to feel the security of grasping something fully understandable. It is clear in this passage that Wagner is concerned, somewhat as he is in *Die Meistersinger* and even in the figure of Erda, with the revelatory power of dreams, with the intuitive access they provide to the truth, but also, perhaps more, with the difficulty of conveying them conceptually. But what he sees as condemned to failure in terms of language and ideas, Hans Sachs and Walther succeed in accomplishing in terms of art.

At the end of the essay, Wagner does give his attention to art and sees it as providing a path to revelation, which is in fact hardly different from providing a translation of religious experience. Like a friendly savior, art takes the place of the seriousness of life, substituting illusion for reality. In this illusion, however, reality itself appears to be illusion. What this may mean can again be understood most readily in terms of *Die Meistersinger.* Drama in general reveals how reality may be transformed into illusion by art, but within this illusion itself Sachs is depicted as viewing the whole compass of reality in a special light: as *Wahn,* or delusion; and it even seems to be implied in the opera that *this* transformation takes place under the influence of art or of the attitude associated with art. Certainly the recognition by Wagner himself of the values of contemplation and resignation, which to a great extent displaced those of action and achievement, was closely bound up with his changing understanding of art and with the ideals embodied in *Die Meistersinger* in particular.

But if art and life are then viewed as a dream, religious revelation is a deeper kind of dream which presents us with truth rather than illusion or really shows us that illusion – since it signifies the nothingness of conventional reality – is in fact an aspect of the truth. At the same time, however, art itself is given a higher value, for it is the illusion of art that enables us to discover both the illusory nature of reality and to re-experience the truth of revelation. Wagner's royal young patron enters his peroration in the third person:

The noblest of artworks will gladly be permitted by him [Ludwig], so that taking the place of the sternness of life, it will in a kindly fashion dissolve reality into illusion. And in this illusion, stern reality itself will finally ap-pear also to be only illusion. And in the transport of his gaze upon this wonderful play of illusion, the inexpressible dream of holy revelation will return to him clear and bright, with a significance that is related to that of the illusion in its very nature. . . . The nothingness of the world – here it is acknowledged openly, harmlessly, as though with a smile; for in willingly allowing ourselves to be deceived, we were led, without any deception, to recognize the reality of the world.[51]

With the religious constituent subtracted, this contains much the same interplay of illusion and reality that we discovered in *Die Meistersinger,* a work of the same period. The essay contains what is actually a com-pact interpretation of the meaning of Sachs's *Wahn* monologue at the opening of act 3 and also a confirmation of what we guessed the larger nature of the opera to be.

In a much later religious essay, "Religion und Kunst," of 1880,[52] Wagner concerns himself with instrumental music, as represented by a mature symphony of Beethoven, rather than with opera, which is clearly what he had in mind in the essay we have just discussed. This in itself reveals a shift in his point of view and at the same time entails a correspondingly more elevated notion of the capacity of art. It is now not art or life but only religious truth that is the realm of the dream. This is a realm, however, that remains inexpressible and beyond any possibility of concrete thought; it can be revealed only by the prophetic tone-poet. In instrumental music, then, art becomes a direct revelation of a kind of deep dream that cannot be formulated or otherwise conveyed or known except by religious experience. Music is thus the adumbration if not the equivalent of religion.

The Romantic response to instrumental music reappears in "Über das Dirigieren" of 1860,[53] as Wagner describes the subject of a Beethoven quartet movement as a phantom arising from the depths of memory – a lovely, tenuous, and scarcely realized dream-image. In conformity with the conception of art as illusion, however, the images are not attributed to the listener's revery but are placed in the music itself. The same year, 1869, witnesses a sudden concentration on the art of the actor and on its nature as play and illusion. This takes place in the essays "Über das Dirigieren," "Die Bestimmung der Oper," and "Über Schauspieler und Sänger";[54] and then, starting in 1870, Wagner gives his attention to an analysis of opera with respect to illusion and to the relative functions, within opera, of visual representation and music. This body of theory supplants the realistic conception of opera in Wagner's main treatises of twenty years earlier, where the cooperation of the arts served the end of perceptual concreteness and emotional impact. There is a forecast of the later outlook in the essay "Zukunftsmusik," which Wagner wrote in 1860 as a preface to a prose translation of his librettos. He undertakes here an explanation of the advantages of legend over history as subject matter for opera, and in the context of this discussion he describes the effect of the kind of scenery and music that are called for:

Through the legendary tone of the music, just as through the characteristic scene, the mind is at once put into that dreamlike state in which it is soon to arrive at complete clairvoyance. Here the world becomes clearly understandable; the mind attests to a new context of phenomena: one that it could not attest to with the usual waking eye, with which it constantly seeks the "why" of things, as though to overcome its fear of the inconceivable. How music is to produce this magical clairvoyance you will now easily understand.[55]

What is perceived in the opera, then, will have the character of the images of a dream and will thus also contain a kind of intelligibility and truth that does not depend upon causality. Other forecasts of the value Wagner was to find in illusion occur in the religious essay of 1864 that we have discussed and in a fragment that probably dates from the same year:

in the finished drama, the corporeal figures of the dream-image that is viewed, the other world, as though projected before us through a laterna magica, corporeal, like the figures of every time and place in clairvoyant visions clearly before us. Music is the light of this lantern.[56]

Conceptions of the dream understandably will play an important part in an illusionistic theory.

Setting aside for the moment the elaborate and fundamental speculative essay on Beethoven of 1870, we can give our attention to three essays written for various purposes in Bayreuth in 1872 and 1873. In the first of these, "Brief über das Schauspielerwesen an einen Schauspieler," Wagner discusses something which had fascinated him as a child but which he now finds distressing: the wardrobe of costumes and masks seen in any chance visit backstage at a theater:

From the inordinately anguished impression that I was subject to on each occasion of this kind, only a sudden magical intervention was able to free me: this occurred when I heard the distant sound of the orchestra. *Then my nearly halting pulse was revived. Everything before me was quickly transported into the sphere of miraculous dreams. All the ghosts of hell seemed released. For now the eye no longer* saw *the horrible distinctness of a thoroughly unintelligible reality.*[57]

This is reminiscent of one of Wagner's early Romantic stories, in which he repeats an attitude expressed by Hoffmann about the disturbing effect of the sight of orchestral performers and musical instruments. Wagner has the listener take by preference a distant seat from which he cannot see the orchestra. In our Bayreuth essay, however, it is not so much the interference and exclusion of visual impressions that are important but rather the transformation and subordination of these impressions under the influence of music and the dreamlike quality they assume. It is not music and hearing along that are valued but the power music has of affecting the visual world, which seems to be connected here with its power of arousing visual imagery.

In the second of the Bayreuth essays that are of interest for our purposes, "Ein Einblick in das heutige deutsche Opernwesen," Wagner deals with the overall unity of effect of the visual aspects of a theatrical production. The goal he has in mind, however, is not realism but the illusion of a dream. Every factor – grouping of figures, painting, lighting, each movement, each exit – contributes to "that ideal deception . . .

which encloses us as though in a twilight fancy, in a prophetic dream of what has never been experienced."[58] The prophetic dream significantly displays a property that distinguishes dream from reality, for it presents us not with a lived-through experience but with the "never experienced."

The third essay, "Das Bühnenfestspielhaus zu Bayreuth," is an extended consideration of Wagner's Bayreuth theater in the form of a speech. If the effect of the structure and arrangement of the auditorium is successful, he tells his hearers,

the mysterious entrance of music will now prepare you for the unveiling and clear presentation of the scenic images, which – as they seem to present themselves before you from an ideal dream-world – will display the full actuality of the meaningful deception of high art.[59]

The concealed orchestra eliminates any visual interference with the visual suggestiveness of the music, so that this will then appear to be consummated by the stage images, more especially because of a peculiar design of the proscenium. This is obviously very different from the cooperation and complementary effect of two independent arts. Wagner has placed his dramatic theory on a completely new footing, in which the notion of illusion is central.

Later in the essay he presents a closer description, telling how his demand for an invisible orchestra had at once led his friend Gottfried Semper to a particular treatment of the space that would be needed between the proscenium and the first row of seats. This space, Wagner says, we called

the "mystic abyss," because it was to divide reality from ideality. And the master terminated it in the forward direction with an expanded, second proscenium, through the effect of which, in its relationship to the narrower proscenium lying behind, he had expected at once the strange deception of an apparent distancing of the actual scene. This consists in the spectator feeling himself far removed from the scenic event, but perceiving it nevertheless with the clarity of an actual proximity. And from this there follows the further deception that the figures on stage appear enlarged and superhuman.[60]

The theater is a true "theatron," Wagner concludes, a space designed solely for viewing; and the relationship between the spectator and the scenic image is unique in its effect.

Between him and the image to be gazed at there is nothing clearly percep-
tible, but only a space between the two prosceniums, maintained in a kind
of floating state through the mediation of architecture. This space shows
the image it has distanced with the unapproachableness of a dream-
manifestation, while the ghostlike music sounding from the "mystic
abyss" – like the fumes arising under the seat of Pythia from the sacred
womb of Gaia – places him into that enraptured state of clairvoyance to
which the image gazed upon now becomes for him the most authentic copy
of life itself.[61]

In Wagner's final theoretical conception, the drama has become a true
image of life that is seen in a clairvoyant dream provoked by music. His
view of "the birth of tragedy" is close to that of Nietzsche, a not unexpected result of their close intellectual collaboration and mutual
influence.

This view remains essentially unchanged through the last decade of
Wagner's life. An essay on *Parsifal* ("Das Bühnenweihfestspiel in Bayreuth") that was written in Venice in 1882 and published in the *Bay-
reuther Blätter* contains the same characteristic reference to a
"wahrtraumhaftes Abbild"[62] of the world. But an intensification of
Wagner's religious feeling has affected his conception of reality; the
world has become totally evil, and he seeks only to flee from its hypoc-
risy and robbery and murder. The essay is thus closely related to "Religion und Kunst," which was written two years before and which equates
religion with instrumental music rather than opera; but while music
was the revelation of truth in the earlier essay, it is now seen in the
somewhat negative light of a salvation and an escape from the world. To
this desire for escape *Parsifal* owes its existence.[63] The encompassing
acoustical and optical atmosphere in this opera, Wagner writes, influences our whole sensibility and conspires to transport us from the everyday world. He refers to the device of moving scenery in particular,
which – combined with music – places us "into a dreamlike transport."[64] It also brings into the drama the legendary inaccessibility of the
temple of the grail, the route to which cannot be discovered by the un-
initiated. Indeed even Wagner's earlier imaginative use of scenery,
which is doubtless a concomitant – as it is in *Parsifal* – of his use of legend and myth, at once suggests the fanciful locations and the illogical
succession of the images of a dream. We may think here, for example, of
his use of a smokescreen to effect rapid and frequent changes of scene in

Das Rheingold – one of the operas that supposedly were to exemplify a realistic aesthetics – and of his fondness for twilight and dawn settings, for darkness and mist.

The extended essay on Beethoven of 1870 is understandably concerned with instrumental music, but the treatment of the subject is at once so ramified and so fundamental that the implications it contains for opera are extremely important. Wagner really develops a general artistic philosophy based on Schopenhauer which conceives music as antagonistic to the other arts and to visual art in particular. Music is connected with our understanding of the inner character of things, he argues, of their *Wesen*. To this we have access because we are part of nature. But we must turn our consciousness inward and seek "to see clearly inwardly."[65] Here the theory of dreams becomes relevant, with its basis in the phenomenon of clairvoyance:

If consciousness turned inward thus succeeds in that phenomenon to actual clairvoyance, that is, to the capacity of seeing where our waking consciousness, turned towards day, only darkly senses the nocturnal foundation of the affections of the will – then tone will be expelled from this night into actual, waking perception as the direct expression of the will. As the dream confirms in every experience, there stands beside the world that is regarded, thanks to the functions of a waking brain, a second world, fully equalling the first in clarity and no less manifesting itself to intuition. But this in any event cannot lie outside us as object, and must therefore be brought to knowledge in consciousness by an inwardly directed function of the brain and only under the peculiar form of perception that Schopenhauer calls precisely the dream-organ.

Now a no less definite experience, however, is this: that alongside the world which presents itself both in wakefulness and in dream as visible, there is at hand for our consciousness a second world which manifests itself through sound and is perceivable only through hearing: in the true sense of the word, then, alongside the world of light a world of sound, of which we can say that it is related to the former as the dream is to the waking state: it is namely exactly as distinct to us as this, even though we must recognize it as entirely different.[66]

The cerebral organ of dreams, Wagner continues, cannot be activated by external impressions but only through inner causes. Here he cites Schopenhauer's evidence of the occurrence of predictive dreams, of prophetic ones that make distant events perceptible, and of those of somnambulistic clairvoyance.

From the most oppressive of such dreams we awake with a scream, in which the troubled will expresses itself with the utmost directness, so that through the scream the will enters immediately and definitely into the world of sound, to manifest itself outwardly.[67]

But the inspired composer is in a similar state of ecstatic clairvoyance.

What he saw there can be conveyed by no language. Just as the dream of the deepest sleep translates only into the language of a second, allegorical dream that immediately precedes awakening, so the will devises for the immediate picture of its self-intuition a second organ of communication, which has one side turned towards the inner intuition, while it contacts with the other, through the uniquely sympathetic and direct manifestation of tone, the external world that now appears with awakening. The will calls out; and in the returning call it recognizes itself once again.[68]

Thus again we come upon a theory of two types of dream, and music is the medium of the allegorical type, which has the crucial function of conveying the ontic insight of the deep dream to the waking consciousness. It is in music, therefore, that the cosmic will manifests itself as personal will. Very much as Shakespeare did with respect to several fields of scientific knowledge, Schopenhauer and Wagner anticipate the results of modern research on sleep, which has demonstrated both a deep, dreamless level of sleep, from which nightmares probably arise, and a lighter stage, often immediately preceding waking, in which dreams appear. This lighter, allegorical state is entered not only in composing, Wagner points out, but also in listening to music, when even though our eyes are open, we are put into a dreamlike state that has the same essential similarity to somnambulistic clairvoyance.

The relationship between music and visual consciousness, which is fundamental to operatic theory, is described in various ways. In general, Wagner holds that the two aspects of consciousness suppress each other mutually, that music cancels out vision and every external perception. But he also offers notions of how the two may be joined, stating early in the essay,[69] in accordance with Schopenhauer, that even the objective character of things, as conveyed by their appearance and grasped by knowledge, would not be understood without some access to their inner nature, which is to say, without the participation of music. And in more detail subsequently, he shows how the analogical speech of music conveys the otherwise unknowable images of the deep dream to the waking consciousness, so that it may hold them fast for itself. This is accomplished through rhythm:

Through the rhythmical arrangement of tones, the musician enters into contact with the intuitively known, material world: namely by means of the similarity of the laws according to which the motion of visible bodies manifests itself intelligibly to our intuition.[70]

But the process seems self-defeating, for music

expresses the innermost nature of gesture with such immediate intelligibility that as soon as we are completely filled with music, it deactivates our vision for the intensive perception of gesture, so that we finally understand it without actually seeing it. But if in doing this, music draws the aspects of the world of appearance which are most closely related to it into what we have called its dream-realm, it does so only so that – through a wonderful transformation – it may turn intuitive knowledge inward, in a sense, where it is now enabled to grasp the nature of things in their most direct manifestation: to interpret the dream image, as we might say, that the musician had discerned in deep sleep itself.[71]

Music draws the world of appearance into its realm of dream in order to turn intuitive knowledge inward at the same time, so that it becomes capable of interpreting the images of the deep dream – of grasping the essence of things directly. Music thus absorbs and transforms objective knowledge, which joins with it in its interpretive task.

But Wagner has here deduced the consequences of his epistemological theories for instrumental music only, since this is his subject. As far as opera is concerned, there would be not only this purely musical dream but also the external world of the stage, unabsorbed and unassimilated. Of this, however, music will reveal the inner nature, as Wagner sought repeatedly to demonstrate. In the operatic situation, however, we would have to alter our normal mode of musical apprehension, for the stage would be completely wasted if music cancelled out vision altogether. Nietzsche's *Birth of Tragedy* suggests that the visual absorbs the musical, becoming in this way more deeply meaningful and more fully understood. But Wagner's illusionistic theory of drama suggests a solution more in keeping with the general tendency of his thought, for if the stage itself is dreamlike, it can easily appear to represent the visual images that can be projected in the normal mode of listening to music. The stage will seem to realize this imagery, so that the full functioning of our open eyes will be in some sense or in some degree suppressed, as is required by Wagner's conception of the action of music. There will thus be three levels of dream: ontic, allegorical, and visual, of which the last furnishes a further specification of music in terms of appearance – a second interpretation that does not involve the absorption and consequent disappearance of the visual world.

The importance of the dream in Wagner's thought seems related both to his own nature and to the outlook of his times. Wagner himself – as is doubtless befitting a dramatist – was fascinated by the interplay of reality and illusion and quite susceptible of confusing the two. There can be little doubt of the autobiographical nature of his art; all of his important dramatic characters have their counterparts in his life, either in how he understood himself or in the people he knew. This gave his life a histrionic quality; he saw himself acting out a role of great consequence, and this consciousness speaks out everywhere in his writings and his deeds. He was also more literally a great actor; it is difficult to imagine a greater one. Acting was his single most outstanding ability, he believed; but he devoted himself to other things because of natural limitations in stature and voice. Nietzsche saw this clearly, although in a negative sense. It is to his acting genius, nevertheless, that Wagner's other accomplishments are ultimately due – in stage production, direction, and dramatic and musical composition.

If Wagner was an actor in life, his most voluminous and comprehensive and characteristic theory of drama is highly realistic. And he experienced the impact and significance of his characters and dramatic action as in no way different from those of real people and events. The ultimate theoretical realization of this interchange of play and life, however, would seem to be an illusionistic aesthetics of drama. A tendency toward such an aesthetics is concealed in the very subject matter which Wagner came to prefer for his operas. He justified his interest in legend and myth by his aim of concentrating the dramatic action on powerful and universally human motives without the distraction and particularity of a specific historical context. But myth was also an intrinsically suitable concern – as later psychological and anthropological theories of the dream have made abundantly clear – for a mind that could not free itself of either the influence or the problems of illusion, with its puzzling combination of deception and revelation. And bound up closely again with an interest in the dream is the significance found in night, which is as much a feature of nineteenth-century thought as it is of Wagner's ideas in particular.

As far as the general tendencies of nineteenth-century thought are concerned, the dream is a natural part of the Romantic interest in fantasy and the miraculous, of the escape from the confines of everyday bourgeois existence. Wagner himself compares the role of music in his illusionistic drama with the role of incense in inducing a mystic cultic state, and the operatic prelude becomes something like a frame narrative that leads from the real world to the dramatic dream. But even more broadly considered, his interest in the dream seems to mark a new conception of inner life that belongs to the development of volitional and existential thought and that is concerned with states of consciousness rather than with faculties of the soul. For one thing, Wagner dethrones the faculty of reason both in his operas and in his major treatises, connecting it with all the evils of civilization that have obscured and corrupted the happier and simple state of natural man. And when he depicts even personal will, as we can see best in the figure of Siegfried, it is no longer merely one faculty among others but has become identical with the entire state of consciousness of his hero. The same can be said of the healthy sensuality that Wagner celebrates in *Das Liebesverbot*, which is grounded in the outlook of Young Germany; it is no longer an appetitive faculty but has expanded to take over consciousness as a whole. And when Wagner refers to will as the object of the dream state of consciousness, he speaks of it in terms that are affective as well as volitional; it clearly includes both spheres, while reason characterizes similarly not a part but the entire state of consciousness that belongs to objective knowledge and the waking world. Wagner's characters tend accordingly to become identified with a single generalized state of consciousness, a fact that is also the outcome in part of his effort to concentrate, intensify, and simplify the motives of the action. Wotan says to Erda, for example, "your wisdom disperses before my will."[72]

Even the individual senses conformably follow the same tendency; they do not cooperate, as the older faculties did, to constitute a total adjustive process of perception, but hearing alone has become the instrument of the dream state, just as vision alone is the instrument of the rational state. This assimilation of the senses to states of consciousness follows a principle directly opposite to that of synesthesia, which is invoked just as frequently throughout the century. In synesthesia, the sensory complement of the broadened and generalized affectivity that belongs to a state of intoxication or of what we now call expanded consciousness or to the dream state is achieved not by the sole reliance on an individual sense but by a fusion of all the senses that deprives them of individuality and constitutes a common sensibility. In the distant predecessors of the nineteenth-century conceptions of the dream, such as Plato's myth of Er and the *Somnium scipionis* of Cicero and of Macrobius, the faculties of the soul are similarly subordinated to a generalized state, although by fusion rather than the broadening of a single faculty, and the senses again follow suit, although by means of synesthesia rather than the operation of a single inherently appropriate sense.

But the symptomatic position of the dream in nineteenth-century thought is not simply that of a state of consciousness; for a special importance resides in the subordination of rationality and in the close connection with creativity and imagination, capacities that cannot be numbered at all among the traditional compartmentalized faculties of the soul. The Platonic notion of creativity makes it a kind of divine madness or ecstatic state; the rhapsode has no knowledge of what he sings. But like the dream and the myth, creative madness also brings us to the truth – through direct insight rather than reason. What we have in dream and myth and creation are products of the poetic imagination, but this is deployed unconsciously; it is the expression, in fact, of a divine agency acting through the inspired artist. The state of the human agent is thus irrational; even though he is put in touch with truth and beauty by a higher power than his own, neither reason nor will nor passion plays a role, but instead all are suspended and deactivated. But this is applicable not only to the *Ion* and the *Phaedrus* of Plato, or to the Tenth Book of the *Republic;* it applies equally to the conceptions Wagner entertained. Even the role of inspiration remains present in the nineteenth century; creative imagination is its secular equivalent, but this is found only in a higher state of consciousness, or at least in a special state that is both conscious and unconscious at once. Here reason is assimilated as workmanship, the feelings are transcended by a generalized joy of creation, and the personal will has been stilled and super-seded by merging with that of the cosmos.

NOTES

From *The Journal of Musicology* 7, no.1 (1990): 54–81. © 1990 by the Regents of the University of California.

1. Hoffmann's influence on Wagner can be seen most readily in *Die Hochzeit.* The text is found in Wagner's *Sämtliche Schriften und Dichtungen,* 5th ed. (Leipzig 1911), vol.11; the score in *Richard Wagners Werke,* ed. M. Balling (Leipzig 1912–ca.1929), vol.12.

2. *Sämtliche Schriften und Dichtungen,* 11:17. (Translations throughout are by the author.)

3. Ibid., 11:20

4. Ibid., 11:51.

5. Ibid., 1:276.

6. Ibid., 11:239.

7. Ibid., 6:209.

8. Loc. cit.

9. Ibid., 6:212.

10. Loc. cit.

11. Ibid., 5:261.

12. Ibid., 6:153.

13. Ibid., 6:155.

14. Ibid., 10:338.

15. Loc. cit.

16. Loc. cit.

17. Wagner here makes use of an aspect of the dream he had discussed in his tract on Beethoven in 1870. See note 67.

18. *Sämtliche Schriften und Dichtungen,* 10:346.

19. Ibid., 1:261.

20. Ibid., 6:42.

21. Ibid., 10:374–75.

22. Ibid., 7:52.

23. Ibid., 7:27.

24. Ibid., 7:26.

25. Ibid., 7:55.

26. Ibid., 7:55–56.

27. Ibid., 12:345.

28. Ibid., 7:235.

29. Loc. cit.

30. Ibid., 7:238.

31. Ibid., 7:252.

32. Ibid., 7:255–57.

33. Ibid., 7:267–68.

34. This has become well known through Alfred Lorenz's work, *Das Geheimnis der Form bei Richard Wagner* (Berlin 1924–33), vol.3 (*Der musikalische Aufbau von* Die Meistersinger von Nürnberg).

35. *Sämtliche Schriften und Dichtungen,* 7:268.

36. Loc. cit.

37. Richard Wagner, *Mein Leben* (Munich 1976), p.36.

38. Ibid., p.37.

39. Loc. cit. See my article on "The Formation of Wagner's Style" in *Music and Civilization* (New York 1984) for a consideration of the role of these fifths in Wagner's musical style (reprinted as chapter 11 in this collection).

40. Loc. cit.

41. Loc. cit.

42. Loc. cit.

43. Ibid., pp.75–76. See also note 1.

44. Ibid., pp.511–12.

45. "Eine Art von somnambulen Zustand." Ibid., p.512.

46. *Sämtliche Schriften und Dichtungen*, 1:129.

47. Ibid., 12:76–77.

48. Ibid., 12:80.

49. Ibid., 1:220.

50. Ibid., 1:156.

51. Ibid., 8:29.

52. Ibid., 10:250–51.

53. Ibid., 8:294.

54. Ibid., vols.8 and 9.

55. Ibid., 7:121.

56. Ibid., 12:279.

57. Ibid., 9:261.

58. Ibid., 9:287.

59. Ibid., 9:327.

60. Ibid., 9:337.

61. Ibid., 9:337–38.

62. An "image like those of a clairvoyant dream" is perhaps the best that can be done with this in English. Ibid., 10:307.

63. Loc. cit.

64. Ibid., 10:305.

65. Ibid., 9:68.

66. Ibid., 9:68–69.

67. Ibid., 9:69.

68. Ibid., 9:73–74. Wagner thereupon presents a poetic description of the more concrete antiphony of the calls of Venetian gondoliers. He had heard these from his balcony during a sleepless night in Venice, and this "tönende Nachttraum" conveyed much more of Venice to him than any daytime visual experience could. See my article on "The Tonal Ideal of Romanticism" in *Festschrift für Walter Wiora* (Kassel 1967) for further consideration of the contrast that was set up between hearing and vision in the nineteenth century (reprinted as chapter 8 in this collection).

69. *Sämtliche Schriften und Dichtungen*, 9:67.

70. Ibid., 9:76.

71. Ibid., 9:76–77.

72. Ibid., 6:156.

Index

Page numbers in italics indicate musical examples.